Trying Again

Trying Again

A Guide to Pregnancy After Miscarriage, Stillbirth, and Infant Loss

Ann Douglas and

John R. Sussman, M.D.

TAYLOR TRADE PUBLISHING

Lanham • New York • Oxford

Published by Taylor Trade Publishing
An imprint of The Rowman & Littlefield Publishing Group, Inc.
4501 Forbes Boulevard, Suite 200
Lanham, Maryland 20706

Distributed by National Book Network

Library of Congress Cataloging-in-Publication Data

Douglas, Ann, 1963–

    Trying again : a guide to pregnancy after miscarriage, stillbirth, and infant loss / Ann Douglas and John R. Sussman.

       p.   cm.

    Includes bibliographical references and index.

    ISBN 0-87833-182-4 (pbk.)

    1. Miscarriage. 2. Stillbirth. 3. Infants (Newborn)—Mortality. 4. Pregnancy. 5. Loss (Psychology). I. Sussman, John R. II. Title.

RG631 .D69 2000

618.3'92—dc21

                                        00-044683

Printed in the United States of America

*To Ian, my subsequent baby,
and Laura, the baby I never
got to take home.*
—A.D.

*To Beth and Stephen, who
tried again, and to
Marybeth and George, who
tried so hard.*
—J.S.

Contents

Foreword

MOST EXPECTANT PARENTS *assume* that their pregnancy will result in the birth of a healthy baby. There probably was a time when you
too thought that foresight, good judgment, living well, being a good person, or religious faith would protect you. Then, when your baby(s) died,
those safe assumptions were shattered. You come face to face with the
fact that you can't always avoid tragedy. Your beliefs about pregnancy and
birth, life and death, fate and justice all come into question. You start to
realize that there are no answers to "Why me? Why my baby?" Your grief
includes painful feelings of anger, guilt, failure, and powerlessness. You
begin to understand that life is unfair and you are *always* vulnerable to
tragedy.

As a result, when you embark on another pregnancy, it is normal for
fear to color every aspect. You may feel uneasy because you know that
even if you do all the "right" things, there are no guarantees. You may
wish you could relax, but you can't forget what happened before. You
may even feel certain that you're unable to have a baby who can survive.
While intellectually you may know that the odds are in your favor, it can
be difficult to convince yourself *emotionally*.

To get through this pregnancy, stay open to all your feelings. While
pessimism and anxiety can be overwhelming, also embrace any optimism
and confidence you feel, however fleeting. Optimism does not make bad
things happen, and in fact, it can help you cope with your anxieties and
your grief.

Make wishes for the new life that stirs within you. Let yourself feel
close to this new baby. Collect mementos and memories, as they would
offer great comfort in any case. You may believe that your detachment

will keep you from getting your hopes up and shield you from having to deal with another tragedy, but this is only an illusion. As you well know, nothing can protect you from the grief that follows the death of a baby.

Recognize the source of your anxiety, and talk or write about your fears. As you grapple with your worries, let go of the ones that arise from your imagination or past experience. You only need to listen to the worries that are based on what's actually happening now. And remember that even if you truly are high-risk, while you may be in the throes of horrific worry, your pregnancy—and the baby—may very well turn out just fine.

Be an informed advocate for this pregnancy. Read books, like this one you have in your hands, because the more information you have, the more empowered you'll feel. This comprehensive book can arm you with knowledge, which can combat your fears and enable you to get the obstetric care you deserve.

Finally, continue to grieve for the baby(s) you miss so much. Accept that having fears is a normal part of your grief, and a natural part of a subsequent pregnancy.

You cannot recapture the innocence and blissfulness normally associated with pregnancy. But you *can* find a balance between anxiety and optimism. You can face your vulnerability and still reach for your dreams. So if you feel your hopes rising, let them flow. Dare to imagine the softness of a baby's skin, and how full your arms will be. Caress little outfits, and enjoy your big belly. Even though you don't *feel* like a normal pregnant woman, you can dare to nest like one. If it gives you hope, do it. With my best wishes,

DEBORAH L. DAVIS, PH.D.
Author of *Empty Cradle, Broken Heart:
Surviving the Death of Your Baby*

Acknowledgments

A BOOK LIKE THIS doesn't come together without the assistance of a huge number of people.

We would like to start out by thanking the people who made this book possible—the large number of bereaved parents who agreed to share their stories with us when we were researching this book: Christi Allard, Jacqueline Alloun, Ann Angel, Aubyn Baker, Caryl Bartholomew, Cathy Bender, Petra Heldt-Bertrand, Lori Bianco, Miriam Blake, Jennifer Blankenship, Anne Boardman, Candy Cure Booth, Michelle Brown, Nancy A. Brown, Becky Burton, April Sayers Caddy, Jennifer Callahan, Nora Callahan, Dawnette Chadwick, Debbie Charles, Caroline Clements, Rhonda Cohen, Leslie G. Collings, Tammy Conner, Pamela Contreras, Birgette D'anna, Sarah Davis, Kim Dawley, Nancy DeWolf, Nancy Feidman, Cheryl Forbes, Tammie Forbes, Cyndie Forget, Lisa Frank, Kim Freeland, Phyllis Fritz, Mary Geitz, Monique Gibbons, Kathy Gomberg, Suzy Gray, Patricia Greenwald, Desirae Gregg, Sara Grimes, Molly Groome, Cindy Grubb, Carla Henoud, Marilyn Hilton, Jennifer Leigh Hucke, Cindy Hughes, Janna Imergoot, Jennifer Irizarry, Jodi Jaffray, Sheri L. Jiron, Sue Jones, Cathie Joseph, M. David Kellin, Cathy King, Julie Blair Lane, Heather Linn, Janis Louie, Lisa Lawson, Francesca Lyons, Gabriela A. Magnuson, Krystyne Mahurin, Tracey Marcyan, Gretchen McDeid, Karen Minner, Laura Moore, Jennifer Morris, Sandra Murphy, Michael Nettleton, Tracy Oak, Tammy L. Oakley, Lisa O'Hearn, Roberta Lee Parry, Linda Peden, Carleen Pena, Terri Geoffrey Penney, Kimberly Petry, Holly Richardson, Janann Rogillio, Bonnie Rudolph, Steve Russell, Laure Schnackenberg, Denice Schneider, Heike Sellers, Julie Simon, Renee Sorensen, Marcella Stark, Grace Stephens, Erica Taylor, Robert

Thompson, Lisa Thompson-Kjesbu, Jeannie Ueno, John Vos, Nicole Vos, Pandora D. Waldron, Janet Wall, Shannon Walters, Karen Howden Weaver, Jayne Webb, Robin Elise Weiss, Laura Yaker, Janice Zimmerman, as well as those parents who preferred to remain anonymous.

We also wish to express our thanks to a number of other people: Sara Grimes and Michael Nettleton of the Subsequent Pregnancy after a Loss Support Group, Janet Estes of the Infant Loss Support Group, Tracy Keleher of Canadian Parents Online, and Jan Pearse of Perinatal Bereavement Services Ontario, for encouraging so many parents to participate in our research; pediatrician Alan Greene, M.D., of Dr.Greene.com, for serving as a resource on issues related to infant death; Pandora Waldron, for graciously allowing us to reprint her beautiful poem, "A Different Child," in the epilogue of this book; and our agent, Ed Knappman of New England Publishing Associates, and our editors, Camille Cline and Delia Guzman of Taylor Publishing, for believing in this project.

Finally, we owe a huge debt of gratitude to Deborah Davis, Ph.D., author of *Empty Cradle, Broken Heart,* for generously agreeing to conduct a detailed technical review of the manuscript. Her comments were tremendously insightful and we sincerely appreciate her contributions to our efforts to ensure that this book is helpful to parents who are weathering the emotional highs and lows of a subsequent pregnancy.

ANN DOUGLAS
JOHN R. SUSSMAN, M.D.
January 1, 2000

Trying Again

Introduction

IT TAKES COURAGE to attempt another pregnancy when you've already experienced the death of a baby through miscarriage, stillbirth, or infant death. You know there's a chance you'll end up experiencing another loss—a risk that any pregnant woman faces—but you're willing to risk heartbreak again for a shot at the ultimate prize: a healthy baby.

No matter where you are in your quest for another baby—whether you're thinking of trying to conceive, actively trying to become pregnant again, or already pregnant—you are likely hungry for information. You may be wondering how long you should wait before you start trying to conceive again, whether you're at higher-than-average risk of experiencing the death of another baby, whether you should seek out the services of a high-risk pregnancy specialist, and how you're going to manage to make it through the months ahead without driving yourself completely crazy!

WHY A BOOK ABOUT PREGNANCY AFTER LOSS?

As you've no doubt discovered by now, most pregnancy books choose to ignore the possibility that anything can go wrong before or after a birth. While these books typically devote entire chapters to such relatively minor issues as equipping the nursery or shopping for maternity clothes, you might not find more than a paragraph or two dealing with miscarriage, stillbirth, or infant death—something that can leave you feeling angry and betrayed if the unthinkable happens to you.

We wrote this book because we wanted to arm pregnant women and their partners with the information and reassurance they need to weather the physical and emotional highs and lows of a subsequent pregnancy. If you're looking for a book that will answer the 1001 pregnancy-related questions that run through your head at 2:00 A.M. (but rarely while the doctor's office is open!) and that acknowledges the unique challenges of embarking on pregnancy after miscarriage, stillbirth, or infant death, you've found it.

We've set out to focus on the types of issues that are of primary concern to couples who are either contemplating a subsequent pregnancy or are already pregnant again. You'll find:

- A detailed discussion of the causes of pregnancy loss and infant death, including the highlights of some important new research in these areas
- Help in deciding whether you're physically and emotionally ready to attempt another pregnancy
- The latest news about genetic counseling
- The facts you need to know about preconception health
- Information about how your reproductive history (e.g., miscarriages, stillbirths, pregnancy terminations, infant deaths, and/or the birth of a child with a disability) may impact on your next pregnancy
- Practical tips on increasing your odds of conceiving quickly
- A frank discussion of the emotions that you may experience when the pregnancy test comes back positive
- Detailed information about prenatal testing, including a discussion of the pros and cons
- Useful advice on coping with the unique physical and emotional challenges of a high-risk pregnancy
- Helpful hints on surviving the emotional highs and lows of the postpartum period, including a detailed discussion of the experience of "regrieving"
- A directory of organizations, Web sites, online support groups, books, and other resources that you and your partner may find useful during the months ahead

What makes the book truly special, however, are the numerous true stories of the joys and challenges of coping with a subsequent pregnancy that are sprinkled throughout the text. We interviewed more than a hundred parents while researching this book. During a three-month period, these parents answered a series of questionnaires that focussed on every imaginable aspect of pregnancy after a loss:

- How they decided that it was time to start trying to conceive again—and how they coped if the two of them didn't agree on that timeline
- How they stayed sane if they didn't manage to conceive as quickly as they wanted
- Whether they decided to stick with the same caregiver they had worked with in the past or whether they decided to switch to another doctor or midwife
- What they decided to do about the prenatal testing issue
- How they coped with their fear that something would happen to this baby, too
- What they did to prepare themselves for the upcoming birth, and so on.

We decided to write this book shortly after finishing work on our first pregnancy book, *The Unofficial Guide to Having a Baby* (IDG Books, 1999). While we are proud of the fact that the book was the first mainstream pregnancy book to tackle the issues of pregnancy loss, infant death, and pregnancy after a loss in great depth, we felt that we still had a lot to say on this subject—an entire book's worth, in fact! The result is the book that you are holding in your hands.

You might be interested to know that we each had very personal reasons for wanting to write this book.

Ann's fourth child, Laura, was stillborn three years ago due to an umbilical cord knot. Her youngest child, Ian, was born healthy eleven-and-a-half months later, after what Ann describes as the most emotionally draining forty-one-and-a-half weeks of her life! Because an earlier pregnancy had ended in miscarriage, she was beginning to wonder if she would ever be blessed with another living child. Ann wanted to write the type of book that she desperately needed, but yet was unable to find during her last pregnancy: a book that focussed on the unique challenges of planning another pregnancy. "I just couldn't relate to mainstream pregnancy books that assume that the biggest crisis you're facing in your pregnancy is whether the Winnie the Pooh wallpaper you ordered will arrive before the baby. I wanted a book that understood that my biggest concern was whether or not I'd end up with a healthy baby in my arms."

John wanted to write a book that would address the types of concerns most often expressed by the couples he encounters in his obstetrical practice, couples who are embarking on pregnancy after miscarriage, stillbirth, or infant death. "My reasons for doing this book have to do with the pain I've shared with so many hopeful would-be parents over the years when I had to sit beside them in the ultrasound room, office, or emergency room, and explain to them that their baby was dead or that they had otherwise lost the pregnancy that they had been so excited about just days, hours, or minutes before."

We think that this book is groundbreaking in many ways and hope that you will agree. Because we want this book to be as helpful as possible to parents experiencing miscarriage, stillbirth, and infant death, we would like to encourage you to write to us, in care of our publisher

Taylor Trade Publishing
1550 West Mockingbird
Dallas, TX 75235

if there's an issue that you'd like us to address in a subsequent edition of the book. You can also E-mail your comments to us at

pageone@kawartha.com.

We hope that you enjoy this book and that you are blessed with the safe arrival of a healthy baby in the very near future.

⚘ 1   *The Quest for Answers*

I had an unyielding yearning to know what had happened and why.
—Roberta, who experienced two first-trimester miscarriages before giving birth to a healthy baby

WHEN YOUR BABY dies, you are often left with more questions than answers. Even if you are able to obtain an adequate explanation of the medical events that led to your baby's death—and, frankly, that isn't always possible—you will likely find yourself struggling with at least one question that can't be answered easily: Why did this happen to me?

This chapter will focus on the hunger for information that many couples experience following the death of a baby: why the desire for information is so strong, where parents tend to turn for information, and why it can be so difficult to come to terms with your baby's death when there is no adequate explanation for what went wrong.

THE HUNGER FOR INFORMATION

Couples who have experienced the death of a baby through miscarriage, stillbirth, or during infancy often feel a powerful need to find out as much as possible about the circumstances surrounding their baby's death. In addition to obtaining as much information as possible from their caregivers, they may turn to other sources in their quest for answers: books, medical journals, the Internet (see Appendix C), and so on. Unfortunately, despite the hours that they spend meeting with doctors and researching the causes of their babies' deaths on their own, many couples still feel dissatisfied by the amount of information that they are able to uncover.

That was certainly the case for Sara, whose first child was stillborn at twenty-three weeks due to a severe infection. "I don't think anyone could have given me enough information about my loss," she admits. "There just isn't any answer to 'Why me?'"

Laure, who has experienced four miscarriages as well as the birth of two living children, was similarly driven to try to uncover clues about what was going wrong with her pregnancies: "I joined E-mail lists, searched the Internet for information, and read any book that might help me to find out what was causing the miscarriages. I left no stone unturned."

Mary found that she was able to work through some of her feelings of grief by attempting to learn as much as possible about the circumstances that had led to her five second-trimester losses. She also felt that she would be in a better position to decide whether to attempt another pregnancy if she had a better idea about what had gone wrong. "It was very therapeutic for me to be on this quest for information," she explains. "I felt that if we found a cause for the losses that was correctable, I would try again; if we found a cause that was not correctable, we would call it a day."

WHEN THERE'S A CLEAR-CUT CAUSE

In some cases of miscarriage, stillbirth, and infant death, the cause of death is obvious; in others, there is simply no clear-cut medical explanation for what went wrong. While it is always difficult to experience the death of a baby, most grieving parents find some measure of comfort to be had in trying to find out what causes some babies to die before birth, and why some babies are born too soon or with life-threatening illnesses.

Kim, whose first baby died at thirty-nine weeks, remembers feeling relieved that there was a concrete medical explanation for her baby's death. "Seeing the knot in the umbilical cord, having that answer, offered a measure of peace—especially since the cause of her death was something that gave me no increased risk of another loss."

Some couples feel that the medical explanation for what happened is just a small part of the puzzle. What they really want to know is why this tragedy happened to them and their babies. Lori lost her son at thirty-nine weeks of pregnancy due to amniotic band syndrome, a condition in which bands of amniotic tissue interrupt the blood flow to all or part of the baby, occasionally resulting in the baby's death. She was relieved that her doctor was able to provide her with a concrete explanation for her son's death, but she was frustrated that he was unable to answer her biggest question: Why had this happened to her baby? "He spent an hour-and-a-half going into detail as to why stillbirths happen in general and what was known about amniotic band syndrome in particular," she recalls. "As he told us, doctors do not know for certain how or why these bands form, so in many ways, he simply couldn't answer our questions to our satisfaction."

Janis, who chose to terminate her pregnancy at five months when her baby was diagnosed with severe heart defects, was also frustrated by the fact that no one could adequately explain why her baby had developed these problems. "The genetic counselor explained everything she could and really went the extra mile for us, but no one knows why our baby had a heart defect or what caused it," she recalls. "It may have been a fluke of nature or a result of pesticides, pollution, food additives, preservatives, and so on. She didn't have the answer and I am not sure who could answer any of these questions."

For Laura, whose second child died during open heart surgery at eight days of age, the biggest challenge came from trying to make sense of all the highly detailed medical information she was given at the time of her baby's death. "For the most part, we were satisfied with the amount of information we were given. We had to absorb so much information about congenital heart problems that we could take in only part of it at a time." The only thing that the doctors weren't able to tell her was the one thing that she really wanted to know: Why her daughter had died during surgery that the majority of babies survived. "As far as the specific causes for Sarah's death, unfortunately they don't really know. She did not survive a surgery that has a high mortality rate (30 percent), but they can't explain why some babies don't make it when others do."

Monique was frustrated by the delay in obtaining an adequate explanation for her daughter's death, especially since the information she was initially given in the hours after her baby's death turned out to be inaccurate. "It took a long time for us to find out exactly what had happened," she explains. "At first there was speculation that damage was done to the brain stem and this was the cause of death. It wasn't until a few months later, after reviewing the autopsy report, that we discovered that Natalie had died because of an intraventricular hemorrhage."

WHEN THERE'S NOT A CLEAR-CUT REASON

As hard as it may be for parents who have lost babies to accept, there's still much that we don't know about miscarriage, stillbirth, and infant death in this era of high-tech medicine. While some significant breakthroughs in both reproductive and neonatal medicine have been reported in recent years, scientists continue to struggle to unlock the mysteries of pregnancy and infant loss.

Many parents find it difficult to accept the fact that they may never receive a satisfactory explanation of the events that led to their babies' deaths. Kelly was devastated when it turned out that the initial explanation for her son's death was incorrect and that the doctors had no idea what had gone wrong. "At first, when the resuscitation failed, the hospital personnel told us he probably had a birth defect, like underdeveloped lungs," she recalls. "This was a relief in a way because we felt like there was nothing anyone could have done to prevent it. But it was also scary because there was the possibility it could happen again. Well, it turned out not to be the case at all, and we were left with no explanation for why he died. There was an autopsy and we consulted with a perinatalogist, but we still didn't find a reason. Not knowing why he died is the hardest thing for me to come to terms with, other than not having him here."

Cheryl was also frustrated by the fact that the doctors weren't able to provide her with more information about the causes of her three pregnancy losses: "A lot of my questions were answered with, 'We really don't know why this happened.' There were a lot of suggestions that could not be confirmed with any certainty."

Like Kelly and Cheryl, Debbie finds it difficult to accept the fact that she doesn't have an adequate explanation for her two pregnancy losses. (Her first child was stillborn at thirty weeks of pregnancy and her second baby was miscarried.) "Sometimes I feel almost jealous when I hear that someone has discovered a reason for their loss, but then I remind myself that everyone asks *why* they lost their baby, even if there is a medical reason."

Some women feel very angry that so little is known about the circumstances that led to their babies' deaths. "I wish more research was done about early pregnancy," says Molly, who has experienced two first-trimester miscarriages. "I get so sick of people saying, 'We really don't know much about this early stage.' It's sort of invalidating, like until you get to be four months along, they won't bother with you because you're not a good risk or investment of their time. In later pregnancy, they seem to know so much about problems and how to fix them. It's very frustrating to have large problems early on and yet no answers—no proactive path to go down."

Lori—whose son was stillborn due to amniotic band syndrome—is also angry that more isn't done to prevent these types of tragedies. She feels that the quality of care offered to women who experience pregnancy loss should be given to every pregnant woman. "This may be awful to say, but I think the medical community gives you one 'free pregnancy'—it's like a throwaway. They don't monitor you closely unless you have experienced a loss because the cost of that additional attention would simply be too great. My husband and I went to a loss support group soon after our loss and met a couple who had lost their first child at twenty-two weeks due to an incompetent cervix. During the next pregnancy, she'll be monitored closely and she'll have a cerclage performed, but the husband's point was, 'Why can't doctors routinely check for these types of problems at the appropriate points in any pregnancy? Why do you first have to suffer a loss?'"

Kim—whose daughter was stillborn at thirty-nine weeks—shares similar feelings. "It continues to bother me that you get extra cautious care only after one baby has died. It's too big a price. Every life is precious enough to be worthy of that level of care. My second baby had her cord around her neck, and thanks to close monitoring, they were able to take the baby at thirty-seven weeks and she was fine. Who knows: If they had monitored me that closely with Molly, she might still be here."

Women who have experienced a series of first-trimester miscarriages can be particularly resentful of the fact that no type of treatment is attempted until after two or three consecutive losses. "I was never offered any explanations for my first three losses," says Jennifer, who has experienced four miscarriages and one live birth. "When they occurred years ago, I was basically told that 'These things happen.' Even after three miscarriages, I was still naïve enough to think it was just bad luck. After my fourth loss, my current obstetrician offered me many tests and was very helpful in trying to find out what was causing my losses. When I think back, I am very angry with my past caregivers. Each loss was handled by a different obstetrician and all were aware of my miscarriage history. Why was no advice or further testing offered? I will never know what caused my previous losses and can only wonder if they were related or each a different problem."

Kathy, who experienced a miscarriage at eleven weeks, felt less guilty than afraid. She was certain that she would experience another loss if the cause of her first miscarriage wasn't determined. "My doctor was very sympathetic and understanding, but explained that she didn't have the answers. She told me that most miscarriages are caused by chromosomal flukes, and that it wouldn't happen again," she says. "Of course, this was probably all true, but it wasn't a good enough answer for me because I was convinced that it would happen to me every time if we didn't find out what had gone wrong."

THE BLAME GAME

In the absence of a concrete explanation for what has gone wrong and why, it's easy for mothers who have experienced a loss to blame themselves for their babies' deaths.

"I wanted answers, and there were none to be had," explains Lisa, whose first pregnancy ended in miscarriage. "That was extremely frustrating because it left me wondering if I was somehow at fault. I knew intellectually that it most likely wasn't the case, but there was still a little part of me that wanted to blame this tragedy on something. If there was no other source of blame, then it must be my fault."

Jennifer, whose first child was stillborn at term, experienced similar feelings: "We had an autopsy as well as chromosomal studies and genetic testing done on Samantha and no cause was found for her death. 'Unexplained fetal demise at term in a normal girl' was the official phrase. I wasn't sure how I felt about this. On the one hand, not having a cause for her loss confirmed for me that she really was as perfect as she appeared. Also, it helped me to feel that we still had the potential for living children if we decided to embark on pregnancy again. On the other hand, babies don't just die for no reason and I wanted to know why this happened to our baby girl. I wanted to have something to rage against. With no cause, there was nowhere to place blame. Except, of course, on myself: I must have done something."

While mothers who have experienced the death of a baby prior to birth have a tendency to blame themselves for an unhappy pregnancy outcome—after all, wasn't it their "job" to keep the baby safe?—fathers can also be racked with feelings of guilt. For a long time, Michael, whose twin daughter Robyn died shortly after birth, felt that he should have been able to do something to prevent his daughter's death.

"I was nagged for months with a feeling I could have done something to prevent Robyn's death. I now know that this is called counterfactual thinking: It's the 'what if' game that fries your intellect and emotions after a loss. During a routine ultrasound two days before Robyn died— where our twins were being measured, among other things, to avoid the possibility of twin-to-twin transfusion—it had seemed to me that the ultrasound technician actually measured the same twin twice," Michael says. "At that ultrasound no appreciable difference in size was recorded. Yet two days later there was a five-hundred-gram difference in their sizes—significant at that point, and indicative of the twin-to-twin transfusion that caused Robyn's death.

"As it happens, two to three years after Robyn's death, I had the opportunity to sit on a discussion panel with the neonatal pediatrician who had cared for our daughters in the hospital," he continues. "I asked the doctor if it was possible that Robyn could have been measured twice, given the facts of our case. He reflected for a moment and then observed that this was possible, and easy enough to happen. At that point, at that time, if we had known about the difference in the babies' sizes [e.g., if Robyn hadn't been measured twice, without her twin being measured at all], Robyn might have survived.

"It took me quite a while to forgive myself," Michael says. "Now I had a new bit of information with which to play the 'what if' game. Could I have saved Robyn's life by mentioning what I observed at the time? Or was I really only a nervous, uneducated father in the ultrasound room, in which case it might have made no difference at all? Sometimes when we find out more, it can be more than what we want to know."

While blaming yourself for your baby's death is a normal part of grieving, it's possible to work through these feelings and let them go as you come to terms with the fact that you don't have total control over what happens to your beloved children. Deborah Davis, Ph.D., author of *Empty Cradle, Broken Heart,* offers these words of wisdom to grieving parents who are struggling to come to terms with feelings of guilt: "Bad stuff happens to good people. If you feel ready to get past your feelings of guilt, try looking in the mirror or writing yourself a letter, telling yourself that you are a good and loving parent. After all, no one loved your baby more than you did—and still do. And without a doubt, if there had been a known and guaranteed way to prevent this tragedy, you would have pursued it with all your might."

2 *The Truth about Miscarriage*

IT'S A SUBJECT pregnancy books tend to gloss over and prenatal classes generally choose to ignore: the possibility that pregnancy will end in anything other than the birth of a healthy baby.

While it's easy to understand why authors and prenatal class instructors are eager to dodge the topic—it's not the most happy or upbeat subject, after all—those who choose to ignore the possibility of pregnancy loss do expectant couples a tremendous disservice. Rather than acknowledging that miscarriage and stillbirth can and do occur, and arming these couples with information that would serve them well if they were to experience the death of a baby before birth, these so-called experts choose instead to leave parents-to-be in the dark. While the majority of couples are fortunate enough to give birth to healthy babies nine months down the road, just as their pregnancy books and prenatal instructor predicted, those parents who end up experiencing the heartbreak of losing a baby are left feeling isolated and alone.

This conspiracy of silence might lead you to conclude that the death of a baby prior to birth is an unusual event—something that happens only in a very small number of pregnancies. Of course, nothing could be further from the truth. Miscarriage and stillbirth are actually far more common than most people realize. Consider these facts:

- Between 20 percent and 25 percent of pregnancies end in miscarriage, ectopic pregnancy, molar pregnancy, or stillbirth. This means that, each year, about one million American women experience the heartache of having a baby die prior to birth.

- Miscarriages (the death of a baby before the twentieth week of pregnancy) are the most common type of pregnancy loss, occurring in between 15 percent and 20 percent of confirmed pregnancies.
- Ectopic pregnancies (pregnancies in which the fertilized egg implants somewhere other than inside the uterus—typically the fallopian tube) occur in one out of every sixty pregnancies in the United States (between 1 percent and 2 percent of pregnancies).
- Stillbirth (the death of a baby after twenty weeks gestation but prior to birth) occurs in about 1 percent of pregnancies.
- Molar pregnancies (pregnancies that result in the growth of abnormal tissue rather than a healthy placenta and embryo) occur in one out of every fifteen hundred to two thousand pregnancies in the United States.

Because it can be so difficult to uncover the facts, you may still have a lot of unanswered questions about your baby's death—questions that may be causing you a great deal of anxiety. You may be wondering what caused your baby to die and what your odds are of ending up with a healthy baby the next time around. Those are the types of issues that will be discussed in the next three chapters. This chapter will zero in on the factors believed responsible for ectopic pregnancies, molar pregnancies, and miscarriages; then we will look at what—if anything—can be done to reduce your chances having another baby die during early pregnancy. Then, in the following two chapters, we'll consider the major causes of stillbirth and infant death.

ECTOPIC PREGNANCY

In an ectopic pregnancy, the fertilized egg implants somewhere other than in the uterus. In 95 percent of ectopic pregnancies, the fertilized egg implants in one of the fallopian tubes (the narrow passageways that are designed to transport the egg from the ovary to the uterus). In the remaining 5 percent of cases, the fertilized egg implants itself in the abdominal cavity, the ovaries, or the cervix.

An ectopic pregnancy is described as being unruptured (or subacute) if it is detected before a tubal rupture, and ruptured (or acute) if it isn't detected until after the tube has burst, causing pain, internal bleeding, and shock.

The Symptoms of an Ectopic Pregnancy

The following are the most common symptoms of an ectopic pregnancy:

- Bleeding, especially bleeding that is either lighter or heavier than what you would normally experience during a menstrual period.
- Abdominal pain, either sudden and acute or sharp and aching, and typically felt more on one side of the abdomen than the other.
- Shoulder pain, caused by the pooling of blood from the ruptured tube in the abdomen—something that can irritate the diaphragm, triggering pain that is felt in the shoulder area.
- Weakness, dizziness, fainting, and/or a weak but rapid pulse, caused by substantial blood loss.

An unruptured ectopic pregnancy is characterized by vaginal bleeding; pain on one side of the abdomen; pain in the shoulder region (if there has been internal bleeding); and fainting (if the blood loss has been substantial). It can be diagnosed through a blood test that measures the level of human chorionic gonadotropin (hCG), an ultrasound, or both. If the condition is detected early enough, it may respond to medication or, if surgery is required, it may be possible to save the tube.

A ruptured ectopic pregnancy is characterized by pain and shock, a weak but rapid pulse, paleness, and falling blood pressure. A blood transfusion as well as removal of the tube may be required.

Some ectopic pregnancies are detected relatively early in pregnancy, while others aren't detected until much later. If an ectopic pregnancy implants in the narrowest part of the fallopian tube, it will become symptomatic and, if untreated, rupture very early—typically within six to eight weeks of implantation. If, however, it implants in a wider section of the fallopian tube, the tube may be able to retain the growing pregnancy for up to fourteen weeks. Either way, it usually won't grow much larger than the size of a walnut.

While it's not possible for a tubal ectopic pregnancy to develop much beyond the fourteenth week of pregnancy without causing a tubal rupture, an abdominal ectopic may, in rare cases, continue until the fetus reaches viability. While this occurs in between 5 percent and 25 percent of abdominal ectopic pregnancies, these types of pregnancies are almost always terminated because of the very high risk of maternal hemorrhage and because of the poor prognosis for the baby. These babies are born extremely premature, and about 20 percent to 40 percent of fetuses who make it past twenty weeks have pressure deformities caused by inadequate levels of amniotic fluid.

An ectopic pregnancy can pose a significant threat to a woman's health, and is one of leading causes of infertility. It can also put a woman's life at risk if the tube ruptures and causes massive internal bleeding.

Some women face a higher-than-average risk of experiencing an ectopic pregnancy. The following are the key risk factors for ectopic pregnancy:

- *Previous tubal infections (medically known as salpingitis).* These are caused by pelvic inflammatory disease, sexually transmitted diseases such as chlamydia and gonorrhea, postpartum endometritis, or post-abortion infections. Tubal infections such as these can damage the mucus surface of the fallopian tube, causing adhesions that can obstruct the movement of the fertilized egg as it attempts to make its way through the tube and into the uterine cavity. Women with a history of pelvic inflammatory disease have a one in four chance of experiencing an ectopic pregnancy if they become pregnant.
- *Previous tubal or pelvic surgery.* Tubal adhesions may be caused by irritation to the mucus surface of the tube. This can happen if blood entered the fallopian tubes during surgery to treat infertility, an infection, or a previous ectopic pregnancy; during an appendectomy; or during a cesarean delivery.
- *A structural abnormality in the fallopian tube.* Women who are born with certain types of fallopian tube abnormalities are at higher-than-average risk of experiencing an ectopic pregnancy than other women.
- *Abnormal hormone levels.* Inadequate levels of progesterone can impair the fertilized egg's ability to make its way through the fallopian tube by weakening the tube's propulsive force. This can prevent the fertilized egg from reaching its destination—the uterus—and cause the egg to implant in the fallopian tube instead. **Note:** Ovulation-stimulating drugs, such as human menopausal gonatropin or clomiphene citrate,

alter the hormonal balance, too, and can also interfere with the fallopian tube's ability to force the fertilized egg into the uterus.

- *Smoking.* Women who smoke more than thirty cigarettes per day are five times as likely to experience an ectopic pregnancy as other women. Scientists say that nicotine's effect on the hormone estrogen may interfere with the fallopian tube's ability to contract and propel the embryo toward the uterus.

- *Douching.* A study conducted by the Centers for Disease Control and Emory University of Atlanta, Georgia, revealed that douching increases a woman's chances of experiencing an ectopic pregnancy.

- *Becoming pregnant with an intrauterine device (IUD) in place.* Approximately one in every two hundred IUD users will experience an ectopic pregnancy. Although IUDs do an excellent job of preventing intrauterine pregnancies, they aren't nearly as effective at protecting against ectopic pregnancies.

- *Becoming pregnant after a tubal ligation (sterilization).* While the vast majority of tubal ligations are successful (e.g., they serve as a permanent method of birth control), pregnancy does occur in a small number of cases. Women who become pregnant after a tubal ligation face significantly higher-than-average odds of experiencing an ectopic pregnancy. A recent study reported in the *New England Journal of Medicine* cited that an ectopic pregnancy rate of 7.3 per 1,000 procedures can be expected over a ten-year period.

- *A history of ectopic pregnancy.* A woman who has experienced an ectopic pregnancy in the past faces higher-than-average odds of experiencing another one in a future pregnancy (a 12 percent risk as opposed to the 1 percent risk faced by pregnant women in general). It's important to put these numbers in perspective, however. Even if you have experienced an ectopic pregnancy, you still have 88 percent odds of *not* experiencing another one the next time around.

MOLAR PREGNANCY

A molar pregnancy (also known in medical circles as a hydatidiform mole or as gestational trophoblastic disease) results in the growth of abnormal tissue rather than a healthy embryo. It is believed to be caused by some sort of genetic error that occurs at the very beginning of pregnancy.

In a complete molar pregnancy, no fetus develops—just thousands of fluid-filled cysts that can reach the size of grapes. (If the pregnancy were developing normally, these cells would eventually develop into a standard-sized placenta.) A partial-molar pregnancy has an abnormal fetus as well as thousands of these fluid-filled cysts. In very rare situations (about one in every 22,000 to 100,000 births) a normal twin may also be present and will continue to develop until the woman goes into extremely preterm labor.

In rare cases, a molar pregnancy will become cancerous. Fortunately, this type of cancer—choriocarcinoma—is almost always curable if it is detected right away. If it's not treated aggressively enough, however, it can spread to other parts of the body, including the lungs and brain. That's why women who have experienced a molar pregnancy need to have their hCG levels tested frequently to ensure that this type of cancer isn't developing. If test results are normal for six months to one year following a molar pregnancy, the woman and her partner may be given the go-ahead to try for another baby. (They need to postpone their next pregnancy because the rising hCG levels of a normal pregnancy would be difficult to distinguish from the rising levels of persistent gestational trophoblastic disease—the medical term for the cancerous form of this disease.)

In most cases, a molar pregnancy is spontaneously miscarried. In some cases, however, it is diagnosed only when a pregnant woman begins to experience some of the symptoms of molar pregnancy (See "The Signs and Symptoms of a Molar Pregnancy" following). Once a molar pregnancy has been diagnosed, it is terminated immediately and the womb is carefully emptied to ensure that no abnormal tissue is left behind.

The Signs and Symptoms of a Molar Pregnancy

The following are the most common signs and symptoms of a molar pregnancy:

- Vaginal bleeding during the first trimester
- A uterus that grows too quickly
- Enlarged ovaries (detected by ultrasound)
- Extremely high levels of hCG (detected through a blood test)
- Severe nausea, vomiting, and high blood pressure caused by unusually high hormone levels

The following are the key risk factors for molar pregnancy:

- *A previous molar pregnancy.* Women who have experienced one molar pregnancy have a 1.3 percent to 2.9 percent chance of experiencing another.
- *A family history of molar pregnancies.* Molar pregnancies tend to be more common in certain families than others, something that has led scientists to conclude that there may be a genetic link.
- *Being of Southeast Asian descent.* Molar pregnancies tend to be more common in women of Southeast Asian descent.

MISCARRIAGE

Miscarriage—the spontaneous death of an embryo or fetus before the twentieth week of pregnancy—is the most common type of pregnancy loss, occurring in between 15 percent and 20 percent of all confirmed pregnancies. (The medical term for miscarriage is "spontaneous abortion," but we've chosen to use the term "miscarriage" throughout this book because couples who have been through such a loss tend to find the term "spontaneous abortion" to be rather insensitive.) Researchers think that miscarriages are actually more common than pregnancies that result in the birth of a healthy baby. They suggest that between 50 percent and 75 percent of all pregnancies are lost, but the majority of these pregnancies are lost so early that a woman often isn't even aware that she was pregnant. Researchers estimate that 75 percent of miscarriages occur during the first eight weeks of gestation (e.g., anytime from two weeks to ten weeks after the first day of your last menstrual period).

While most women going through a miscarriage experience bleeding and other symptoms (see Symptoms of Miscarriage following), a woman may not realize her baby has died until her doctor or midwife is unable to detect a fetal heartbeat at her next prenatal checkup. (*Note:* An ultrasound can detect the fetal heartbeat as early as six weeks after the first day of your last menstrual period, but a doppler stethoscope won't pick up a fetal heartbeat until ten to twelve weeks, and a fetal stethoscope won't pick up a fetal heartbeat until eighteen to twenty weeks.) When the woman has no symptoms, this is medically known as a missed abortion (the baby has died, but has not been expelled from the mother's body). (See "How Miscarriages Are Classified" following for a list of other important miscarriage-related terms.)

Symptoms of Miscarriage

The following are the most common symptoms of miscarriage:
- Spotting or light bleeding that isn't accompanied by any pain (although not all first-trimester bleeding is necessarily an indication that you're having a miscarriage)
- Heavy or persistent bleeding—with or without clots—accompanied by abdominal pain, cramping, or pain in the lower back
- A gush of fluid from the vagina that is not accompanied by pain or bleeding (an indication that your membranes may have ruptured)
- The sudden disappearance of all pregnancy symptoms, such as morning sickness or breast tenderness.

How Miscarriages Are Classified

The medical profession uses the following terms to classify miscarriages:
- *Threatened abortion.* A term used to describe a situation in which miscarriage is possible, but not inevitable. A woman who is having a threatened abortion is probably experiencing vaginal bleeding and possibly some pain as well.
- *Inevitable abortion.* A term used to describe a situation in which the cervix has begun to dilate and the pregnancy will inevitably be lost.
- *Incomplete abortion.* A term used to describe a situation in which some of the products of conception (the medical world's term for the gestational sac, fetus, umbilical cord, and placenta) are left in the uterus after a woman has miscarried. In other words, the woman has experienced a partial miscarriage. A dilation and curettage (D&C) or suction curettage is usually performed to remove the remaining material.

- *Complete abortion.* A term used to describe a situation in which all of the products of conception are expelled from the uterus during a miscarriage.
- *Missed abortion.* A term used to describe a situation in which the pregnancy has been lost, but the fetus and the placenta have not been expelled from the uterus. Pregnancy symptoms begin to disappear, but because she hasn't experienced any of the typical symptoms of a miscarriage, the mother may not realize there is a problem until a doppler or ultrasound fails to detect the fetal heartbeat during a prenatal checkup. **Note:** Sometimes the term "blighted ovum" is used instead of "missed abortion," but "missed abortion" is the preferred term. "Blighted ovum" is both old-fashioned and medically inaccurate—to say nothing of offensive!
- *Early miscarriage.* A term used to describe a miscarriage that occurs before twelve weeks gestation.
- *Late miscarriage.* A term used to describe a miscarriage that occurs between twelve and twenty weeks gestation. (Sometimes miscarriages at this stage of pregnancy are referred to as second-trimester losses, or fetal deaths.)

THE CAUSES OF MISCARRIAGE

Even though miscarriage is the most common type of pregnancy loss, occurring in 15 percent to 20 percent of all confirmed pregnancies, medical science still doesn't know a lot about the causes and possible treatments for miscarriage. In this section, we'll look at what pieces of the miscarriage puzzle scientists have managed to put together in recent years.

Chromosomal abnormalities The leading cause of miscarriage is chromosomal abnormalities. In fact, recent studies have indicated that as many as 60 percent of miscarriages are caused by a nonrecurring genetic abnormality in the developing embryo. These randomly occurring genetic errors happen prior to conception (if there is a defective egg or sperm cell) or during the earliest stages of pregnancy, when cell division is occurring.

Because there's little room for error at this stage of human development, most of these pregnancies are miscarried. (If miscarriages didn't occur, the number of babies born with congenital anomalies would increase significantly, jumping from the present rate of 2 percent to 3 percent of live-born infants to a considerably higher 12 percent.)

Here's some good news for couples who have experienced a miscarriage of this type: Most miscarriages caused by chromosomal abnormalities are random occurrences. They are therefore less likely to recur during subsequent pregnancies than other causes of miscarriage. (If, however, you have repeated miscarriage of this type, an underlying genetic problem could be to blame. Such a problem could potentially recur in subsequent pregnancies.)

Maternal disease   Certain types of medical conditions are associated with higher-than-average miscarriage rates. They include:

- Immune system disorders, such as lupus
- Congenital heart disease
- Severe kidney disease
- Uncontrolled diabetes
- Thyroid disease
- Intrauterine infection

We will discuss these and other types of maternal diseases in Chapter 3.

Hormonal imbalances   A hormonal imbalance can cause a woman to miscarry. If, for example, the corpus luteum that develops during the early weeks of pregnancy fails to secrete enough progesterone to maintain the endometrial lining of the uterus and to sustain the pregnancy, a woman may miscarry. (*Note:* The corpus luteum—or "yellow body"—is the structure that is created in the ovary when the egg is released from the follicle. Its purpose is to secrete progesterone, a substance that is vital to sustaining a pregnancy.) This condition, which is known as a luteal phase defect, is believed to be responsible for as many as one-third of recurrent pregnancy losses.

A luteal phase defect can be diagnosed through testing—either by measuring progesterone levels in the blood or by doing an endometrial biopsy during the second half (or luteal phase) of the menstrual cycle. This test involves inserting a narrow catheter through the cervix and into the uterus so that a small sample of tissue can be scraped from the uterine lining.

If a luteal phase defect is diagnosed, progesterone suppositories or vaginal cream may be prescribed. They are started at the time of ovulation and continued until the tenth to twelfth week of gestation. (At this point in a pregnancy, the placenta will take over the task of producing adequate quantities of progesterone.) Some doctors also treat this condition by prescribing clomiphene citrate—a fertility drug that can assist with the manufacture of progesterone during those critical first few weeks of pregnancy.

Luteal phase defect isn't the only hormonal disorder that a pregnant woman needs to be concerned about, of course. Increasing evidence shows an association between a hormonal disorder known as polycystic ovarian syndrome (PCOS) and recurrent miscarriage. A recent British study showed that between 44 percent and 56 percent of patients experiencing recurrent miscarriage suffer from PCOS, which is characterized by irregular menstrual periods (or even the absense of menstrual periods altogether) as well as excessive hair growth. PCOS occurs in 6 percent to 10 percent of premenopausal women and is more common in overweight than normal-weight women. It is a proven cause of infertility. (See Chapter 8 for a more detailed discussion on infertility.)

Rhesus (Rh) disease   Rh incompatibility occurs when the mother's blood is Rh-negative and the father's is Rh-positive. This is a relatively common combination, given that 15 percent of the population is Rh-negative. If the baby also has Rh-positive blood and some of its blood cells get into the mother's bloodstream during pregnancy, the mother can become Rh-sensitized. (In other words, she can develop antibodies that may attack a baby's red blood cells, causing anemia and a series of potentially life-threatening problems, collectively known as Rh disease, in the current or any subsequent pregnancy).

Rh disease was once a leading cause of pregnancy loss, but it can usually be prevented by ensuring that an Rh-negative woman with an Rh-positive partner receives shots of Rh Immune Globulin (e.g., Rhogam®) following each delivery or miscarriage; whenever there is any sign or possibility of bleeding in the womb during pregnancy (e.g., after amnio-centesis and in the case of either placenta previa or a placental abruption); and during the twenty-eighth week of each pregnancy. (The Rh Immune Globulin helps to prevent a woman from producing antibodies to Rh-positive cells—something that could lead to problems in a future pregnancy.)

As amazing as Rh Immune Globulin is, it has two main weaknesses: It isn't capable of destroying existing antibodies, and it doesn't work for everyone.

If the Rh Immune Globulin shot isn't administered before the woman's body has the chance to start forming antibodies (generally within seventy-two hours of the episodes previously noted), she may develop anti-Rh antibodies. In such a case, her next pregnancy will have to be monitored very closely. A blood transfusion may be necessary for the baby before or after delivery in order to prevent severe anemia. If untreated, this ane-mia can lead to oxygen deprivation and heart failure which can result in either stillbirth or neonatal death. Also, the baby may need to be deliv-ered prematurely if it develops a life-threatening condition called hydrops fetalis, in which the baby becomes extremely swollen as a result of severe anemia and heart failure. Babies with severe hydrops fetalis may be still-born or die shortly after birth. Those who are less severely affected often respond to treatment, but the treatment (intrauterine blood transfusion) involves risks as well.

Immune system disorders   Immune system disorders are believed to be responsible for between 5 percent and 10 percent of recurrent miscar-riages. They occur when a pregnant woman's immune system—which has been carefully programmed to fight such foreign invaders as bacteria and viruses—makes a mistake and starts attacking normal cells in her body.

A condition known as antiphospholipid antibody syndrome (APA) is one of the most common of these types of immune system disorders. It occurs when the body mistakenly decides that phospholipids (the parts of a cell's membrane that function as a nerve insulator) are, in fact, foreign material. The antibodies that are produced in response to this perceived threat are believed to cause clots in the placental blood vessels—something that interrupts the flow of oxygen and nutrients from mother to baby.

Women with APA aren't just at higher risk of experiencing miscarriage: they're also more likely to experience fetal growth restriction (when the developing baby's growth lags behind what might be expected for a particular stage of pregnancy), preeclampsia (a potentially serious condition of pregnancy characterized by high blood pressure), and placental abruptions (the premature separation of the placenta from the uterine wall). All of these can lead to the death of the baby.

Fortunately, much can be done to treat APA. According to a study reported in the *British Medical Journal* (1997), the pregnancy loss rate for women with this condition who receive no form of treatment is 90 percent, women who take one baby aspirin a day before conception and during their next pregnancy have a 42 percent live birth rate; and women who are treated with both aspirin and heparin (a blood-thinning drug that prevents clots from forming in the placental blood vessels that supply nourishment to the fetus) have a 71 percent live birth rate. (Other studies have reported success rates of between 75 percent and 93 percent.) The only downside to treating this condition with heparin is that heparin use can lead to bone loss. That's why women who take heparin are advised to counter the effects of bone loss through exercise and by getting enough calcium and Vitamin D.

Not all cases of APA are treated this easily, unfortunately. Some women with this syndrome also require treatment with prednisone, a steroid that is believed to suppress the activity of antibodies. This treatment is controversial, however, because of the potential for side effects in both the baby and the mother.

Another possible course of treatment is intravenous immunoglobulin (IVIg), in which the mother is injected with donor antibodies, which function as decoys. These decoys distract the harmful antibodies, keeping them from wreaking havoc on the placenta. The key downfall to this treatment is its price: A pregnant woman can expect to pay between $10,000 and $30,000 for IVIg over the course of her pregnancy.

Allogeneic factors Some women develop antibodies to their partner's leukocytes (white blood cells), which can lead to miscarriage. This condition can sometimes be treated by immunizing a woman with paternal or third-party leukocytes, a technique that tricks the woman's body into producing the blocking antibodies that prevent her body from rejecting the developing baby.

Other causes　　Scientists have identified some other common causes of miscarriage as well:

- *Anatomical problems of the uterus and cervix.* Certain types of anatomical problems involving the uterus and the cervix can lead to miscarriage. Congenital uterine abnormalities are believed to be responsible for about 10 percent of recurrent miscarriages. Uterine adhesions or fibroids may interfere with implantation and lead to miscarriage. And an incompetent cervix (a grossly insensitive gynecological term that simply means that your cervix opens too early in pregnancy, leading to pregnancy loss) may open prematurely, leading to a second-trimester miscarriage.
- *Viral and bacterial infections.* Viral and bacterial infections are thought to play a role in miscarriage, although in many cases the cause-and-effect relationships are not totally clear.
- *Recreational drug and alcohol use.* Women who use recreational drugs or consume large quantities of alcohol during pregnancy are at increased risk of experiencing a miscarriage.
- *Exposure to harmful substances.* Exposure to certain types of harmful substances can increase your chances of experiencing a miscarriage. Substances that should be avoided include high-dose radiation, dangerous chemicals, such as those used by drycleaners or photofinishers, cytotoxic (chemotherapeutic) drugs, cocaine, alcohol, cigarette smoke, and moderate-to-heavy doses of caffeine (more than five cups a day, according to an article in the *New England Journal of Medicine*). Even something as apparently harmless as tap water may pose a possible threat to developing babies. A study reported in the medical journal *Epidemiology* revealed that women who drank more than five glasses of tap water per day that contained at least 75 micrograms per liter of trihalomethane were at increased risk of experiencing a miscarriage. (Trihalomethane—a substance that is formed when chlorine reacts with acids from plant matter—is believed to damage the placenta and the embryo.)
- *Increasing maternal age.* Your chances of experiencing a miscarriage increase as you grow older. While women in their twenties have just a 10 percent risk of experiencing a miscarriage during any given pregnancy, the risk for women in their forties is believed to be approximately 50 percent.

SOLVING THE PUZZLE OF RECURRENT MISCARRIAGE

The medical profession used to wait until a woman had experienced three consecutive losses before doing any type of testing to try to determine the cause. At that point, she was labeled a "habitual aborter"—a dreadful term that simply meant she had experienced repeated losses.

These days, the American College of Obstetricians and Gynecologists recommends such tests after a second consecutive loss—particularly if the woman in question is over the age of thirty-five. The reason for doing the test sooner rather than later is obvious: to minimize the number of times that a particular woman goes through the trauma of losing a baby. (It's good to see that the medical profession is starting to come around on this particular issue. As the comments in Chapter 1 indicated, many couples feel tremendously angry about being forced to endure a series of miscarriages before their losses are taken seriously and testing is commenced.)

If you've experienced two consecutive losses, you should have a complete preconception health workup done before you start trying to conceive again. (You'll find detailed information on preparing for pregnancy in Chapter 6.) Your doctor may want to conduct some tests to try to determine the reasons for your losses.

Tests Used to Determine the Causes of Recurrent Miscarriage

Your doctor may recommend one or more of the following types of tests to try to determine what's causing you to miscarry repeatedly.

TYPE OF TEST	PURPOSE
Blood tests	To detect any hormonal or immune system problems that could be causing you to miscarry.
Genetic tests involving you and your partner and/or chromosomal testing of tissue from a miscarriage	To determine if you or your partner are carriers of any genetic disorder that could be causing you to miscarry.
Genital tract cultures	To look for the presence of infection.

TYPE OF TEST	PURPOSE
Endometrial biopsy (the removal and analysis of a small sample of endometrial tissue)	To determine whether the endometrial tissue, which lines your uterus, is sufficiently hospitable to allow an embryo to implant and grow.
Hysterosalpingography (an X ray of the uterus and the fallopian tubes)	To look for blockages and other problems in the uterus and the fallopian tubes.
Hysteroscopy (an examination of the inside of the uterus using a telescopelike instrument that is inserted through the vagina and cervix)	To look for blockages and other problems in the uterus and the fallopian tubes. This test is generally performed if something unusual is picked up during a hysterosalpingography or sonohysterography.
Ultrasound and sonohysterography (imaging techniques that involve bouncing high-frequency sound waves off the reproductive organs to create a corresponding image on a computer screen)	To look for structural problems with the uterus and to detect fibroids or adhesions that could be causing you to miscarry.

Depending on what is discovered from these tests, your doctor may recommend one of the following courses of treatment:

- Surgery to remove large, grapefruit-sized fibroids or smaller fibroids that are located just under the uterine lining, or to correct any uterine abnormalities that have been identified. If a structural problem seems to be causing you to miscarry repeatedly, surgery will up your odds of taking home a live baby at the end of your next pregnancy to somewhere between 70 percent and 85 percent.
- The insertion of a stitch in your cervix (a procedure known as cerclage) to keep the cervix from opening prematurely. This will be recommended if you have been diagnosed with an incompetent cervix.
- A course of antibiotics to cure any infections that may be causing you to miscarry.

- Improved management of any chronic diseases, such as diabetes or lupus, that may be triggering your losses.
- Hormone therapy to correct any imbalances (e.g., a luteal phase defect or PCOS) that may be making it difficult for your body to sustain a pregnancy. The aim is to get your hormones back to their appropriate levels to create the most embryo-friendly uterine environment possible.
- Treatment for immune system problems, such as antiphospholipid antibody syndrome (APA), that may be causing you to miscarry. This may involve treatment with aspirin, heparin, prednisone, and even injections of antibodies.
- Treatment for allogeneic factors that may be causing you to miscarry. One experimental treatment involves injecting the female partner with leukocytes (white blood cells) from the male partner.

You'd think that with all these tests, it would be possible to determine the causes of all recurrent miscarriages. Unfortunately, that's simply not the case. For as many as 50 percent of couples, the causes of recurrent miscarriage remain unexplained.

Part of the problem, of course, is that a series of miscarriages may be caused by a series of different factors. For example, a woman's first miscarriage may have been caused by a random chromosomal abnormality, while her second may have been the result of an unknown cause.

Fortunately, the news is not all doom and gloom when it comes to recurrent miscarriages. Despite the fact that they have experienced losses in the past, couples who have a history of unexplained miscarriage have a 52 percent to 61 percent chance of giving birth to a live baby at the end of their next pregnancy. While these odds are considerably lower than the better than 75 percent odds enjoyed by couples with no history of pregnancy loss, they're still high enough to encourage a significant number of couples to pursue their dream of taking home a healthy baby.

3 *The Truth about Stillbirth*

WHILE MOST PREGNANT women tend to breathe a huge sigh of relief when the first trimester comes to a close, putting the peak risk period for miscarriage behind them, mothers who have experienced stillbirth realize that they're not necessarily out of the woods yet.

While stillbirth is far less common than miscarriage, it does occur in approximately 1 percent of pregnancies. It tends to be more common in women over the age of thirty-five and under the age of fifteen; in pregnancies that extend beyond the forty-second week; in multiple pregnancies; and in pregnancies involving a male fetus.

Stillbirth is typically diagnosed after a pregnant woman becomes concerned about an absence of fetal movement or when a heartbeat can't be picked up by doppler or ultrasound during a routine prenatal checkup.

While approximately 60 percent of stillbirths are unexplained, doctors have managed to identify eight key causes for the remaining 40 percent of stillbirths: chromosomal abnormalities; maternal health problems; infection; problems with the placenta; problems with the uterus; umbilical cord problems; complications resulting from a multiple pregnancy; and intrapartum death (fetal death that occurs during labor). See the following chart for details on tests that can be done to try to determine the cause of stillbirth. We will discuss these causes in this chapter.

Tests That Can Determine the Cause of Stillbirth

TYPE OF TEST	WHEN IT IS PERFORMED	WHAT INFORMATION IT CAN PROVIDE
Genetic amniocentesis	Prior to delivery	Cells obtained from the amniotic fluid can provide clues to the cause of death for up to two weeks following the death of the fetus; cells obtained from fetal tissue after the delivery are rarely able to provide this type of information.
Amniotic fluid culture	Prior to delivery	Samples of amniotic fluid can be tested for organisms such as cytomegalovirus and listeria.
Blood test	Prior to delivery	Blood tests can help to rule out the possibility that the stillbirth was caused by diabetes; syphilis; toxoplasmosis; human parvovirus; drugs such as cocaine; a feto-maternal hemorrhage (when fetal blood from the placenta enters the mother's bloodstream); or antibody problems.
Urine test	Prior to delivery	A urine test can help to identify any sources of infection that might have contributed to the stillbirth.
Culture and pathology examination of the placenta	After delivery	The placenta should be examined for signs of infection and/or abnormalities that might have caused the stillbirth. **Note:** This type of examination should be conducted by a placentologist or other expert in fetal/placental pathology, since he or she is likely to have more specialized

TYPE OF TEST	WHEN IT IS PERFORMED	WHAT INFORMATION IT CAN PROVIDE
		knowledge of this field than a general pathologist.
Autopsy	After delivery	A fetal autopsy can sometimes help to identify the cause of death. Unfortunately, deterioration of the fetus following death sometimes makes it difficult to obtain any useful information from an autopsy.
Photographs of the stillborn baby	After delivery	Photographs can be useful in diagnosing chromosomal abnormalities and other problems in the baby that was stillborn.

NOTE: Studies have shown that the cause of fetal death can be determined in 80 percent to 90 percent of cases if the battery of tests outlined in the previous table is performed before and after the delivery. This provides a rate of unexplained stillbirth of just 10 percent to 20 percent—a figure that is significantly lower than the 60 percent unexplained stillbirth figure, which is the generally accepted norm.

CHROMOSOMAL ABNORMALITIES

Chromosomal abnormalities are responsible for approximately 60 percent of miscarriages. They also play a significant role in stillbirth: Between 6 percent and 13 percent of stillborn babies as opposed to 2 percent to 3 percent of liveborn infants have chromosomal abnormalities. As the following table indicates, chromosomal abnormalities are an important factor in both stillbirths and neonatal deaths (deaths that occur during the first twenty-eight days of life).

Incidence of Chromosomal Abnormalities in Newborns vs. Babies Who Are Stillborn or Who Die Shortly After Birth

CHROMOSOMAL ANOMALY	INCIDENCE PER 1,000 NEWBORNS	INCIDENCE PER 1,000 STILLBORN BABIES OR BABIES WHO DIE SHORTLY AFTER BIRTH
Trisomy 21 (Down Syndrome)	1.2	7.0
Trisomy 18	1.0	18.0
Trisomy 13	0.1	5.0
Sex chromosome abnormalities	3.9	12.0
Balanced structural anomalies	1.9	3.5
Unbalanced structural anomalies	0.5	5.0

Adapted from *Williams Obstetrics,* nineteenth edition by F. Gary Cunningham, M.D.; Paul C. MacDonald, M.D.; Norman F. Gant, M.D.; Kenneth J. Leveno, M.D.; and Larry C. Gilstrap III, M.D. (Norwalk, Connecticut: Appleton and Lange, 1993).

MATERNAL HEALTH PROBLEMS

Certain types of medical conditions can increase a pregnant woman's chances of experiencing stillbirth. A pregnant woman may already have health problems when she becomes pregnant or she may develop health problems during pregnancy. The fact that a pregnant woman has one of these conditions doesn't necessarily mean that she will be unable to carry her baby to term, however; it simply means that her pregnancy will need to be managed more carefully in order to increase her odds of giving birth to a healthy baby.

Here's a summary of the types of maternal health conditions that are most often associated with stillbirth.

Diabetes   Diabetes is one of the most common medical complications of pregnancy. In fact, studies have shown that approximately 2 percent to 3 percent of pregnancies are complicated by diabetes. While 90
percent of these cases involve gestational diabetes, approximately 10 percent of pregnant diabetics were diabetic before pregnancy.

During pregnancy, the amount of glucose in the blood stream increases naturally. This poses problems for diabetic mothers and their babies. Unlike glucose, insulin cannot cross the placenta to help to bring the
baby's blood sugar levels down to normal range. The baby's pancreas
gland responds by producing high levels of insulin—something that can
stimulate growth and cause the baby to become very large. Larger babies
require greater quantities of oxygen and nutrients than smaller babies. If
the placenta is unable to meet the baby's needs in these areas, the baby
may be stillborn.

Some additional factors can explain why babies of diabetic mothers are
more likely to be stillborn. These babies tend to be "large for dates"
(greater than the ninetieth percentile for weight for their gestational age),
putting them at greater risk for birth-related trauma including shoulder
dystocia (when the shoulders are too wide to allow for a nontraumatic
vaginal delivery) and asphyxia (suffocation). They also tend to have im-
mature lungs because elevated blood sugar levels appear to interfere with
the normal maturation of the lungs. Pregnant women with diabetes are
more likely to develop urinary tract infections (which, if left untreated, can
cause infections in the developing baby and preterm labor), pregnancy-
induced hypertension, and polyhydramnios (a condition in which there is
an excessive amount of amniotic fluid). Finally, babies born to mothers
with uncontrolled or poorly controlled diabetes are four times more likely
to have congenital abnormalities—something that increases their chances
of being stillborn. This may be due to the effects of high blood-glucose levels during the period of organ formation in the early weeks of pregnancy.

Common fetal anomalies in infants born to diabetic mothers include
skeletal and central nervous system defects, congenital cardiac anomalies,
gastrointestinal malformations, and congenital renal anomalies. These
anomalies are directly related to diabetes control during the three-month
period leading up to conception and the first two months of pregnancy.

Epilepsy   Pregnant women with epilepsy face a higher-than-average
risk of losing babies through miscarriage and stillbirth, and of giving birth

to babies with congenital defects. Some of these risks are particularly high for mothers who take anticonvulsant drugs. Unfortunately, many epileptic mothers have no choice but to continue to take these drugs during pregnancy: The risk to the baby may actually be greater if a pregnant woman stops taking the drugs and starts experiencing severe seizures. A baby who is deprived of oxygen during severe epileptic fits may be miscarried or stillborn. While the most common side effects of these drugs are poor fetal growth, cleft lip, and cleft palate, in rare cases congenital heart defects and other more serious (or even fatal) developmental abnormalities may result.

If you have already had a stillborn baby and you are epileptic, you should talk with your doctor about the best course of action for treating your condition during your next pregnancy. It may be possible to switch from your current "cocktail" of epilepsy medications to a relatively low dose of a single medication—something that may help to increase your chances of having a healthy baby.

High blood pressure (hypertension)   High blood pressure puts an added strain on a pregnant woman's heart, arteries, and kidneys—all of which are already operating at increased capacity in order to meet the needs of the developing baby. High blood pressure can cause the blood vessels supplying the placenta to narrow and become constricted—something that can lead to a condition known as placental insufficiency, which basically means that the placenta isn't capable of meeting the baby's needs for nutrients and oxygen. In severe cases, the baby will be stillborn.

If high blood pressure during a previous pregnancy contributed to the death of a baby, your caregiver may recommend both bed rest and the use of antihypertensive drugs during your next pregnancy. If your blood pressure is extremely high (160/105) or your condition is complicated by either kidney disease or heart disease, your doctor may recommend that you reconsider your plans to attempt another pregnancy, due to the potential of life-threatening risks that might affect you and your baby.

Note: Please see the related section on preeclampsia in this chapter. Women who have had problems with high blood pressure in the past are at increased risk of developing preeclampsia.

Heart disease   Between 0.5 percent and 2 percent of pregnant women have cardiac disease—something that can increase their odds of experiencing miscarriage or stillbirth, or of giving birth to a premature infant. During pregnancy, the amount of blood being pumped by the body increases significantly. By the start of the third trimester, a pregnant woman's body is pumping 45 percent more blood a day than it was before she became pregnant. If a woman already has problems with her circulatory system, uterine blood flow may be severely reduced, something that can lead to fetal growth restriction or pregnancy loss, or that may necessitate the immediate delivery of a premature baby. While women with mitral valve prolapse (a disorder in which the heart valve clicks and murmurs) don't face any significant risk during pregnancy, women with more serious types of heart problems face significantly higher fetal and maternal mortality rates.

Kidney disease   Women with a history of kidney disease face an increased risk of miscarriage, stillbirth, and of giving birth to a premature infant. They may develop high blood pressure during pregnancy, something that can cause damage to the placenta and either injure the baby or result in stillbirth. They are also at increased risk of developing kidney infections—something that can trigger premature labor or lead to an infection of the fetal membranes. If the pregnant woman's kidneys are unable to cope with the added strain of pregnancy, it may be necessary to deliver the baby right away in order to save the mother's life.

Note: Kidney transplant patients who have had very little protein in their urine, normal blood pressure, and no evidence of kidney rejection over the past two to five years are considered to be good candidates for pregnancy.

Liver disease   While mildly to moderately severe liver disease doesn't appear to pose a particular risk to a pregnant woman or her baby, liver failure from severe viral hepatitis, drug toxicity, or acute fatty liver of pregnancy (a rare condition affecting one out of 10,000 to 15,000 pregnancies) can be associated with maternal and fetal death as well as prematurity and fetal distress during labor.

Another more common condition, intrahepatic cholestasis of pregnancy, affects about one in five hundred to a thousand pregnant women. It is characterized by a build-up of bile acids in the liver and bloodstream, associated with severe generalized itching. Some studies have found a disproportionately high rate of stillbirth, preterm labor, fetal distress, and postpartum hemorrhage in affected pregnancies. It is believed that close monitoring of these pregnancies and early delivery after fetal lung maturity is confirmed can minimize risks to mother and baby. Researchers at the University of Birmingham in England believe that the disorder is underdiagnosed and may actually be responsible for as many as 4 percent to 5 percent of unexplained stillbirths.

Lung disease   According to the U.S. Department of Health and Human Services, approximately 1 percent of pregnant women have chronic asthma and another 1 percent will develop the condition during pregnancy. Women with severe asthma face increased risks of miscarriage, preterm labor, and of giving birth to a low birthweight baby (e.g., a baby under five-and-a-half-pounds) or an infant with neonatal hypoxia (low oxygen levels). Also, it's dangerous for any woman to develop pneumonia during pregnancy, since a pregnant woman's respiratory system is already working extra hard to meet the needs of both her and her growing baby.

Parathyroid disease   The parathyroid—which is situated behind the thyroid gland—plays a key role in regulating calcium levels in the body. Women with too much parathyroid hormone—a condition known as hyperparathyroidism—are at increased risk of experiencing a stillbirth or neonatal death or of giving birth to a baby with tetany (severe muscle spasms and paralysis caused by inadequate levels of calcium). Fortunately, this condition is rare in pregnancy.

Sickle-cell disease   Sickle-cell disease is an inherited blood disorder that affects people of African, Caribbean, and Eastern Mediterranean descent. It affects the hemoglobin in the red blood cells, something that can interfere with blood flow to the placenta. The baby may die because of a lack of oxygen and nutrients. Pregnant women with sickle-cell disease are also more prone to infection and more likely to develop pregnancy-induced hypertension than pregnant women who do not have the disease. If your last baby was stillborn due to complications resulting from sickle-cell anemia and you are thinking of attempting another pregnancy, your doctor may recommend that you have blood transfusions every few weeks after you conceive.

Systemic Lupus Erythematosus (Lupus)   Lupus is a chronic auto-immune disease in which the body's immune system attacks its own connective tissue and organs. Women with lupus face a higher-than-average risk of both miscarriage and stillbirth, because, researchers believe, they are likely to have high levels of an antibody called anticardiolipin, a substance that results in blood clotting and that can cause clots to form in the blood vessels leading to the placenta. Women with lupus are also at risk of experiencing a variety of pregnancy-related complications, including preeclampsia, HELLP syndrome (a potentially life-threatening form of preeclampsia that is characterized by hemolysis, the destruction of red blood cells; elevated liver enzymes; and low platelets), and preterm labor. Most doctors suggest that women with lupus postpone pregnancy if their disease is active and affecting the heart, lungs, or kidneys.

Preeclampsia (toxemia)   Approximately 6 percent to 8 percent of pregnant women develop a condition known as preeclampsia. The symptoms of this condition—which tend to develop during the last half of pregnancy—include swollen hands and feet, sudden weight gain, high blood pressure (140/90 or higher), increased protein in the urine, and headaches. It's most likely to occur in women under the age of nineteen or over the age of forty, first-time mothers, women who are carrying multiples, women with certain types of pregnancy complications (e.g., Rh incompatibility or molar pregnancy), and women with chronic high blood pressure, diabetes, kidney disease, or a family history of preeclampsia. The condition can develop into eclampsia—a life-threatening condition that occurs in approximately one in 2,300 pregnancies.

Note: You will find more detailed information on many of these medical conditions in Chapter 13.

INFECTION DURING PREGNANCY

Certain types of infections can cross the placenta and cause harm to the developing baby, either by causing stillbirth or by triggering labor before a baby is ready to be born. Here are the types of infections that are most commonly associated with the death of a baby prior to or shortly after birth:

Cytomegalovirus (CMV)   Cytomegalovirus is a virus that is transmitted through casual human contact. In most cases, it doesn't have any lasting effects on the developing baby, but in some cases it can result in a severe handicap, stillbirth, or neonatal death. It is most likely to cause a problem if a woman contracts CMV for the first time when she is pregnant; it is less likely to cross the placenta during subsequent pregnancies. There is no vaccine or treatment available for CMV yet.

Human parvovirus B19 (Fifth disease)   Human parvovirus is an infection common in children. While it is relatively harmless when contracted by children or adults—it is typically characterized by bright red cheeks, low-grade fever, flat or raised rash on the arms and legs, headache, sore throat, and joint pain—it can cause severe anemia in the developing fetus by disrupting the production of red blood cells. This can lead to heart failure, miscarriage, or stillbirth.

Listeriosis   Listeria is a form of bacteria that is carried by approximately 5 percent of the population and that is most commonly contracted from food. If a mother contracts listeriosis during pregnancy, she may experience few, if any, symptoms or she may develop a severe illness that is characterized by a high fever and symptoms similar to food poisoning. Listeriosis can lead to miscarriage, stillbirth, or premature labor, or cause pneumonia, septicemia (a bacterial blood infection), and meningitis in a newborn baby.

Because of the potentially devastating effects of listeriosis, pregnant women are advised to avoid soft cheeses such as brie and Camembert, pate, and ready-cooked poultry, because these foods are most likely to carry the bacteria.

Note: Previous exposure to listeriosis may provide some measure of immunity against future exposure to the diseases, so if you have had a baby die because of listeriosis, you are unlikely to lose any more babies for the same reason.

Rubella (German measles)   Rubella is a relatively minor disease in children and adults, causing nothing more serious than a rash and a slight fever, but if it is contracted by a pregnant woman—particularly during the first trimester of pregnancy—it can be harmful, or even fatal, to the developing baby. Rubella is contracted through contact with an infected person. Because rubella is contagious for about two weeks, starting five to seven days before the rash shows up, you may not find out you were exposed to the disease until after the fact. That's why it's routine practice to ensure that you've got sufficient antibodies to the disease before you become pregnant. If you had rubella as a child, you're probably immune to the disease, but it's still a good idea to have your caregiver check your immunity to be sure. If it is determined that you are not immune to rubella, you should be vaccinated at least three months before you start trying to conceive again. (You should have a follow-up blood test done just to be sure that the vaccination worked.)

Toxoplasmosis   Toxoplasmosis is usually contracted by handling or eating raw or undercooked meat, or by coming into contact with cat feces. It is most dangerous if contracted during the first trimester of pregnancy, but exposure should be avoided at all times, since toxoplasmosis is known to cause hydrocephalus, eye problems, miscarriage, stillbirth, premature labor, and neonatal death. If you have had a baby die because of complications resulting from toxoplasmosis, you may have developed some immunity that will help to protect any future babies you carry.

Sexually transmitted diseases   Sexually transmitted diseases can be passed on to the developing baby during pregnancy or at the time of birth. Chlamydia, syphilis, and herpes are associated with higher-than-average rates of stillbirth as well as other complications such as preterm labor. Syphilis is also known to cause birth defects in the developing baby, including structural bone damage, nervous system problems, and lung, spleen, liver, and pancreatic failure. The risk of the fetus contracting HIV from an HIV-positive mother is approximately 30 percent to 40 percent, although recent studies have indicated that this risk can be reduced to approximately 8 percent if a woman takes the drug zidovudine during her pregnancy.

PROBLEMS WITH THE PLACENTA

The placenta is the developing baby's life support system during pregnancy. It carries oxygen, nutrients, and antibodies to the fetus; returns waste products to the mother for disposal; and produces hormones that help to maintain the pregnancy. Problems with the placenta are believed to be responsible for between 15 percent and 25 percent of all stillbirths and neonatal deaths.

Three major types of problems can arise with the placenta.

Placental insufficiency and placental failure   As their names imply, placental insufficiency and placental failure mean the placenta is unable to meet the baby's needs for nutrients and oxygen. These conditions are more likely to occur during a first pregnancy than in subsequent pregnancies. They can occur if the placenta hasn't developed properly, if it isn't functioning properly, if it fails to keep growing as the baby grows, or if the pregnant woman is experiencing high blood pressure or other diseases that interfere with the operation of her circulatory system. These conditions are most likely to occur after the twenty-eighth week of pregnancy, a time when the baby's growth is particularly rapid and his need for oxygen and nutrients is particularly high. Unfortunately, there is often little warning that something is going wrong.

Still, if you have previously had a baby die as a result of placental insufficiency or placental failure, your doctor may want to follow your next pregnancy more carefully. More frequent ultrasounds may be ordered and blood flow studies that measure the flow of blood through the umbilical cord and the placenta may be conducted as well as regular fetal heart rate monitoring (nonstress testing).

Placental abruption   A placental abruption occurs when the placenta becomes partially or wholly separated from the wall of the uterus as a result of bleeding between the placenta and the uterine wall, reducing or cutting off the supply of nutrients and oxygen to the baby. Placental abruptions occur in one in 150 pregnancies. They are most likely to occur in mothers who have had two or more children, who have pregnancy-induced or chronic high blood pressure, who have experienced a previous abruption, who experience trauma to the abdomen during pregnancy, who smoke (a factor that is responsible for 40 percent of placental abruptions), who use cocaine, or whose membranes rupture prematurely.

A partial abruption can cause bleeding on and off during pregnancy. A full abruption is a medical emergency that can put the life of both mother and baby at risk. If you have experienced an abruption during a previous pregnancy, you face one in eight odds of it happening again (as opposed to the one and two hundred odds faced by any pregnant woman). Unfortunately, there is usually no way to predict an abruption ahead of time, even with careful monitoring.

Placenta previa   Placenta previa occurs in one in two hundred pregnancies and is more common in women who have had several children. It happens when the placenta implants low in the womb, partially or fully blocking the cervix. As the lower portion of the uterus begins to stretch in late pregnancy, the placenta may begin to separate from the uterine wall, causing bleeding. The placenta may continue to separate from the wall of the uterus as the cervix opens, cutting off the supply of oxygen to the baby and exposing the mother to the risk of hemorrhaging.

Researchers have identified some risk factors for placenta previa: endometrial scarring from a previous episode of placenta previa; a history of abortion; a previous cesarean delivery; having given birth a large number of times before; having closely-spaced pregnancies; having such medical conditions as high blood pressure, diabetes, and uterine fibroids; carrying multiples; being a smoker or a recreational drug user; and being over forty. If you have had a baby die as a result of placenta previa, your caregiver will likely perform an ultrasound during your next pregnancy to confirm the placenta's location. If the ultrasound reveals that you have developed placenta previa again, a cesarean will likely be scheduled at thirty-seven weeks of pregnancy (generally after confirming maturity of the baby's lungs through amniocentesis).

PROBLEMS WITH THE UTERUS

Problems with the uterus can also lead to a baby's death. In some cases, they cause a woman to go into premature labor, something that may result in the birth of a baby who is too young to survive. (We'll discuss this issue in greater detail in Chapter 4.) Some of these babies die prior to or during labor; others die shortly after the birth.

There are three major types of uterine-related problems.

Incompetent cervix   Incompetent cervix—the premature opening of the tight ring of muscle and connective tissue between the vagina and the uterus—is responsible for approximately 15 percent of second-trimester deaths. (If these deaths occur before the twentieth week of pregnancy, they are classified as miscarriages; if they occur after that point, they are classified as stillbirths.) The peak risk period for losses due to an incompetent cervix is sixteen to twenty-four weeks of pregnancy. A woman is more likely to have problems with an incompetent cervix if: she has had a number of previous miscarriages and D&Cs (because repeated dilation of the cervix can weaken the muscles and connective tissue fibers and cause them to lose some of their elasticity); she has had multiple second-trimester abortions, including pregnancy terminations; she has experienced a difficult forceps delivery in the past or the rapid delivery of a large baby; she is carrying multiples (the added weight can cause the cervix to open prematurely); she had a cone biopsy performed to remove cancerous or precancerous cells in the cervix; her cervix was affected by some sort of congenital anomaly; and her mother took an antimiscarriage drug called diethylstilbestrol (DES) during pregnancy. (DES was subsequently found to cause uterine defects in some daughters of women who took the drug.)

The first symptom of an incompetent cervix is generally a premature rupture of the membranes. This may be accompanied by some bleeding. The woman then experiences a short and relatively painless delivery.

If you have had a previous baby die as a result of incompetent cervix, your doctor will examine you early in your next pregnancy to see if the cervix is beginning to dilate or thin. Somewhere between fourteen and sixteen weeks of pregnancy, a cerclage (stitch) will be inserted at the upper end of your cervix to try to hold the cervix closed until the baby is ready to be born. (You will be put under a general or spinal anesthetic while the cerclage is being inserted.) The procedure is relatively simple: your doctor will probably prescribe bed rest and some medications to help prevent contractions and infection from becoming a problem. The stitch may be left in place permanently if you're planning to have a cesarean section. (The presence of a stitch in your cervix won't prevent you from conceiving any subsequent babies.) If you're planning to have a vaginal delivery, the stitch will be removed before or during early labor. (You won't be allowed to labor for long with the stitch in place because it may tear your cervix.) The success rate for cerclage is somewhere between 85 percent and 90 percent.

Fibroids Fibroids are noncancerous growths of smooth muscle tissue that occur in the wall of the uterus. They can be as small as a pea or as large as an orange or grapefruit. They are extremely common, affecting approximately 20 percent of premenopausal women, and often don't cause any problems during pregnancy. In some cases, however—particularly if there are a lot of fibroids or the fibroids are particularly large—they can lead to pregnancy loss. Because the high levels of estrogen during pregnancy can cause fibroids to grow rapidly, they can distort the inside of the uterus, preventing proper implantation of the embryo, interfering with the blood supply to the developing baby, and/or causing a woman to go into premature labor. Fibroids are more common in older women and women of African and West Indian descent.

If you've had a baby die because of the quantity or size of the fibroids in your uterus, your doctor may recommend that you have surgery to remove your fibroids before attempting another pregnancy. There is a small risk that the scar tissue that results from this surgical procedure will weaken the wall of the uterus, something that could lead to a uterine rupture in a subsequent pregnancy. Fortunately, this risk is considered to be quite small, but it's something you and your doctor should talk about when you're deciding on a course of treatment.

Uterine abnormalities   Some women are born with uterine abnormalities that may make it difficult for them to carry a pregnancy to term. If, for example, a woman has a womb that is divided in half (a bicornate uterus) or almost completely divided in half (a septate uterus), there might not be enough room in the uterus for the baby to grow. This can lead to premature labor before the baby is old enough to survive. There is also an increased chance that the placenta will implant on a part of the uterus that has a poor blood supply, something that can cause placental insufficiency.

Uterine abnormalities are most likely to cause problems during the fourth to sixth months of pregnancy. Unfortunately, these abnormalities are often not detected prior to pregnancy. A mother with a history of second trimester losses may be sent for a hysterosalpingogram (HSG)—a special type of X ray that involves injecting dye into the uterus—prior to her next pregnancy. If the HSG reveals structural problems with the uterus, corrective surgery may be recommended.

Unfortunately, not all of these types of surgeries are successful. What's more, they may leave a large scar, which can prevent fertilized eggs from implanting in the uterus. There's also a small risk that the scar tissue could rupture during a subsequent pregnancy. Some doctors recommend that their patients attempt a subsequent pregnancy to see if the uterus will stretch the next time around, allowing the baby to grow until it is mature enough to survive in the outside world. If you decide to attempt a subsequent pregnancy without having surgery to correct your bicornate uterus or uterine septum, you'll need to plan for the possibility of a premature birth. This may mean hooking up with a high-risk pregnancy specialist and choosing to give birth in a hospital with state-of-the-art neonatal intensive care facilities.

UMBILICAL CORD PROBLEMS

The umbilical cord serves as a lifeline between the mother and baby during pregnancy. It carries oxygen and nutrients to and waste products away from the baby. If anything disrupts the flow of oxygen and nutrients to the baby, the baby will be miscarried or stillborn.

A normal umbilical cord is made up of two arteries plus a vein. While some healthy babies are born with a cord that has just one artery and one vein, this type of structure sometimes indicates a problem with the baby (e.g., a congenital defect that is incompatible with life). The arteries and the vein are encased in a thick jellylike substance known as Wharton's jelly. The role of the Wharton's jelly is to protect the blood vessels in the cord and prevent them from being compressed. Umbilical cords with too little Wharton's jelly are more prone to compression, twisting, and knotting—something that can lead to stillbirth.

The following are the most common types of umbilical cord problems resulting in stillbirth:

- *Two-vessel cords.* Normal umbilical cords have one vein and two arteries. In 1 percent of pregnancies, one of the arteries is missing—something that may indicate a problem with the baby. Two-vessel cords are more likely to be associated with intrauterine growth restriction and preterm delivery, and stillbirth is six times as likely to occur with a two-vessel cord than with a three-vessel cord.
- *Straight umbilical cords.* Straight umbilical cords (as opposed to healthy, telephone-cord-like umbilical cords) tend to have inadequate quantities of Wharton's jelly—the substance that helps to prevent compression and other types of cord accidents.
- *Abnormalities of cord insertion.* The umbilical cord is usually inserted at or near the center of the placenta. Sometimes it is inserted into the membranes (the large sac that is filled with amniotic fluid) rather than the placenta—something that is known as a velamentous insertion. While velamentous insertions are fairly common—they happen

in about 1 percent of pregnancies—they lead to stillbirth only in a small number of cases, usually due to the tearing of placental blood vessels when the membranes rupture.

- *Vasa previa.* Vasa previa is a rare condition that occurs when umbilical cord vessels from a velementous insertion cross the cervix. Because there is no Wharton's jelly to protect them, they are easily compressed or ruptured by the presenting part of the baby at the time when the membranes rupture, something that can lead to immediate fetal distress or death.

- *Prolapsed cord.* A prolapsed cord occurs when the umbilical cord slips into the vagina ahead of the baby during labor. This can happen if the baby's head is not fully engaged in the pelvis before the woman's membranes ruptured. A prolapsed cord is dangerous for two reasons: the cord can be compressed as the baby's head squeezes against the mother's pelvic bone during labor, and the baby's blood supply may be cut off if the umbilical cord's jellylike case comes into contact with air and begins to harden. Most cases of cord prolapse are detected by monitoring changes to the fetal heart rate during contractions. In most cases, an emergency cesarean section will be performed. Umbilical cord prolapse is more likely to occur during breech deliveries or when the umbilical cord is exceptionally long (more than the average length of 55 centimeters).

- *Umbilical cord knots.* An umbilical cord knot can occur as a baby moves around in the womb. True knots (as opposed to false knots, which are mere bunchings of blood vessels within the cord) occur in approximately 1 percent of pregnancies, and only cause problems for the baby only in approximately 6 percent of these cases. In these cases, the true knot interrupts the flow of oxygen to the baby, resulting in stillbirth. True knots are particularly common in monoamniotic twins (when twins share the same amniotic sac) and in pregnancies in which there is a particularly long umbilical cord.

- *Cord around the neck (nuchal cord).* It's not at all unusual for a healthy baby to be born with the umbilical cord wrapped around his neck. In an exceedingly small number of cases—particularly if the cord has been wrapped around the neck a number of times—a cord accident may occur, causing the death of the developing baby or fetal distress in labor. It's not possible to detect or prevent these types of cord accidents prior to birth.

- *Torsion of the umbilical cord.* It's not unusual for the umbilical cord to become a bit twisted as the baby moves around inside the womb, but in rare situations the twisting (or torsion) cuts off the flow of oxygen from the mother to the baby.
- *Cord strictures.* Cord strictures can occur when there is a shortage of Wharton's jelly at a particular point in the umbilical cord, resulting in an interruption to the flow of oxygen from the mother to the baby.
- *Amniotic band syndrome.* Amniotic bands (bands of constricting tissue that cut off the blood supply to all or part of the baby) often result in limb abnormalities in the developing baby, but if the bands occur on the umbilical cord, they can prevent oxygen from reaching the baby, resulting in death.

COMPLICATIONS RESULTING FROM A MULTIPLE PREGNANCY

Women who are carrying multiples are at increased risk of losing one or more of their babies. Although most pregnancy losses involving multiples occur during the first trimester of pregnancy, they can also occur in the second or third trimesters or shortly after birth.

Women carrying multiples can lose one or more of their babies due to placental abruptions, cord accidents (which are particularly common when two babies share the same amniotic sac), and twin-to-twin transfusion syndrome (a condition in which one baby grows at a faster rate than the other baby, something that can result in the death of one or both babies). They are also at increased risk of developing a variety of pregnancy-related complications—pregnancy-induced hypertension, preeclampsia, polyhydramnios (excessive amniotic fluid), intrauterine growth restriction, giving birth prematurely, and having a baby with birth defects.

Studies have shown that between 0.5 percent and 1 percent of multiple pregnancies result in the death of at least one baby. The incidence is even higher when two babies share the same amniotic sac.

INTRAPARTUM DEATH

Most stillborn babies die before labor begins, but a few die during labor. Fetal distress can occur if a baby isn't receiving an adequate supply of oxygen during labor. It is more likely to occur during a long labor, a labor in which there are excessively frequent contractions, when there are problems with the placenta or the umbilical cord, or when the baby is in fragile condition for other reasons (perhaps due to a congenital anomaly). The baby becomes deprived of oxygen, which leads to acidosis (an abnormally low blood pH), fetal heart rate abnormalities, and—if uncorrected—fetal death.

One of the key signs that a baby may be experiencing fetal distress is the presence of meconium in the amniotic fluid. When a baby is in distress, its body focuses on ensuring a steady flow of oxygen to the brain. As a result, muscles in other areas of the body relax. This can cause the baby's bowels to release meconium—the baby's first stool—into the amniotic fluid. Other signs of fetal distress are an unusually fast or slow heartbeat, decelerations in the heart rate that occur in certain relation to uterine contractions, or a decrease in the normal variability of the heart rate over time. Severe fetal distress can result in damage to or even the death of the baby.

Up until now, we have focused on the factors that can lead to the death of a baby prior to birth. In the next chapter, we will consider deaths that occur after birth—particularly those that occur during the neonatal period.

4 *The Facts About Infant Death*

WHILE THE MAJORITY of parents who give birth each year end up with healthy babies in their arms, not every birth leads to a happy ending. As hard as it may be to believe, given all the amazing breakthroughs in neonatal medicine that we've witnessed in recent decades, just under 1 percent of the nearly four million babies born in the United States each year—7.25 out of every 1,000 babies—don't live long enough to celebrate their first birthdays.

In this chapter, we will examine the most common causes of infant death and consider what, if anything, can be done to prevent these types of deaths.

WHAT CAN GO WRONG

Despite all the high-tech tools that medical science currently has at its disposal, there are still certain types of problems that can't be fixed. If a baby is born with serious abnormalities or a life-threatening health condition, or develops these types of problems during the first year of life, it may not be possible for even the most highly trained specialists to find a way to save the baby's life.

When you consider all the things that can go wrong during a baby's first year of life, the fact that so many babies are born healthy seems all the more miraculous. Appendix A summarizes the causes of the 28,045 infant deaths that were recorded in the United States during 1997, the most recent year for which comprehensive infant death data is available.

Causes of Death during the Neonatal Period

According to the National Center for Health Statistics, infant deaths are most likely to occur during the neonatal period (the first twenty-eight days of life). In 1997, 18,524 of the 28,045 infant deaths in the United States occurred during this period.

It's not difficult to figure out why the first few weeks of life are such a high-risk period for infants. After nine months of relying on its mother's body to keep it alive, a newborn baby suddenly finds itself having to rely on its own body systems. Most of the time, babies make the transition to life outside the womb remarkably well: Their lungs fill with air and their various body systems start functioning, just as they were designed to do. Things don't always go this smoothly, however; sometimes a baby is born with a serious birth defect or medical condition that leaves him or her ill-equipped to survive beyond the first hours or days of life.

As you can see from the following data, congenital anomalies (problems with the baby that are present at birth) are responsible for almost 25 percent of the 18,524 infant deaths during the neonatal period. Pregnancy- and birth-related complications, breathing problems, infections, and Sudden Infant Death Syndrome (SIDS) are responsible for the majority of other infant deaths that occur during these early weeks of life.

Ten Leading Causes of Infant Death during the First Twenty-eight Days of Life

Number and rate per 100,000 live births

	NUMBER	RATE
1. Congenital anomalies	4,476	115.3
2. Disorders relating to short gestation and unspecified low birthweight	3,867	99.6
3. Newborn affected by maternal complications of pregnancy	1,237	31.9
4. Respiratory distress syndrome	1,226	31.6
5. Newborn affected by complications of placenta, cord, and membranes	946	24.4
6. Infections specific to the perinatal period	737	19.0
7. Intrauterine hypoxia and birth asphyxia	422	10.9

8.	Neonatal hemorrhage	336	8.7
9.	Birth trauma	182	4.7
10.	Sudden Infant Death Syndrome	182	4.7

SOURCE: *National Vital Statistics Report,* vol. 47, no. 19, June 30, 1999.

Causes of Death during the Post-Neonatal Period

The risk of having a baby die drops considerably once a baby enters the post-neonatal period (from twenty-eight days through eleven months of age). SIDS is the most common cause of deaths of babies in this age group. Other significant causes of death during the post-neonatal period include congenital anomalies, accidents and adverse effects, and, to a lesser extent, pneumonia and influenza.

Ten Leading Causes of Infant Death between Twenty-eight Days and Eleven Months of Age

Number and rate per 100,000 live births

		NUMBER	RATE
1.	Sudden Infant Death Syndrome	2,809	72.4
2.	Congenital anomalies	1,702	17.9
3.	Accidents and adverse affects	678	17.5
4.	Pneumonia and influenza	324	8.3
5.	Homicide and legal intervention	281	7.2
6.	Septicemia	196	5.1
7.	Bronchitis and bronchiolitis	105	2.7
8.	Malignant neoplasms	82	2.1
9.	Meningitis	77	2.0
10.	Respiratory distress syndrome	75	1.9

SOURCE: *National Vital Statistics Report,* vol. 47, no. 19, June 30, 1999.

Now that we've talked about what types of problems are most likely to occur during the neonatal and post-neonatal period, let's look in greater detail at the causes of infant death.

CONGENITAL ANOMALIES

According to the National Center for Health Statistics, the leading cause of death during the first year of life is congenital anomalies. In fact, 6,178 of the 3,880,894 babies born in the United States in 1997 died as a result of a congenital anomaly. (See "Ten Leading Causes of Infant Death in 1997" following.) These anomalies include neural tube defects such as anencephaly, spina bifida, and hydrocephalus; heart and other circulatory system defects; problems with the respiratory, digestive, genitourinary, and musculoskeletal systems; and chromosomal anomalies such as Down's syndrome.

Ten Leading Causes of Infant Death in 1997

Number and rate per 100,000 live births

		NUMBER	RATE
1.	Congenital anomalies	6,178	159.2
2.	Preterm/low birthweight	3,925	101.1
3.	Sudden Infant Death Syndrome	2,991	77.1
4.	Respiratory Distress Syndrome	1,301	33.5
5.	Problems related to complications of pregnancy	1,244	32.1
6.	Complications of placenta, cord, and membrane	960	24.7
7.	Accidents	765	20.0
8.	Perinatal infections	777	19.7
9.	Pneumonia/influenza	421	11.6
10.	Intrauterine hypoxia and birth asphyxia	452	10.8

SOURCE: *National Vital Statistics Report,* vol. 47, no. 19, June 30, 1999.

Note: Approximately 3 percent of newborns are born with some type of congenital anomaly. The severity can range from minor imperfections that have little, if any, effect on the baby's health, to life-threatening problems. While some congenital anomalies are detected before birth through prenatal testing (e.g., AFP, ultrasound, amniocentesis, and CVS), not every pregnant woman knows ahead of time that she will be giving birth to a baby with a congenital anomaly.

Neural Tube Defects

The term "neural tube defect" is used to describe malformations of the spinal cord and the brain. (The spinal cord and the brain are collectively referred to as the "neural tube" when they first begin to form between fifteen and twenty-five days postconception.) Neural tube defects were responsible for the deaths of more than five hundred U.S. babies in 1997: 344 of these babies died as a result of anencephaly and other similar anomalies; 48 because of spina bifida; and 146 because of congenital hydrocephalus.

There are three basic types of neural tube defects:

- *Anencephaly.* Anencephaly occurs when the upper part of the brain and most of the lower part does not develop during the first few weeks of pregnancy. In some cases, the skull bones are also malformed and the top of the baby's head may be misshapen. Some anencephalic babies are miscarried and others are stillborn. Those who survive until delivery die within a few hours or days of birth.
- *Spina bifida.* Spina bifida occurs when the vertebrae in the spinal column fail to close properly around the spinal cord. In some cases, a portion of the spinal cord protrudes outside the body. This can result in paralysis below the point on the spine at which the defect occurs. If the spinal defect is high enough in the column, it will not be possible for the respiratory muscles to function.
- *Hydrocephaly.* Hydrocephaly occurs when there is a buildup of spinal fluid in the brain. The baby's head becomes enlarged because the pressure of the spinal fluid causes the brain tissues to swell and the soft bones of the skull are pushed out. Some hydrocephalic babies are miscarried, stillborn, or die shortly after birth, but others survive. Hydrocephalus is frequently found in babies with chromosome abnormalities or spina bifida and may be caused by infections such as toxoplasmosis. Bleeding in the brain in premature babies can also lead to hydrocephalus. In a small number of cases (particularly when there's a male fetus involved), there can be a genetic component to hydrocephalus.

Risk factors   Neural tube defects are more likely to occur when parents have a family history of the defect. They are more likely to occur in people of European and Scandinavian origin and less likely to occur in people of African or Afro-Caribbean origin.

Parents who have previously given birth to a baby with either spina bifida or anencephaly face one in twenty-five odds in each future pregnancy that the next baby will have one of these problems. Parents who have previously given birth to two babies with these types of neural tube defects face one in seven odds of a recurrence.

In most cases, parents who have given birth to a baby with hydrocephalus do not face a higher-than-average risk of having a hydrocephalic baby during their next pregnancy.

Prevention and treatment   Studies have shown that consuming adequate quantities of folic acid during the two to three months prior to conception and during pregnancy can reduce a couple's chances of giving birth to a baby with a neural tube defect by 50 percent to 70 percent. While all women of childbearing age are advised to consume at least 0.4 mg of folic acid per day, particularly if they are planning to conceive in the near future, mothers who have had a baby with a neural tube defect are advised to consume ten times that amount, or 4 mg per day.

If you have had one or more babies die because of a neural tube defect, you may wish to consider prenatal testing during your next pregnancy. Most severe neural tube defects can be detected prior to birth through alpha feto-protein testing (AFP), amniocentesis, and/or ultrasound. (See Chapter 11 for a detailed discussion of the pros and cons of prenatal testing.)

Heart and Other Circulatory System Anomalies

Congenital heart problems were responsible for the deaths of 1,760 U.S. babies in 1997.

The heart is a remarkably complex organ and one on which a newborn baby's very survival depends. It starts out as a hollow tube in the developing embryo, and then divides into two sides and folds over on itself twice.

Some babies with heart problems, such as hypoplastic left heart syndrome (HLHS), thrive during their time inside the uterus, but die within a few days of birth. This is because a baby's circulatory system functions differently inside the womb than after birth. A baby with serious heart problems may be ill-equipped to make the transition to life outside its mother's body.

There are a number of congenital heart defects, including the following:

- *Hypoplastic left-heart syndrome.* Hypoplastic left-heart syndrome is the most common type of fatal congenital heart condition. Babies with this problem have a very small and underdeveloped left ventricle. Consequently, very little oxygenated blood is able to pass from the lungs through the heart and out to the rest of the body. While a newborn with this condition initially appears to be healthy, the baby typically dies within one to two days after birth because he or she isn't receiving enough oxygen.
- *Transposition of the great arteries.* Transposition of the great arteries is another common congenital heart defect. It involves a transposition (or "reversal") of the pulmonary artery, which is responsible for carrying blood to the lungs, and the aorta, which carries oxygenated blood throughout the body. Since both the pulmonary artery and the aorta come out of the opposite side of the heart than what you would usually expect (the aorta comes off the left ventricle and the pulmonary artery comes off the right ventricle), the body is divided into two separate circulatory systems. Blood to and from the lungs flows into the left side of the heart, but oxygenated blood is unable to reach the baby's other organs. Sometimes a baby with this condition can be saved through emergency surgery, but often babies with transposition of the great arteries die shortly after birth.
- *Pulmonary valve atresia.* Pulmonary valve atresia (also known as hypoplastic right-heart syndrome) involves a blockage in the flow of blood to the baby's lungs.
- *Tricuspid atresia.* Tricuspid atresia is an anomaly in which there is no opening to allow blood to pass through the right side of the heart.
- *Fallot's tetralogy.* With Fallot's tetralogy, there is a hole in the baby's heart as well as a blockage that prevents the blood flow from reaching the baby's lungs.

Risk factors   Women who have previously given birth to a baby with a heart defect face 2 percent to 3 percent odds of giving birth to another baby with a heart defect. If the mother has heart disease herself, the odds of giving birth to a baby with a heart defect rises to 5 percent.

Prevention and treatment   The only types of congenital heart anomalies that can be prevented in subsequent pregnancies are those that have been caused by prenatal exposure to certain types of teratogenic substances (e.g., drugs that are known to cause heart defects in developing babies) or diseases. Other types of heart anomalies are unpreventable.

If you have previously given birth to a baby with a heart defect, your doctor may recommend that you go for a special type of ultrasound called a fetal echocardiogram. This test—given at approximately twenty-one weeks of pregnancy—can be used to detect heart problems in the developing baby.

Unfortunately, not all heart problems can be detected with a fetal echocardiogram. Some heart problems become evident only after a baby is born, when his or her circulatory system has fully kicked into gear. While surgery can help to correct some types of heart problems, some are inoperable or are associated with a host of other serious birth defects or chromosomal anomalies. What's more, some babies undergoing risky heart operations are too ill or too young to survive the rigors of surgery.

Other Congenital Problems

Infant deaths due to congenital anomalies involving the respiratory, digestive, genitourinary, and musculoskeletal systems aren't as common as those deaths caused by congenital anomalies involving the heart and circulatory system, but they are important to mention nonetheless, since they lead to a significant number of infant deaths each year. (See Appendix A.)

Some—but not all—of these anomalies can be diagnosed prior to birth and, in certain cases, potentially life-saving surgery may be performed on the fetus or newborn baby. For example, it may be possible to close the abdominal wall, to repair a diaphragmatic hernia, or to relieve a urinary tract obstruction, if the baby is born with these types of deformities.

Tragically, in some cases, the problems with the baby are too far-reaching to be corrected. Babies with Potter's syndrome, for example, are born without kidneys and with underdeveloped lungs. Ill-equipped for life outside the womb, these babies die from respiratory failure within one to two days of birth.

Chromosome Abnormalities

When everything goes according to plan, a developing baby ends up with cells that contain twenty-three pairs of two chromosomes each—a total of forty-six chromosomes. One chromosome in each pair is inherited from the mother and the other from the father. If things don't go as nature intended, however, the developing baby can end up with an abnormal number of chromosomes (e.g., forty-five, forty-seven, or sixty-nine) or with chromosomes that are defective (either incomplete or that may have extra pieces of chromosomal material attached to them).

Incidence of Chromosomal Abnormalities in Newborns

CHROMOSOMAL ABNORMALITY	APPROXIMATE INCIDENCE PER 1,000 BIRTHS
Autosomal Trisomies	
Trisomy 21	1.0
Trisomy 18	0.1
Trisomy 13	0.1
Total	**1.2**
Sex Chromosome Abnormalities	
Male	2.6
Female	1.3
Total	**3.9**
Structural Rearrangements	
Euploid (balanced)	1.9
Aneuploid (unbalanced)	0.5
TOTAL	**2.4**

Adapted from *Williams Obstetrics,* nineteenth edition, by Cunningham et al. Norwalk, Connecticut: Appleton and Lange, 1993.

Most babies with abnormal chromosomes are miscarried during the first few weeks of pregnancy. In fact, noted in Chapters 2 and 3, researchers believe that at least half of first-trimester miscarriages are caused by chromosomal abnormalities. Not all babies with severe chromosomal abnormalities are lost during early pregnancy, however. Some survive until the time of delivery, but die shortly after birth as a result of problems with the heart, kidneys, digestive system, or other organs.

The following are a few of the most common types of chromosomal disorders:

Autosomal Trisomies (when an extra non-sex chromosome is present)

- *Trisomy 13 (Patau's syndrome).* A baby with Trisomy 13 has an extra thirteenth chromosome. Trisomy 13 results in severe heart, intestinal, and urogenital abnormalities, and a severe mental handicap. Most babies with Trisomy 13 are miscarried or stillborn. The majority of those who do survive until after birth die during their first year of life. Trisomy 13 occurs in one in 10,000 newborns.

- *Trisomy 18 (Edwards' syndrome).* A baby with Trisomy 18 has an extra eighteenth chromosome. Trisomy 18 is characterized by heart and kidney defects and a severe mental handicap. Most babies with Trisomy 18 are miscarried or stillborn. The majority of those who survive until after birth die during their first year of life. Trisomy 18 occurs in one in 10,000 newborns.

- *Trisomy 21 (Down's syndrome).* A baby with Trisomy 21 (more commonly known as Down's syndrome) has an extra twenty-first chromosome. While Down's syndrome is generally not fatal, babies with Down's syndrome are more likely to have congenital defects of the heart, gastrointestinal system, and so on, and so may be at increased risk of dying as a result of these additional complications. Down's syndrome occurs in one in one thousand newborns.

Sex Chromosome Abnormalities. Sex chromosome anomalies are usually the result of an extra X or Y chromosome or a missing sex chromosome. An example of the former would include Klinefelter syndrome, in which a male infant has an extra X chromosome, causing infertility and often mild mental deficiency. However, only the latter, known as Turner syndrome, is associated with an increased rate of miscarriage. There is no increased risk of stillbirth or neonatal death with any of the common sex chromosome anomalies.

Structural Rearrangements. Structural abnormalities include deletions of chromosome parts and rearrangements of genes in abnormal sequences or locations within chromosomes. The effect of each of these abnormalities depends on the specific chromosome involved and how big the involved area is. In some cases, the pregnancy will continue normally; in other cases, miscarriage or stillbirth will result. Some of these abnormalities are inheritable and some arise spontaneously.

Risk factors The risk of giving birth to a baby with a chromosomal problem (particularly the trisomies) increases as a woman ages.

The Risk of Giving Birth to a Liveborn Child with Down's Syndrome or Another Chromosomal Anomaly

AGE OF MOTHER	RISK OF DOWN'S SYNDROME	TOTAL RISK FOR ALL CHROMOSOMAL ABNORMALITIES
20	1/1,667	1/526
21	1/1,667	1/526
22	1/1,429	1/500
23	1/1,429	1/500
24	1/1,250	1/476
25	1/1,250	1/476
26	1/1,176	1/455
27	1/1,111	1/455
28	1/1,053	1/435
29	1/1,000	1/417
30	1/952	1/384
31	1/909	1/384
32	1/769	1/323
33	1/625	1/286
34	1/500	1/238
35	1/385	1/192
36	1/294	1/156
37	1/227	1/127

AGE OF MOTHER	RISK OF DOWN'S SYNDROME	TOTAL RISK FOR ALL CHROMOSOMAL ABNORMALITIES
38	1/175	1/102
39	1/137	1/83
40	1/106	1/66
41	1/82	1/53
42	1/64	1/42
43	1/50	1/33
44	1/38	1/26
45	1/30	1/21
46	1/23	1/16
47	1/18	1/13
48	1/14	1/10
49	1/11	1/8

SOURCE: *Merck Manual*, sixteenth edition

As frightening as these numbers may initially appear to be, it's important to put them in perspective: The majority of mothers giving birth in their forties do deliver healthy babies. In fact, even a forty-five-year-old woman has excellent odds (95 percent) of giving birth to a chromosomally normal baby.

Age isn't the only risk factor when it comes to chromosomal abnormalities, however. Certain types of chromosomal problems run in families. Some people inherit the tendency to produce a large proportion of abnormal chromosomes. One particular type of condition—a balanced chromosomal translocation—occurs when a person produces the correct amount of genetic material, but this material is incorrectly distributed ("translocated") so that some chromosomes end up with too much genetic material while others end up with too little.

Prevention and treatment   While it's impossible to prevent chromosomal abnormalities, certain types of chromosomal problems can be detected prior to birth, thereby giving expectant parents the option of deciding whether they wish to terminate their pregnancy prematurely rather than carrying their baby to term. This is a subject that we'll return to in Chapter 11, when we talk about the pros and cons of prenatal testing.

Preterm/low Birthweight

Prematurity is another major cause of infant death. It was responsible for the deaths of 3,925 U.S. babies in 1997 alone. Unfortunately, prematurity is a growing problem: According to the National Center for Health Statistics, the number of babies being born prematurely has risen by more than 20 percent since 1981.

Approximately 7 percent of babies arrive prematurely, that is, before the end of the thirty-seventh week of pregnancy. These babies are at risk of experiencing such prematurity-related complications as respiratory distress syndrome (a subject that we'll discuss later in this chapter), bleeding of the fragile blood vessels in the brain, and infection.

Risk factors   Certain women are more likely to give birth prematurely than others. A woman is more likely to go into labor prematurely if:

- She is under the age of twenty or over the age of thirty-five
- She has had a cone biopsy (the removal of a cone-shaped portion of tissue from the cervix) performed on her cervix at some point in the past
- She is carrying more than one baby (labor typically starts at thirty-two to thirty-four weeks in a multiple pregnancy)
- The baby she is carrying has severe congenital anomalies
- She has experienced preterm premature rupture of the membranes (PPROM), placenta previa, or a placental abruption
- She has been diagnosed with an incompetent cervix, fibroids, uterine abnormalities, or polyhydramnios (excess amniotic fluid)
- She is a DES daughter (a woman whose mother took the antimiscarriage drug diethylstilbestrol during pregnancy)
- She has a urinary tract infection or other type of infection (with or without a fever)
- Her lifestyle is unhealthy (e.g., she eats poorly, is under a lot of stress, and/or smokes or uses illicit drugs)
- She has preexisting health conditions that put her at increased risk of

experiencing a premature birth (e.g., diabetes, kidney disease, or cardiovascular disease)

- She has history of premature birth (Mothers who have previously given birth to a premature baby have a 15 percent chance of giving birth to another baby prematurely—three times as high as a woman who has never given birth to a premature baby. After two premature deliveries, the risk climbs to 32 percent.).

Unfortunately, in at least of 50 percent of cases, the cause of preterm labor cannot be explained.

Prevention and treatment   While it isn't possible to prevent all cases of premature labor, you can increase your odds of carrying your baby to term by:

- Avoiding sexually transmitted organisms that are known or suspected to trigger premature labor (mycoplasma, ureaplasma, and the bacteria that cause bacterial vaginosis)
- Promptly seeking treatment for urinary tract infections
- Not allowing your temperature to go too high before you seek medical treatment for a fever (a high temperature at any point in pregnancy can cause your uterus to start contracting)
- Avoiding injuries and wearing seat belts properly
- Leading a healthy lifestyle during pregnancy (e.g., not smoking or taking illicit drugs).

Your doctor may decide to monitor your next pregnancy extra closely, relying on one or more of the following four tests that can help to predict whether you will go into premature labor again:

- *Bacterial vaginosis screening test.* Studies have shown that women who have bacterial vaginosis (a thin, milky discharge with a fishy odor that is caused by the presence of anaerobic bacteria in the vagina) are at increased risk of experiencing preterm labor, premature rupture of the membranes, and/or a preterm delivery.
- *Fetal fibronectin (fFN).* The fetal fibronectin test (fFN), which is performed at twenty-four to thirty-four weeks of pregnancy, is similar to

a pap smear. It can be performed on mothers whose membranes are still intact and whose cervixes have dilated no more than 3 cm.

- *Salivary estriol (SalEst).* The salivary estriol test is a saliva test. Performed between twenty-two and thirty-six weeks of pregnancy, it helps to rule out the possibility of premature labor in mothers who would otherwise be considered high risk (e.g., mothers who are carrying multiples or who have a history of preterm labor). It's highly accurate at predicting who won't go into labor prematurely, but not particularly accurate in pinpointing those who will.

- *Cervical length.* Your caregiver may order an ultrasound or manual examination to assess the length of your cervix, since mothers who have shorter-than-average cervixes are at increased risk of going into premature labor.

SUDDEN INFANT DEATH SYNDROME (SIDS)

Sudden Infant Death Syndrome (SIDS) is the name given to the sudden death of an infant that remains unexplained after a complete investigation. SIDS is the leading cause of death of infants between one month and one year of age, taking the lives of approximately one in one thousand liveborn infants. In 1997, it was responsible for the deaths of 2,991 U.S. babies.

Scientists are currently hard at work trying to unlock the SIDS mystery. Some researchers believe that a brain abnormality may play a role in SIDS—a theory that appears to be supported by a recent study that showed 70 percent of babies who die from SIDS have some sort of brain abnormality. Other researchers believe that circulatory system disorders, biochemical imbalances, metabolic problems, and/or an overactive immune system may be responsible for SIDS, too. Unfortunately, because there is still so little known about SIDS, parents who experience the heartbreak of having a baby die because of this mysterious syndrome are often left with more questions than answers.

Risk factors The risk factors for SIDS include prematurity (especially babies with birthweights of less than 4.4 lbs); being a multiple; abnormal or irregular breathing patterns in the newborn (particularly if the baby periodically goes for long stretches of time without breathing, a condition known as apnea); having a slight cold (one-third of infants who die of SIDS had a runny nose or slight cough two to three days prior to their deaths); maternal smoking or drug use during pregnancy (especially heroine, methadone, or cocaine use); and being born to parents who have previously lost a baby to SIDS.

Here are some additional risk factors that you need to know about:

- *Sex.* Male babies are more likely to die from SIDS than female babies.
- *Ethnicity.* African-American and Native-American babies are at higher risk of dying from SIDS than the babies of caucasians. (African-American babies are two to three times as likely to die from SIDS while Native-American babies are three times as likely to die from SIDS.)
- *Age.* The peak risk period for SIDS is between one and four months of age. The risk of having a baby die because of SIDS drops dramatically after the baby reaches six months of age and virtually disappears once the baby reaches one year of age.
- *Time of year.* SIDS is more common during the winter months than at other times of year.
- *A history of pregnancy complications.* Researchers at the Kaiser Foundation Research Institute in Oakland, California, have discovered that placental abruptions and placenta previa double a baby's risk of experiencing SIDS. They suspect that these problems with the placenta may affect the nervous system of the developing fetus, which may, in turn, predispose certain babies to SIDS.

Prevention and treatment   The number of SIDS cases has declined by 42 percent since the American Academy of Pediatrics initiated its Back to Sleep campaign in 1992. The campaign has been designed to stress the importance of placing babies to sleep on their backs or sides, not on their stomachs—the position that is associated with the greatest number of SIDS cases. (Wonder why infants who are allowed to sleep on their stomachs face an increased risk of SIDS? Researchers at the University of Sydney in Australia suspect that infants who are placed on their stomachs may have more difficulty swallowing. Infrequent swallowing may trigger a reflex that causes the heart to slow and breathing to stop when unswallowed fluid from the mouth or throat escapes into the breathing passage.)

While putting your baby to sleep in the safest possible position (on his back or side) is the most important thing you can do to reduce your baby's risk of experiencing SIDS, there are other important steps you can take to minimize the risk to your baby:

- Make sure that your baby's sleeping environment is safe. The sleeping surface should be firm rather than soft, and the crib, bassinet, or bed should be free of pillows and other soft bedding that could increase the risk of suffocation or cause excessive quantities of carbon dioxide to pool around your baby's head. (Some researchers believe that a lack of oxygen and/or an excessive carbon dioxide intake may be responsible for some SIDS cases. This can occur if a baby has a respiratory infection that hampers breathing or if a baby rebreathes exhaled air when the baby is sleeping on his or her stomach or under a blanket.)
- Don't smoke during pregnancy or allow anyone to smoke near your newborn baby. Second-hand smoke doubles a baby's chances of experiencing SIDS and babies whose mothers smoked during pregnancy are three times as likely to succumb to SIDS.
- Watch your caffeine intake during pregnancy. Researchers in New Zealand recently reported that babies whose mothers consumed large quantities of caffeine during pregnancy are twice as likely to experience SIDS. They discovered that pregnant women who consume four or more cups of coffee per day (400 mg of caffeine) place their babies at an increased risk of SIDS. The researchers theorize that caffeine's stimulant effect may leave the baby with "an inadequate respiratory drive"—something that may leave the baby unable to meet sudden demands for more oxygen. (*Note:* Not everyone believes that caffeine is a risk factor for SIDS, however. A recent Swedish study concluded that caffeine intake during pregnancy is not linked to an increased risk of SIDS, but that heavy postnatal alcohol consumption—five or more drinks per day—might be.)
- Don't allow your baby to become overheated. Studies have shown that infants who are overdressed are more susceptible to SIDS.
- Breastfeed your baby. Some studies have shown that babies who are breastfed face a lower risk of SIDS than bottlefed babies. Don't be afraid to offer your baby a pacifier, however; a recent British study confirmed that pacifier use is not linked to an increased risk of SIDS.
- Obtain adequate prenatal care. Babies who are born to mothers who

receive little or no prenatal care are more susceptible to SIDS than other babies.

RESPIRATORY DISTRESS SYNDROME (RDS)

Respiratory Distress Syndrome (RDS) is the term used to describe serious breathing problems experienced by newborn and premature babies. It was responsible for the deaths of 1,301 U.S. babies in 1997.

RDS is usually caused by a lack of surfactant—the greasy liquid that prevents the hollow sacs in the lungs from collapsing and sticking together each time the baby exhales. Premature babies are most likely to be born without adequate amounts of surfactant if their births are unexpected (in other words, if there is little advance warning that a premature birth may occur and it is therefore not possible to accelerate the maturation of the baby's lungs in utero by administering steroids).

Some of the specific types of problems that can be associated with RDS include:

- *Pneumonia.* Pneumonia is the term used to describe an infection of the tiny, hollow sacs in the lungs. It is usually caused by an infection contracted by the baby while in the womb, during delivery (especially if the baby inhales meconium), or on a ventilator (a particular risk if the baby is on the ventilator for a prolonged period of time). If a baby develops pneumonia, these sacs become filled with fluid—something that can prevent oxygen from passing through them and entering the baby's bloodstream.
- *Persistent pulmonary hypertension/persistent fetal circulation.* This condition occurs if the pressure in the blood vessels of the lungs doesn't drop after birth, thereby restricting the amount of blood that flows through them. It is most likely to occur in babies who have inhaled meconium, who have developed severe RDS and/or an acute infection, or who experienced a shortage of oxygen, at the time of delivery. A baby with this condition will become increasingly ill and short of oxygen, and will ultimately experience heart failure if he or she doesn't receive appropriate treatment.
- *Bronchopulmonary dysplasia.* Bronchopulmonary dysplasia is most likely to occur in babies who have been on ventilators for a prolonged pe-

riod of time. Babies with bronchopulmonary dysplasia have abnormally developed lungs and bronchial tubes. The lungs become scarred and less efficient at allowing oxygen to pass into the baby's bloodstream. The baby's heart must work extremely hard to ensure a sufficient flow of oxygen to the body's organs. This can lead to heart failure.

- *Intraventricular hemorrhage.* An intraventricular hemorrhage can occur if pressure changes during the delivery cause blood vessels in the brain to bleed into the central ventricles (the fluid-filled spaces) of the brain or the brain itself. It is most likely to be a problem in severely premature infants and in babies who were deprived of oxygen during the delivery. In 10 percent of cases, an intraventricular hemorrhage will lead to brain damage or death. It is a common complication of RDS and is also associated with hydrocephalus.

Babies who are born prematurely and who are believed to be at risk of RDS are typically given one or more of the following treatments:

- *Oxygen hood.* The baby is placed under an oxygen hood (so that oxygen—and sometimes warm, moist air—can be pumped into the baby's lungs).
- *Nasal cannula.* The baby is attached to a nasal cannula (a plastic tube that supplies prescribed amounts of controlled oxygen).
- *Continuous Positive Airway Pressure (CPAP).* The baby is given Continuous Positive Airway Pressure (CPAP) treatment (oxygen and moist air are forced through the pharynx, vocal cords, and trachea, and then into the lungs).
- *Respirator.* The baby is hooked up to a respirator so that the respirator can breathe for the baby until the baby is able to assume total responsibility for breathing on its own.
- *Synthetic surfactant.* The baby is treated with synthetic surfactant (a substance that is present in the lungs of full-term babies, but that is often missing from the lungs of premature babies). Synthetic surfactant can help to prevent or lessen certain complications, such as chronic lung disease, respirator dependence, and some retinal disease and hemorrhages, and can help to reduce the amount of time a baby spends in the hospital.

- *Liquid ventilation.* The baby is given liquid ventilation (fluids are pumped into the baby's lungs to create an "underwater" environment similar to what the baby experienced before birth).
- *Nitric oxide.* The baby is given nitric oxide along with oxygen in an attempt to prevent blood vessel constriction problems that can develop in the lungs.

Note: Some babies die as a result of another breathing-related problem: failure to breathe. They may either be too ill to breathe or their breathing reflex may have been depressed as a result of fetal distress experienced during labor. (A lack of oxygen during the delivery may depress the breathing reflex that should kick in after birth.) While attempts are made to resuscitate babies who fail to breathe, these attempts aren't always successful. In some cases, babies will be placed on ventilators to see if they recover and learn to breathe on their own. If they don't, however, their parents are faced with the heartbreaking choice of deciding when to turn off the respirator and allow the baby to die.

Risk factors   Premature infants are at greater risk of developing RDS and other respiratory system disorders.

Prevention and treatment   The key strategy for avoiding RDS is to prevent preterm labor. A baby's lungs aren't fully mature until the last few weeks of pregnancy. If a woman is at an increased risk of delivering before thirty-four weeks gestation, steroid shots may be given to encourage the lungs to mature before the baby is born.

CONDITIONS ARISING BEFORE AND IMMEDIATELY AFTER BIRTH

In 1997, complications arising during the perinatal period (the period prior to delivery as well as the first month following the birth) resulted in the deaths of 12,935 U.S. infants. These problems included maternal complications of pregnancy (e.g., gestational diabetes or preeclampsia); problems with the placenta, umblical cord, and membranes; complications of labor and delivery; slow fetal growth and fetal malnutrition; birth trauma; intrauterine hypoxia and birth hypoxia (when the baby is deprived of oxygen while in the uterus or during the delivery); infections acquired in the uterus, at the time of delivery, and during the newborn period; hemorrhage; and perinatal jaundice.

Since we talked at great length about pregnancy- and birth-related complications in Chapters 2 and 3, we won't repeat that discussion here. What we will talk about, however, is the threat posed by infection during the newborn period.

While maternal antibodies protect newborns against certain types of infections, not all types of antibodies are able to cross the placenta. Consequently, a newborn is susceptible to infection during and after delivery. The risk of infection during the delivery increases if there is a significant delay between the time when the membranes rupture and the onset of labor—particularly if there is a delay of eighteen to twenty-four hours or more. Once the membranes rupture, it is possible for infection to travel from the vagina into the uterus, something that can result in the pregnant woman developing an infection of the uterine lining (amnionitis) or the placenta (placentitis), and her baby contracting sepsis (blood poisoning) or pneumonia, both of which may prove fatal to the baby.

The following types of infections can result in infant death:

- *Group B streptococcus.* Group B streptococcus (GBS) is the most common source of fatal infection in newborns: 10 percent to 30 percent of pregnant women carry GBS in the vagina or rectum and 5 percent of babies who become infected die. Group B strep is capable of causing sepsis (blood poisoning), pneumonia, and, in some cases, meningitis in the newborn baby. The GBS bacteria can reach the baby during or just before delivery. While fewer than 5 percent of all babies whose mothers are GBS carriers become infected with GBS, premature babies, babies who are small for their gestational age, and babies with compromised immune systems are at increased risk of being infected. The American Academy of Pediatrics recommends that pregnant women be tested for GBS between thirty-five and thirty-seven weeks of pregnancy, and that all women who have risk factors prior to being screened for GBS (e.g., mothers who go into labor before they have been tested) be treated with antibiotics during labor. (See Chapter 13.)
- *Herpes.* Herpes increases a woman's chances of going into premature labor. What's more, a baby who becomes infected with herpes during the delivery can develop a potentially fatal infection of the brain and the membranes surrounding the brain, and/or develop hydrops fetalis,

a condition that can result in heart failure. A baby is most likely to contract herpes if the mother has just developed it for the first time (e.g., she is experiencing a primary infection) or if she has open sores at the time of delivery. In either of these cases, a cesarean section would be recommended.

- *AIDS.* The baby of an HIV-positive mother has a 30 percent to 40 percent risk of contracting HIV. This risk can be reduced to 8 percent if the mother takes a drug called zidovudine during her pregnancy.

- *Listeriosis.* As noted in Chapter 3, listeria (the cause of listeriosis) is a form of bacteria carried by approximately 5 percent of the population, and is commonly contracted from food. Newborns who contract listeriosis can develop pneumonia, blood-poisoning, and meningitis.

- *Chicken pox.* A pregnant woman who develops chicken pox within five days of delivery runs the risk of giving the infection to her baby. A newborn baby's system can be overwhelmed by the virus, and may develop such potentially fatal complications as meningitis or encephalitis (a brain infection).

- *Meconium aspiration.* If a baby experiences fetal distress prior to the onset of labor, meconium may be released into the amniotic fluid. Because a shortage of oxygen can trigger reflex breathing or gasping movements in the baby, the baby may breathe in meconium and permanently damage his or her lungs. Meconium prevents oxygen from passing through the lungs into the bloodstream and can cause an infection in the lungs. It can also lead to pneumothorax—a life-threatening condition in which a hole develops in the baby's lungs and air escapes into the baby's chest.

- *Meningitis.* Meningitis is an infection of the membranes surrounding the brain. It can be fatal and was responsible for the deaths of forty-six U.S. infants in 1997.

- *Blood poisoning (septicemia or sepsis).* Blood poisoning refers to an overwhelming infection of the entire body that results in a collapse of blood vessels, a fall in blood pressure, and possibly heart failure.

- *Necrotising enterocolitis.* Necrotising enterocolitis is an infection of the walls of the large and small intestines. It occurs when the blood supply to the intestines is reduced and results in small sections of tissue dying. Over time, the baby's stomach becomes swollen and the intestines become full of holes. The condition, which can cause death, is most common in very premature newborns and low-birthweight babies, and in infants who have experienced birth hypoxia; who have developed RDS, blood poisoning, or hypoglycemia (low blood sugar); or who have congenital heart disease.

Risk factors   Babies who are in less-than-optimal health (either because of extreme prematurity or low-birthweight, poor health, or other factors) are at increased risk of contracting an infection prior to or during delivery.

Prevention and treatment   The key to minimizing the number of infection-related infant deaths is prevention.

Prevention is particularly important when it comes to managing Group B strep—the leading type of infection causing infant death. According to the Centers for Disease Control, the number of GBS cases that appear during the first week of life could be reduced by 75 percent if all pregnant women were screened for GBS at thirty-five to thirty-seven weeks of gestation, and if those mothers who were found to be carriers were treated with antibiotics during labor.

As you can see, there are a number of factors that can lead to infant death, both factors that originate before birth as well as factors that arise during the newborn period. While there are still a number of problems that can't be prevented or corrected, some significant breakthroughs have been made in the field of neonatal medicine in recent years—research that has given new hope to parents who have experienced the heartbreak of having a baby die.

Now that we've talked about the medical factors that cause some babies to die before or after birth, it's time to shift focus and consider the factors involved in planning your subsequent pregnancy. We'll tackle one of the most difficult questions of all: how to go about deciding when it's "the right time" to start trying to conceive again.

5 *Are You Emotionally Ready for Another Pregnancy?*

WONDERING HOW LONG you should wait before you embark on another pregnancy? There's not any single right answer. Some couples are eager to start trying to conceive just as soon as they are physically ready; others want more time to work through their grief about the death of their previous baby and to mentally prepare themselves for the challenges of a subsequent pregnancy.

In this chapter, we will consider the emotional factors involved in deciding whether you're ready to start trying to conceive again. (You'll find some guidelines that will help you to decide whether your body is physically ready to support another pregnancy in Chapter 6.) We'll start out by talking about how you may be feeling, how your partner may be feeling, and what to do if the two of you don't agree about the timing of your next pregnancy. Then we'll discuss the pros and cons of plunging into another pregnancy right away, as opposed to waiting awhile. We'll wrap up the chapter by talking about how other people may react when you tell them that you're ready to start trying again.

HOW YOU MAY BE FEELING

Don't be surprised if the mere thought of embarking on another pregnancy makes your head spin. You may find yourself hit with a flood of conflicting emotions—everything from joy to worry to outright terror!

Here are just a few of the emotions that may come washing over you as you start thinking about another pregnancy.

Fear and anxiety   You may find yourself coming up with a lengthy list of things to worry about: How will you cope if you have trouble conceiving? How will you cope if you become pregnant? Will your concerns about your pregnancy be taken seriously by your caregiver? Will you confuse the new baby with the baby who died? Will having another baby cause you to forget about your other baby? If the unthinkable happens and this baby dies too, will you be able to cope? Would having another baby die place too much of a strain on your relationship with your partner? Should you simply be happy with your life "as is" rather than tempting fate by spinning the roulette wheel again? These are just a few of the many thoughts that may rush through your head as you contemplate another pregnancy.

Hopelessness   It's not unusual to find yourself thinking very negative thoughts, even if you're normally a very optimistic person. After all, your faith in the world around you has recently received a major blow. You may feel convinced that your odds of ever having a healthy baby in your arms are, at best, slim to none.

Nancy remembers experiencing these feelings of hopelessness after her daughter was stillborn: "I feared that even if we were successful in conceiving again one day, that we were destined to lose that child, too. It was such a feeling of hopelessness. No one could convince me that the odds were in my favor. I had never imagined that I could lose my first baby and it had happened. Nothing could convince me that it wouldn't happen again."

Guilt   You may find yourself feeling guilty about wanting to try for another baby—as if doing so somehow means that you are being "disloyal" to the memory of the baby who died. Some parents find that they have to work through these feelings of guilt before they can even think about trying to conceive again.

Tracy, whose first child died as a result of amniotic band syndrome, remembers spending some time at the cemetery one day, talking to her son: "I made sure that he understood that I love him with all my heart and that no matter what, he will always be my little boy—my firstborn."

Likewise, Sarah, whose second child was stillborn, felt a need to scatter her baby's ashes before she could move on with her plans for another pregnancy.

Frustration and anger   You may feel frustrated and angry that you have to worry about trying to conceive again. After all, if your last pregnancy and birth had gone according to plan, you would already have a healthy baby in your arms. You may resent the fact that you have to go through the entire process of trying to conceive again, and that you have to do so with no guarantee that you'll end up with the storybook ending that you so desperately want.

Resentment   You may feel resentful toward people in your life who seem to be able to give birth to healthy babies without any difficulty at all: your neighbor who's had a whole string of unplanned pregnancies, your college roommate who got pregnant "the first time," and your cousin who's pregnant right now, and not all that happy about it!

Marie, whose fourth pregnancy ended in miscarriage and whose fifth ended in stillbirth, found it difficult to be empathetic toward a close friend who was struggling about whether to abort an unwanted pregnancy. "I couldn't believe she had the gall to turn to me for support when I was still trying to get over my miscarriage and my daughter's stillbirth."

Powerlessness   You may feel powerless—like your entire life is out of your control. You may resent the fact that you have no control over the one thing in your life that matters most to you right now: ending up with a healthy baby in your arms.

Marilyn says that she spent more time praying after her miscarriage than during any other time in her life, and that she also began physically and emotionally preparing herself for her next pregnancy, as a way to regain some control over her life. "In general, I felt more fragile about life and less in control of things, and therefore I felt like I needed to be better prepared physically, emotionally, and spiritually for the future," she said.

Inadequacy   It's not at all uncommon to find yourself experiencing feelings of inadequacy as you contemplate another pregnancy. According to Deborah Davis, Ph.D., author of *Empty Cradle, Broken Heart*, this can be a particular problem for mothers: "Thinking about trying again can really dredge up feelings of betrayal by your body. You may feel that you can no longer trust your body's ability to conceive or deliver a healthy baby. You may even feel asexual—like you no longer feel at home in your body. You may not want to be touched in any way that's even remotely sexual—a feeling that's particularly common if you had a D&C, a therapeutic abortion, or a traumatic delivery. You may still be healing from enduring those invasive procedures."

Cautious excitement You may feel excited about the prospects of conceiving another child—of having something to be happy about again. On the other hand, you may be too frightened to allow yourself to experience these feelings for too long, out of fear that doing so might "jinx" your chances of conceiving or of ending up with a healthy baby in your arms.

Don't be surprised if the cocktail of emotions cascading through your brain changes from day-to-day, or even moment-to-moment. According to Davis, it's not the least bit unusual to go from feeling euphoric about your decision to start trying again one moment to feeling panic-struck the next. "Especially early on, it is normal to have these mixed and painful feelings about trying again. These emotions can be closely tied to the normal grieving process for the baby or babies who died," she says.

According to Davis, giving yourself the time and opportunity to grieve can help to reduce the intensity of these feelings. "Grieving is what enables you to heal. If you don't allow yourself to grieve, you'll continue to feel raw and unsettled. What's more, by stifling any negative feelings, you may dampen any feelings of peace or happy anticipation that you might otherwise be capable of experiencing. Remember that working through your feelings of anxiety, hopelessness, inadequacy, and guilt is what will free you from the grip of these powerful and painful emotions."

Davis points out, however, that you could end up waiting forever if you waited for these feelings to disappear entirely. "They won't disappear, but they can diminish," she explains. "If your pain is still too overwhelming to allow you to even contemplate a subsequent pregnancy, you may simply need more time to come to terms with the death of your baby—to spend more time focusing on the baby you're missing rather than thinking about having another baby."

MORE FOOD FOR THOUGHT

If you're still undecided about whether or not you're ready to embark on another pregnancy, you might find it helpful to ask yourself the following questions:

Have you had a chance to work through some of your grief?

Grief can be an exhausting emotion—one that demands far more of your time and attention than you may want to give it. If it hasn't been very long since your baby died, you may still be going through a very rough time emotionally and might not be ready to embark on another pregnancy just yet.

As eager as you may be to fast-forward through this particular chapter of your life, there are definite disadvantages to attempting to move on too quickly—a lesson that Desirae learned after the death of her baby daughter (a full-term baby who died as a result of complications from congenital heart disease and other anomalies). "I desperately wanted to get pregnant immediately after losing Katherine, thinking that it would help me in my grief. I know now that it was a mistake," she says. "I should have taken the time to come to terms with her death and allowed myself to grieve. Instead, I went on to have two miscarriages before what would have been her first birthday, and then a third loss after that. Grieving her death on top of the other losses just about did me in. I went on to suffer from panic attacks for about six months and finally had to seek out counseling to deal with my grief."

Marilyn, on the other hand, took a short break before she started trying to conceive after her miscarriage. She used that time to work through her grief and to consider how much having a baby meant to her. "When the miscarriage happened, I felt a deep and profound sadness, not just for me and my husband, but for the child who would never know the beauty of this world. I realized then that a child who makes it into this world is indeed a miracle and has perhaps performed the greatest feat of his or her lifetime just by growing into a complete human being in nine months and being born without mishap," she says.

How would you cope if you were to experience fertility problems?

As much as you might hate to even consider the possibility that you could have difficulty conceiving when you start trying again, some grieving parents do experience this added heartbreak.

Kim found that the fertility problems that she experienced for more than a year after her daughter was stillborn merely added to her grief: "Trying to conceive is its own emotional rollercoaster that, when coupled with grieving, may prove overwhelming. It can be like having another loss each month."

If you don't think that you could cope with the frustration and heartbreak of dealing with fertility problems on top of the stress of working through your grief, you might want to wait a little longer before you start trying to conceive again. While the fact that you have conceived in the past increases the likelihood that you'll be able to do so again, there are no guarantees when it comes to fertility.

How would you cope if you experienced the death of another baby?

It's also important to ensure that you're emotionally strong enough to cope with the possibility of a less-than-happy outcome to your next pregnancy.

Tracy—whose first child died as a result of amniotic band syndrome and who then experienced a miscarriage—remembers weighing the pros and cons of risking more heartbreak when she was trying to decide whether to start trying again. "For me personally, the desire to have a child had to outweigh the fear of losing another one. When I could say that I wanted a child so badly that I was willing to risk the pain of another loss, I knew that I was ready."

Karen, who made the decision to terminate her first pregnancy when prenatal testing revealed that she was carrying a child with Down's syndrome, also had to face her fears head on: "You're ready to try again when your faith in the future is greater than your fear of the future."

*Are you ready to cope with the stress of a
subsequent pregnancy?*

The worry doesn't end when you manage to conceive. In fact, in
many ways, it's just beginning. That's why it's important to ensure that
you're up to coping with the stress of what could very well be the most
nerve-wracking forty weeks of your life.

Nancy decided to postpone her plans to try again, because she didn't
feel that she was ready to cope with the emotional highs and lows just
yet. "Six months after my loss, I was just starting to really emerge from
the fog I'd been in after Jacob died. I wasn't ready to get back on the
roller coaster. I wanted to just be me—to feel stable for a while longer. I
was finally starting to feel good more often than bad, and I wanted to
keep feeling that way."

*Do you want another baby—or do you want the baby
who died?*

According to Davis, author of *Empty Cradle, Broken Heart,* many grieving parents worry that their decision to try again may mean that they're
trying to "replace" the baby they lost. She offers these reassuring words:
"While your next baby might never have been considered or conceived if
it were not for the death of your previous baby, having another baby because your previous baby died does not necessarily mean that you're trying to 'replace' that baby; it simply means that you're trying to create the
family that you have hoped for. You're not in danger of experiencing 'replacement child syndrome' unless you start to actually confuse the new
baby with the baby who died—if you allow yourself to become convinced
that you're going to become pregnant with the baby who died, or if you
start to idealize your beloved deceased baby and then expect that the new
baby will be just as ideal."

Some bereaved parents feel there's an the advantage to giving themselves time to process the fact their previous baby has died before they
start planning another pregnancy. Marilyn feels, in retrospect, that waiting a few months before she started trying again did her a lot of good:
"I'm grateful to my obstetrician for advising us to wait three months before trying to conceive again, because it took at least that long for us to
start looking forward with hope. I think that if we had tried any earlier,

it might have been for the wrong reasons, possibly to 'try and get it right this time' or to 'replace' the baby we'd lost."

Nancy also found that there were advantages to giving herself time to work through her feelings about having a baby die, before she began trying to conceive again. "Even though my heart ached for a baby in my arms, I knew the only child I wanted at first was Jacob. I had to allow myself to get to the point where I could see myself holding another child—another child of mine—and that meant allowing myself to grieve as I saw fit."

Davis stresses that becoming pregnant again isn't the miracle cure that some grieving parents expect it to be. "Becoming pregnant doesn't erase your need to grieve," she stresses. "No other baby can take the place of the baby you miss so much. You cannot expect your new baby to completely fill the void in your heart."

How do your partner and living children feel about another pregnancy?

You're going to need as much support as possible during your subsequent pregnancy. That's why it's important to be sure that your partner and living children share your desire for another baby. If they haven't had enough chance to work through their own emotions, they might be too frightened to risk the possibility of experiencing another heartbreak.

Jennifer was ready to start trying to conceive again right after her baby died, but her husband wasn't. She had to give him the opportunity to work through some of his fears before he decided that he was ready to commit to another pregnancy.

"Immediately after we lost our daughter, my husband and I were at different places with the idea of having more children," she recalls. "I realized for the first time in my life how meaningful it was to be a mother and I wanted to have the opportunity to mother a child on a day-to-day basis, not just to be the mother of a baby who had died. My husband was too scared. Since I was found to lack immunity to rubella [not related to her daughter's death], we decided to take the vaccination and continue a dialogue about whether to have more children.

"One day, my husband came home from work and said that he realized that he had never made a decision in his life based on fear, and he did not want to start now. So we decided that once the vaccine had cleared out of my system, we would start trying to conceive again. We also decided that this was it: If we lost another child, we would not try again. Our hearts and minds would not be able to continue."

Julie and her husband went through a similar experience after their first child was stillborn due to a tight nuchal cord: She wanted to try again, but her husband wasn't quite ready yet. "My arms ached to hold a child, to bring a baby home from the hospital," she recalls. "I felt like I had failed as a mother, even though I knew it wasn't my fault that Bryan had died. I wanted another chance.

"My husband didn't want to try again at first. He was scared and concerned that it would appear that we were trying to replace Bryan. Of course, that is impossible, but I understood his fears and waited until he was ready, too. Fortunately, I didn't have to wait long for him to come around."

Cathy and her husband made the decision to try again because they knew how eager their children were to have a baby brother or sister. "The biggest factor in our decision to try again were my living children. They wanted to have a baby brother or sister so much," she says. "They had been through a miscarriage and the loss of their brother and I really wanted them to experience a happy, successful pregnancy and delivery."

If you find you and your partner are on difficult timetables when it comes to embarking on a subsequent pregnancy, you should make a point to listen—really listen—to one another's concerns. That means exploring your hopes and your fears together. You may find, for example, that your partner is terrified that something may happen to you during pregnancy or birth, or that he simply feels overwhelmed by your "obsession" with becoming pregnant again.

Sometimes all that's holding the reluctant partner back is the need to have his or her concerns taken seriously and to be given the time he or she needs to resolve those concerns. You can't force anyone to deal with their emotions on your timetable. If anything, pushing the issue may work against you. As Davis notes in *Empty Cradle, Broken Heart,* "By simply easing off, you may give your partner the space he or she needs to feel comfortable."

HOW LONG SHOULD YOU WAIT TO START TRYING AGAIN?

As noted at the beginning of this chapter, there's no "right" time to start trying to become pregnant again. Some grieving parents are eager to start

Emotional Factors to Consider in Timing Your Next Pregnancy

	ADVANTAGES	DISADVANTAGES
Conceiving right away	• You may be able to achieve a pregnancy sooner if you start trying to conceive sooner. • Trying again may give you something else to focus on other than your grief.	• You might not have an adequate opportunity to work through your grief before you're confronted with the stress of a subsequent pregnancy. • Friends and family members may assume that you no longer have the same need for support. They may assume that your eagerness to become pregnant again means that you're ready to "move on." • There may be an increased chance of pregnancy loss if you conceive too soon (e.g., if you wait for less than two to three normal menstrual cycles before you start trying to conceive).
Postponing your next pregnancy	• You will have more time to work through your feelings of grief about the death of your baby.	• You will have longer to worry about your fertility and your chances of ending up with a living baby.

ADVANTAGES	DISADVANTAGES
• You are more likely to continue to receive emotional support from family members and friends who might mistakenly assume that you're ready to "move on" if you were to become pregnant right away. • There may be some health advantages to postponing your next pregnancy. (See Chapter 6.)	• Your biological clock will continue to tick. The longer you wait to start trying to conceive again, the greater your risk of experiencing infertility or having another baby die, or giving birth to a baby with chromosomal problems.

trying as soon as they get the go-ahead from the doctor or midwife. Others prefer to take things a little more slowly.

As you can see from the Emotional Factors chart, there are some definite emotional advantages and disadvantages to becoming pregnant right away as opposed to postponing your next pregnancy. (*Note:* You'll find a detailed discussion of the physical factors involved in planning another pregnancy in Chapter 6.)

Now let's consider the key factors that lead couples to choose one or the other alternative.

Trying Again Right Away

The majority of grieving parents who decide to start trying again do so because:

- They feel an overwhelming need to be pregnant again.
- They feel that their lives will continue to be on hold until they give birth to a healthy baby.
- They need something to look forward to again.
- They fear that they'll miss out on their opportunity to become parents if they don't move quickly.

The need to be pregnant again right away   Nancy and her partner, Les, hadn't even left the delivery room after their daughter's stillbirth when they decided that they wanted to try again. "I think we both had a huge need, a desire, to have a baby in our lives," Nancy recalls. "I will never forget when Les was holding Kali and he said, 'You are so beautiful. You would've been so much fun. Why did you have to go,' and then turned to me and said, 'We have to try again someday. I want to know what it's like.' I quickly agreed. We had barely said good-bye to her and we were already expressing a need to try again."

Laure also felt driven to try to conceive right away after each of her five losses: "I had such a strong need to try again. Even though I was crushed and very scared, something deep inside of me wanted to try again. My desire for another child outweighed my fear. My husband was willing to try again as long as I was. By the fifth loss, he was getting quite concerned about me. My depression and ability to function got worse with each loss. Before the sixth pregnancy, we had agreed that this would be our last try. I don't think I could have taken another loss."

Cathie still feels this same powerful drive to become pregnant again, despite the many difficulties she has faced in her quest for a living child. Despite the fact that her first baby was born prematurely and died as a result of complications resulting from a lung anomaly, that her second baby was miscarried, and that she also has a history of infertility, she admits to being "more determined than ever" to have a baby. "I know what it feels like to be pregnant and deliver a child," she explains. "I want that again more than ever."

The desire to get on with life   Some grieving parents are eager to start trying again right away because they feel that their lives will continue to be "on hold" until they give birth to another baby. This was certainly the case for Sheri, whose first child died as a result of a placental abruption caused by the sudden onset of preeclampsia. "The main factor in our decision to try again was our feelings. We just felt like our lives were on hold. We were so ready for a baby after going through the entire nine months of pregnancy, only to come home with empty arms. We felt so disoriented now that our life was not what we were expecting it to be. In fact, it was the exact opposite: Instead of being filled with the joy of a new baby, our lives were filled with such overwhelming sadness," she says.

The desire to have something to look forward to again   It's not unusual for parents who have experienced the death of a baby to decide to
embark on another pregnancy right away, because they desperately want
something to be happy about again. While they are still in the midst of
grieving for the baby who died, they may feel strongly that becoming
pregnant again will give them a reason to go on during what would otherwise be an unbearably dark time in their lives.

Petra and her husband, who experienced a miscarriage and a stillbirth
between the births of their two living children, were eager to start trying
again right away for this very reason. "I guess we probably needed another pregnancy to help us bear the loss of our baby son," she admits.

Molly was similarly motivated by a desire to restore some joy to her
life: "I think that being pregnant is about as much of a cure for [the overwhelming feelings of sadness] as there is. It's very nerve-wracking to be
pregnant after a loss or two, but at least you have hope at the same time."

The fear of never being able to have another child   Marilyn started
trying to conceive again after her miscarriage as soon as the three-month
waiting period recommended by her doctor was up. She admits to being
obsessed with the idea of becoming pregnant again because she was desperately afraid that she would never be able to conceive again or carry a
healthy baby to term. "Things I'd never thought about haunted me during that 'waiting period.' I wondered why I had lost the baby and why
other women seemed to have no problem with their pregnancies. I was
even afraid that my husband would leave me if I could never 'produce'
a child for him. (My husband assured me that this would never happen
after I talked to him about it.) I wanted to know why I lost the baby: Was
there something inherently wrong with my body? Was there some great
reason why this had happened?"

Laura experienced similar fears after her baby was stillborn but, in
her case, she felt a strong need to start trying to conceive right away because of her age: "The greatest factor I had to weigh was my age. I was
thirty-nine when I became pregnant with the child I lost. I am now forty-
one and feel tremendous pressure due to my age. I know of women who
became pregnant for the first time at forty-three and forty-five, but now
that I have suffered a loss, I am aware of all that can go wrong."

Petra was similarly motivated to start trying again right away: "We
couldn't give ourselves time to grieve for our stillborn son before getting

ready for another pregnancy because I was almost forty-three at the time and the ticking of the biological clock added to our anxiety."

Deciding to Wait

The majority of grieving parents who decide to wait a while before they start trying to conceive again do so because:

- They want more time to deal with their grief before embarking on another pregnancy.
- Their anxiety, fear, and pessimism about their next pregnancy may be too overwhelming.
- There are other factors that can affect the timing of a pregnancy.

The need to grieve   Like many parents, Tammy wasn't ready to start trying to conceiving right away, because she wanted time alone so that she could work through her feelings about the death of her premature son. "Dealing with my grief was the number one factor in the decision to wait to try again after our first loss," she recalls. "Emotionally, it was just too much to think of another baby when all I really wanted was Adam, the baby who was born too soon and who was just too tiny to live. I felt I owed it to him to grieve for him and not move on too quickly." In fact, she owed it to herself to give herself this time, too.

The fear of having another baby die   Immediately after her miscarriage, Kathy wasn't sure that she was ever going to be ready to start trying to conceive again. She was too afraid of having another miscarriage. "Because we didn't know what caused the missed miscarriage, I was pretty convinced that it was going to happen again. I felt that there was something wrong with me and I didn't want to cause any more babies to die, so I didn't want to get pregnant again," she says. "Brad, my husband, was more willing to try sooner and wasn't as convinced as I was that we would lose every baby that we conceived.

"By the time I got my period back, I had decided that we should try again, because we really did want to have children, and if we didn't keep trying, we would never get to have any."

The desire to let certain milestones pass before becoming pregnant again   While some women experience a strong need to be pregnant by the time certain milestone dates roll around (e.g., their original due date or the anniversary of their child's birth or death), others feel a strong need to let these milestones pass before they start planning another pregnancy.

Nancy—whose baby died shortly after birth, due to severe prematurity—decided to wait until her due date had passed: "Once I got past my original due date, I felt an emotional relief and was ready to try again."

Other considerations   Sometimes practical matters can affect the timing of a subsequent pregnancy: the needs of other children in the family, financial matters, and the fact that a pregnancy may have to be delayed for medical reasons.

Here are a few examples of the types of factors you may have to consider.

- If you have living children, you will have to keep their needs in mind as you plan your subsequent pregnancy. Gretchen, for example, had to consider the needs of her surviving twin, who has some special needs, when she was deciding when to start trying to conceive again.
- If your pregnancy is likely to be classified as high risk because of your history, you may need to consider whether you'll be able to hold down a job throughout the duration of your pregnancy and, if not, how you will deal with the resulting financial fallout. This was a major consideration for Janna in timing her subsequent pregnancy: "We knew that it was very likely that I would be on bed rest for a large part of the pregnancy."
- You may also have to delay your next pregnancy for medical reasons. Jennifer, for example, found out at her preconception checkup that she had lost her immunity to rubella. "I was revaccinated and told that I needed to wait three to six months before trying again. We opted to wait six months in order to be absolutely certain that my system was free from possible problems from the vaccine," she says. You could run into similar problems if you needed to postpone your pregnancy in order to obtain treatment for a particular health-related problem that could not easily be treated during your next pregnancy—one of many reasons why you might want to schedule your preconception health checkup before you're actually ready to start trying to conceive. (*Note:* You'll find a more detailed discussion of

the physical factors involved in planning a subsequent pregnancy in Chapter 6.)

Go with Your Instincts

While it may seem like there are a lot of factors to weigh in deciding whether it's a good time to start trying to conceive again, your best bet is to listen to your heart, says Marilyn, who has experienced two miscarriages. "I think all couples known when it's the right time for them to start trying again," she explains. "For example, I know one couple who waited only one period after the miscarriage before trying again, and they conceived and had a healthy baby, and I know another couple who were so heartbroken after their miscarriage that they never tried again. It seemed that their miscarriage took them to the threshold of their pain and they didn't want to risk crossing the line if it happened again. Both couples did what they felt was best for them."

Cynthia—who experienced a series of miscarriages before giving birth to her second living child—also feels that it's important to go with your gut feeling. "If you have to consciously decide, then it's probably the wrong time. It's kind of like being in love. You always wondered how you would know when you were, but when you were, you just knew it. I think it's the same. When you're ready to try, you'll want to try. It's really that simple," she says.

The Best-Laid Plans

Of course, sometimes there's no time for planning at all. Lisa was shocked to discover that she had managed to conceive again about two-and-a-half weeks after her miscarriage. "We hadn't decided to try again," she recalls. "We hadn't even begun discussing it because we were both so devastated we couldn't fathom risking the hurt again."

Despite her desire to end up with a baby in her arms, conceiving this quickly proved to be a mixed blessing. Lisa was very worried about the fact that she had conceived without waiting the generally recommended two to three months. "When I found out I was pregnant again, my first question was, 'Am I considered a high-risk pregnancy now?' On the one hand, I wanted my doctor to say 'no' so that I could feel that there was a good chance that this would be a healthy pregnancy," she says. "On the other hand, I wanted to be admitted to the hospital immediately and given round-the-clock attention!" She remembers being "worried for a million reasons that I couldn't even put into words," even though her doctor reassured her that the odds of ending up with a baby in her arms this time around were decidedly in her favor.

TELLING OTHERS ABOUT YOUR DECISION TO TRY AGAIN

Once you and your partner have decided to start trying to conceive again, you will need to decide whether you're prepared to share this news with other people. Some couples feel quite strongly that they want to keep this news to themselves; others gladly share it with their closest friends and relatives in the hope that they'll be given plenty of support and encouragement.

Jennifer and her partner decided to let their friends and family members know about their plans to start trying to conceive again, because they realized that a lot of people had been devastated when their baby died during labor. Their experience with sharing their news was generally positive, but Jennifer does have one regret about the way friends and family members responded. "Everyone was very supportive and happy to see that we decided to embark on another pregnancy. Many were afraid that we wouldn't, in fact," she says. "However, they also seemed to think that our decision to start trying again meant that they no longer needed to ask us about our first child, Samantha, anymore. We love to talk about her and tell people about her, and yet no one asks anymore. It makes me sad that people are pretending that she never existed. She is a very real part of me and the world has lost much without her here. I just wish people would continue to acknowledge her."

Others had considerably less positive experiences than Jennifer when they decided to share their news with others. Jodi's mother strongly discouraged her from trying again, because she was concerned about the effects of another pregnancy on Jodi's health. Lisa discovered that her parents were less than enthusiastic about the idea of her becoming pregnant again. And Gretchen's grandmother started crying when Gretchen spoke of her plans to start trying to conceive again—not because she was happy, but because she didn't think she'd be able to cope if Gretchen had another baby die. Gretchen was furious with her grandmother at first, but then realized that her reaction was more a reflection of her love for

Gretchen than anything else. "It took me some time to stop feeling angry with her for that reaction," she recalls. "Who the hell was she to be looking to me for support? I mean, it was my husband and I who had suffered the loss of our child, not her. I think it was at that moment, however, that I realized just how many people Isaac's death had affected."

Given the fact that some people's reactions can be less than supportive, some couples choose to keep their news under their hats until after a pregnancy has been achieved. This was certainly the way Suzy and Laure chose to handle the situation.

"We don't really talk about it, but some people do ask," says Suzy about her decision to try again after her losses. "After the first loss, we decided not to talk about it at all. When people would ask if we were trying for another, we would lie and say no. Since then, we have experienced a total of four losses. We still prefer not talking about it, but if we feel that the person asking will be supportive, sometimes we will talk about what we have been through. We have never announced that we are trying again."

"We told no one," admits Laure, who experienced five losses before the birth of her first living child. "I did not want to hear what they thought as my family was tired of hearing about my losses. They would not have been supportive. My friends—although they would not have voiced it—would have thought I was crazy to try again."

Some parents chose to keep the news from their living children, too, but others, like Laura (whose second daughter died at eight days of age during open heart surgery), find that it's better to be upfront with their children about their hopes of having another baby. "Our daughter Elizabeth was just about four when we started trying again," she recalls. "We didn't plan to tell her, but we needed an answer to give her when she asked (frequently), 'When can we have another baby?'

"Little did we know that we would have to keep answering that question for a full year. We eventually took to answering the question by explaining that we were trying to have another baby. We used planting seeds as an analogy because Elizabeth had planted a bunch of flower seeds in the spring and only some of them germinated."

In the end, their garden reaped the ultimate of harvests: the birth of a healthy baby.

6 Preparing for Another Pregnancy

A GENERATION AGO, pregnant women didn't visit the doctor to have their pregnancies confirmed until they had missed at least two periods. Today, a growing number of women are choosing to pay their initial visit to their doctors long before that—before they even start trying to conceive, in fact.

In this chapter, we will talk about what's involved in preparing for your next pregnancy, and will start out by considering the advantages and disadvantages of sticking with the same doctor or midwife who cared for you when your baby died, as opposed to switching caregivers. Then we'll talk about the importance of scheduling a preconception checkup with your doctor or midwife before you start trying to conceive. Finally, we'll talk about the pros and cons of genetic testing so that you can decide for yourself whether going this route is the right choice for you and your partner.

SHOULD YOU CHANGE CAREGIVERS?

To change or not to change, that is the question. It's an issue that every mother who has experienced the heartbreak of miscarriage, stillbirth, or infant death needs to decide for herself: whether or not to change caregivers.

Sticking with the Same Caregiver

Women who decide to stick with the same doctor or midwife who cared for them during the pregnancy that resulted in the death of their baby typically do so for three reasons: they feel that they have been treated with compassion and that they received the best possible care, and because they want a caregiver who knows their history.

Lisa decided to stay with the same doctor who cared for her when her baby was stillborn, because the doctor was very compassionate and because he seemed to understand the depth of her pain.

"My doctor is a wonderful human being and doctor," she explains. "He cares so much and was there for us during our darkest hour, during our recovery period and while we were trying to conceive again. I stayed with him because he seems to understand what we have gone through. He has done whatever he could to make this pregnancy as stress-free for us as possible. He offered to provide us with a home doppler to allow us to hear the baby's heartbeat. I have had weekly appointments throughout my pregnancy and monthly ultrasounds, too. He constantly checks on how we are handling things emotionally. I don't think I could dream up better care from a physician."

Nancy was similarly touched by the amount of compassion shown to her by the midwife who cared for her during and after her son's birth and death. "She came to my house to check on me every week for the first few months after Jacob died," she recalls. Since Nancy's pregnancy had been obstetrically uncomplicated (the cause of her son's death was an inborn error of metabolism rather than any pregnancy-related complication), she decided to go back to the same midwife when she became pregnant again, rather than switch to a medical doctor.

Renee didn't see any point in changing caregivers, because even though her previous child had died as a result of a cytomegalovirus (CMV) infection (a virus that is usually harmless to the developing baby, but that occasionally results in severe congenital anomalies, stillbirth, or neonatal death—see Chapters 3 and 10), she had complete confidence in the care she had received from her doctor. "I didn't blame him for my son's death," she stresses. "The CMV infection went undetected during the pregnancy. I think he made the decisions that he thought were best for me and both babies."

Sarah, whose second child was stillborn, had entirely different reasons for staying with the same caregiver during her next pregnancy, reasons that had little to do with the quality of care she received and more with her own need for some sort of closure. "It was important to do it again the 'same' way and to 'get it right' this time—sort of to set things straight," she says.

Cheryl decided to stick with the same doctor, even though her husband, Tom, had initially wanted her to make a change. "Tom wanted me to consider switching doctors after we lost Ethan—not because he had bad feelings toward the doctor, but because he had a hard time returning to the same building where we'd experienced so much pain. I wanted to stay with the same doctor since he was—and continues to be—so caring and responsive. He acknowledges my fears and anxieties and is very open to my questions," she says. "In the end, we decided to stay with the same doctor, but agreed that Tom would limit the number of trips he made with me to the doctor's office."

Changing Doctors

Not every mother who has had a baby die wants to stick with the same doctor or midwife during her next pregnancy, however. Some are eager to make a change, either because of concerns about the quality of care they received during their previous pregnancy or when their baby died, or because they simply find it too painful or scary to go back to the same caregiver again.

Cindy knew she would change doctors even before she had made it through the trauma of delivering her stillborn child. "He was working on his Visa bill while explaining to us how our dead child would be delivered, and then he took a personal phone call to boot!" she says. In the end, she decided to switch to the kind and caring doctor who had offered her support during her amniocentesis. (It was during the amniocentesis she learned that her baby had died.)

Kim had equally compelling reasons for switching from the obstetrician who had treated her so callously after her daughter's stillbirth. "I couldn't even go back to the doctor's office for the six-week follow-up, let alone stay with him for another pregnancy," she says. "When I saw this doctor at the hospital the day after the loss was confirmed, he actually said, 'I'm glad I didn't worry you for nothing.' He was obviously completely inept at dealing with us." Kim's primary-care physician referred her to another obstetrician, who saw her the next day after learning about her situation. "He was so compassionate that my husband and I decided immediately that he was our new doctor."

Rather than go back to her own doctor, whom she also found to be callous and unfeeling during her ordeal, Nancy chose to switch to the doctor who had been present at her daughter's stillbirth. "I had never met her until she delivered Kali, but felt that she was really there for us. At my six-week postpartum visit, I asked her if I could become a patient of hers if we ever conceived again, and she happily agreed. I felt so relieved, even though the thought of another pregnancy seemed so scary. I felt it was important to stick with her because she had been there and had seen firsthand what we'd been through. I wouldn't have to explain my fears to a new doctor. I could feel secure that she would do whatever was humanly possible to see me through another pregnancy. I felt a sort of bond with her that I almost can't explain. I guess it has something to do with the fact that she held my little girl, and not very many people got to do that," she says.

As difficult as it may be to think about switching caregivers, it's important to do so if you're less than happy with your current doctor or midwife. After all, you'll have enough stress to deal with during your subsequent pregnancy. If you haven't been lucky enough to find "Dr. Right" the first time around, keep looking. He or she is out there.

Consider these words of wisdom from Kim, who experienced a miscarriage and a stillbirth before the birth of her first living child. "Doctors seem to have widely different views on handling subsequent pregnancies," she explains. "First, you need to figure out the level of care that you want (e.g., do you want to be treated as normally as possible or do you want to be treated with kid gloves?). Then, you need to grill your provider on specifics. If you're not comfortable with that doctor, you should interview other doctors until you find one who will match your style."

Then, once you've decided on a doctor or midwife, you'll be ready to take the next important step toward planning a subsequent pregnancy: scheduling your preconception checkup.

YOUR PRECONCEPTION CHECKUP: WHAT TO EXPECT

Before Pamela started trying to conceive again after her miscarriage, she scheduled a preconception checkup with her doctor. In addition to performing a physical examination to ensure that she was healing properly after the miscarriage, Pamela's doctor talked to her about the emotional challenges of a subsequent pregnancy. Pamela left the appointment with the green light to start trying again whenever she was ready. "She basically told us to be sure that we grieved and not to pressure ourselves," Pamela recalls. "She didn't see any reason why we wouldn't conceive again soon or why we would be likely to experience another pregnancy loss."

Jennifer—whose daughter, Samantha, was stillborn at term for unknown reasons—also checked in with her obstetrician before embarking on another pregnancy. "Talking with the obstetrician about our plans made them feel more real," she recalls. "We really *were* going to embark on the journey of pregnancy again."

As eager as you may be to start trying to conceive again, you may have some concerns that need to be addressed before you're ready to take that step. You may wonder how soon it's safe to start trying to conceive again, how your history may affect your pregnancy outcome or the health of your baby this time and whether your next pregnancy will be classified as "high risk," and what you should be doing now to get your body in the best possible shape for another pregnancy. You may also wonder if your next pregnancy will be managed any differently this time around: Will you be sent for more frequent ultrasounds? Will your prenatal visits be scheduled at more frequent intervals? Will the delivery be handled in a different manner?

The best way to obtain answers to these questions is to schedule a preconception checkup with the doctor or midwife who will be caring for you during your next pregnancy. Not only will you be able to obtain answers to any specific medical questions that you may have, you'll also have the opportunity to let your caregiver know that you'll be looking for plenty of support and reassurance during the months ahead, whether or not you manage to conceive.

In addition to obtaining answers to any questions that remain about the circumstances that led to your baby's death, you'll also want to talk to your doctor or midwife about what lies ahead. Here are some points that you'll definitely want to raise during your preconception checkup.

When can we start trying again?

Your doctor or midwife will probably recommend that you wait at least two to three menstrual cycles before you start trying to conceive again if you've experienced a miscarriage, stillbirth, or full-term delivery, and at least six months if you've experienced a cesarean delivery.

As eager as you may be to become pregnant right away, your body needs a chance to recover from your previous pregnancy before it embarks on another one. It takes time for your uterus to heal (particularly if you had a D&C) and for your endometrial lining to build back up to healthy levels. Conceiving too quickly can actually work against you: If your body isn't ready to support a pregnancy by the time that you become pregnant again, you face an increased risk of experiencing another miscarriage, stillbirth, or infant death.

You need to be particularly careful about planning your next pregnancy if you required a cesarean delivery in your previous pregnancy. You face an increased risk of experiencing a uterine rupture if the incision from your cesarean hasn't had the chance to heal properly before your uterus has to start expanding again to accommodate your next baby.

Even if you had a thoroughly uncomplicated pregnancy and delivery, you will still need to give your body a bit of a break before you become pregnant again. It needs to have a chance to replenish its stores in order to take the best possible care of your next baby.

It's particularly important to give your body time to heal if you carried you previous baby to term or near-term. Some studies have shown that becoming pregnant within a year of giving birth may put your next baby at increased risk for stillbirth, low birthweight, prematurity, and Sudden Infant Death Syndrome. (*Note:* It's important to stress that these conditions are thought to be more of a problem in economically disadvantaged groups, where nutrition and access to healthcare are less than ideal, but if you do decide to space your pregnancies less than a year apart, you'll want to ensure that you are in the best possible health.)

Here are some more factors to consider if you carried your last pregnancy to term (or near-term):

- A recent study conducted by the U.S. Centers for Disease Control and Prevention concluded that the optimal gap between births is eighteen to twenty-three months. Women who become pregnant again within six months of a previous delivery face a 30 percent to 40 percent chance of giving birth to a premature or underweight baby, likely because the mother is still recovering from her previous pregnancy.
- A study conducted at the University of Chicago revealed that infants conceived less than one year after their mother's previous pregnancy

face a 39 percent increased risk of death during infancy as compared
to infants who were spaced further apart, and that infants conceived
within six months of the previous delivery face double the risk of
death. (*Note:* As compelling as these survey results may be, it's worth
noting, however, that many of these deaths were related to accidents,
abuse, or Sudden Infant Death Syndrome. There was a modest increase—or no increase at all—in such factors as maternal complications during pregnancy, obstetrical and delivery complications, and
birth defects.)

- Your physical health aside, there can be compelling psychological reasons for postponing your next pregnancy: A study reported in the
  British Medical Journal revealed that women who conceive quickly after
  losing a child in late pregnancy had higher levels of depression and
  anxiety than women who allowed themselves more time to mourn
  before embarking on another pregnancy.

You can't just go by a bunch of medical studies, no matter how sci-
entifically sound they may be. You also need to consider your own indi-
vidual circumstances. Here are some other points you'll need to consider:

- *Your reproductive history.* You might want to start trying again sooner
  rather than later if you have had trouble conceiving in the past. As
  you know only too well, there's no guarantee that you'll be able to
  conceive right away once you decide that you're ready for another
  pregnancy.
- *Your age.* You won't want to postpone your subsequent pregnancy too
  long if you're approaching the end of your reproductive years. Not
  only can it be more difficult to conceive, since your fertility declines
  steadily as you age, you also face an increased risk of pregnancy loss,
  chromosomal abnormalities, and certain pregnancy-related complications such as preeclampsia and gestational diabetes.
- *Your overall health.* You should plan to start conceiving relatively soon
  if you have a health condition that is likely to worsen as you age. This
  was the case with Laura, whose second child died during open-heart
  surgery at eight days of age: "I was thirty-five-and-a-half and had
  high blood pressure. Delaying the pregnancy for a year or two could
  have meant more problems with my blood pressure, since it tends to
  increase with age."

In the end, the decision about when to plan your next pregnancy is one that has to be made by you and your partner, perhaps with a little input from your caregiver.

When should I expect my first period?

If you have experienced a miscarriage, you can expect your menstrual period to resume within approximately four to six weeks. Because you ovulate approximately two weeks before your period begins, it may therefore be possible for you to conceive before your get your first post-miscarriage period, although this is generally not recommended. Not all women follow this pattern, however. Some women experience an anovulatory menstrual cycle after a miscarriage (a cycle in which ovulation does not occur). Others experience a lengthier delay before the resumption of their menstrual periods. Certainly, if you haven't resumed your usual menstrual pattern within three months of your miscarriage, you should discuss this with your caregiver.

If your baby died later on in pregnancy or shortly after birth, it may take a little longer for your menstrual periods to resume. After all, you've just completed a term pregnancy and your body has a lot of work to do to get back to its prepregnant state. While some women will get their menstrual periods back right away (within four to six weeks of the delivery), others may experience a lengthier delay of eight to twelve weeks before their fertility returns.

If you are eager to start trying to conceive again, but your menstrual cycles have not yet resumed, you might want to talk with your doctor about your treatment options. Sometimes a single injection of a progestin is all that it takes to jump-start your fertility. You'll find a more detailed discussion of fertility-related issues in Chapter 7.

What are our chances of having another baby die?

While you no doubt want your doctor or midwife to guarantee that your next pregnancy will result in a happy ending, she simply can't do that. After all, she's a midwife or medical doctor, not a fortune teller!

Instead, she'll try to reassure you that the fact that you've experienced a miscarriage, stillbirth, or infant death in the past doesn't necessarily mean that all future pregnancies and births will result in a similarly unhappy outcome—nor does it necessarily mean that you face higher odds of having your next baby die as compared to someone who is pregnant for the very first time. What's more, even if you *do* face an increased risk (as is the case with parents who have a history of such recurring medical conditions as genetic problems or uterine abnormalities), that risk might not be nearly as high as you think.

Consider these facts:

- A mother who has had four miscarriages, but who has previously given birth to a living child, has a 70 percent to 75 percent chance of carrying her next pregnancy to term. What's more, even a mother who has had two or more miscarriages and who has never given birth to a living child has better than 50-50 odds (a 55 percent to 60 percent chance, actually) of having a happy outcome to her next pregnancy.

- Certain types of pregnancy losses can be prevented in a subsequent pregnancy once the problem has been identified and treated. If, for example, you experienced a second-trimester miscarriage because of an incompetent cervix, the insertion of a stitch in your cervix (cerclage) may enable you to carry your next baby to term. Similarly, if your baby was stillborn or died shortly after birth as a result of poorly managed diabetes, you may be able to improve your odds of taking home a healthy baby the next time around by ensuring that your diabetes remains under control both prior to and during pregnancy. (See Chapters 2, 3, and 4.)

- The fact that you have experienced a pregnancy termination or elective abortion doesn't necessarily mean that you're at increased risk of miscarriage or stillbirth the next time around. If you're concerned that you may be at increased risk of experiencing an incompetent cervix or other pregnancy-related complication, either because your last pregnancy was terminated or because you had an elective abortion at some point in the past, here are some reassuring words: The majority of women who have had pregnancy terminations or elective abortions do not experience complications in subsequent pregnancies. When a problem arises, it's typically because the procedure was poorly done or because the mother subsequently developed a pelvic infection. Still, it's not unusual for mothers who have been through a termination or an abortion to feel anxious about the effects that these procedures may have on their future fertility. In some cases, this is because they have unresolved guilt feelings about having had the procedures performed. If you find yourself experiencing extreme anxiety about the way a pregnancy termination or elective abortion may have an impact on your ability to conceive another child, you might wish to seek out the services of a counselor who specializes in helping women to work through their feelings about the death of a baby.

Will my next pregnancy be classified as "high risk"?

You might be surprised to hear your doctor's or midwife's answer to this question. Unless there are some clearly defined medical reasons why your next pregnancy should be treated as "high risk" (e.g., you're epileptic or you have a history of premature labor), chances are your caregiver will classify your pregnancy as "low risk."

Jennifer was shocked to discover that her insurance company considered her second to be low risk, even though her first child's stillbirth remained unexplained. "Astonishingly, we were still considered 'low risk' going into another pregnancy," she recalls. "The insurance company explained that we would have to have another baby die before they would consider us high risk and authorize any visits with a perinatalogist. Our obstetrican's office said that, because no cause was found for Samantha's death, we were not statistically any more likely to lose a child than anyone else and they also did not consider us to be high risk."

As with many parents who have experienced the heartbreak of having a baby die, Jennifer felt anything but "low risk." She was petrified that something would go wrong again and frustrated that her insurance company didn't seem to take her concerns seriously.

Hers was not an isolated case. Most parents who have had a baby die are treated as "low-risk" patients during their subsequent pregnancies. In other words, despite their history, they may not necessarily be considered to be at any increased risk of having a subsequent pregnancy end in tragedy than couples who are embarking on pregnancy for the very first time. This can be a little hard to accept—particularly if you feel tremendously anxious about your chances of ending up with a healthy baby this time.

The best way to resolve your concerns about this matter is to speak frankly with your doctor or midwife about how you are feeling. You need to let her know that while you may technically be "low risk" in the eyes of the medical profession, emotionally you feel anything but. Let her know that you will require plenty of additional reassurance during your next pregnancy, and ask her if she's prepared to be there for you when you need her. If she seems uncomfortable or unwilling to treat you as anything but a low-risk patient, perhaps it's time to consider switching caregivers.

What can I do to increase my chances of having a healthy baby?

Your doctor will no doubt tell you that while there's nothing you can do to guarantee a healthy outcome to your next pregnancy, there's plenty that you can do to put the odds in your favor, starting right now.

Many women view this preconception period as a period of "training" for pregnancy—a chance to get your body in the best possible condition for the ultimate of marathons: motherhood. Jenny was already leading a healthy lifestyle prior to her subsequent pregnancy, but decided to make some improvements nonetheless: "I began eating mostly organic vegetables, purified my water, and cut out all junk food."

Here are some specific steps you can take right now if you're ready to start planning for a healthy pregnancy.

Watch your weight—but not too carefully. While it's always a good idea to try to get to a healthy weight, crash-dieting is not the way to go if you're planning to become pregnant in the near future. Not only do you risk depleting your body of the very nutrients it will need to build a healthy baby: you also risk disrupting ovulation, something that can cause your period to go on an extended vacation. A better approach to losing any unwanted pounds is to eat sensibly and exercise regularly. It may not be particularly glamorous advice, but it's a much healthier alternative for both you and your baby-to-be.

Do a nutrient check. If you're in the habit of skipping meals, it's possible that your body could be missing out on some important nutrients, including folic acid and iron. Since a number of different studies have shown a link between folic iron deficiencies and neural tube defects (such as spina bifida), you'll want to ensure that you're getting the recommended 0.4 mg of folic acid each day. For most women, that means eating plenty of foods that are naturally high in folic acid—oranges, orange juice, honeydew melon, avocados, dark green vegetables (broccoli, brussel sprouts, romaine lettuce, spinach), asparagus, bean sprouts, corn, cauliflower, dried beans, nuts, seeds, bran cereals, whole-grain products, wheat germ, and fortified breakfast cereals—and possibly taking a folic acid supplement as well.

Since your iron requirements double during pregnancy, if you start out your pregnancy by being anemic (low on iron), you will make it that much more difficult for your body to create the additional red blood cells needed to carry oxygen from your lungs to various parts of your body as well as your growing baby. If you feel draggy a lot of the time, it could be because you're not getting enough iron. In this case, you might want to up your intake of such iron-rich foods as whole-grain and enriched cereals, lean meats, dried peas and beans, dark green vegetables, and dried fruits. Here's another important point to note: Vitamin C assists in the absorption of iron, so you might want to enjoy a great big glass or orange juice or a fresh bowl of strawberries along with your breakfast cereal.

Kick any bad habits you haven't managed to break yet. Chances are, you stopped smoking long ago and you wouldn't think of drinking while you were trying to conceive, but just in case you aren't aware of the dangers that these substances pose to the developing baby, here are the facts. Smoking decreases fertility, on average, by 25 percent. Smoking during pregnancy increases your chances of delivering a low-birthweight baby and of having a child die from Sudden Infant Death Syndrome, and it also interferes with the absorption of vitamin C, something that can contribute to iron-deficiency anemia.

Drinking during pregnancy can have equally disastrous consequences for the developing baby: It can lead to serious medical problems, including fetal alcohol syndrome. And don't assume that this advice just applies to mothers-to-be: Preconception health experts are now advising that fathers-to-be give up these vices as well. (While your partner can safely resume drinking alcohol after conception has been achieved, he should plan to kick his smoking habit permanently: Exposure to second-hand smoke is thought to be one of the major contributors to Sudden Infant Death Syndrome.)

Just say no to coffee. While it's hard to get the experts to agree on whether coffee does, in fact, pose significant risks to the developing baby, skipping that morning coffee will give you one less thing to worry about during what could easily shape up to be the most nerve-wracking forty weeks of your life. Caffeine is believed to be harmful to the developing baby because it constricts blood vessels and cuts off the flow of blood to the uterus. Some studies have also linked caffeine with both fertility problems and miscarriage. Bottom line: Why take the chance?

Take a look inside your medicine chest. If you're currently taking any prescription and nonprescription drugs, you'll want to check with your doctor about the advisability of taking them while you're trying to conceive. The most critical period of fetal development takes place during those first few weeks of pregnancy—a time when most women aren't even aware that they're pregnant. (You can find out about the risks that various prescription and non-prescription drugs pose to the developing baby by consulting the drug charts found in Appendix A.) Be sure to ask your doctor if there's a "waiting period" involved after you stop taking a particular drug; if, for example, you're taking Acutane (an acne medication), you should stop taking the drug at least one month before you start trying to conceive.

Make sure you're not getting too much of a good thing. Vitamins are healthy, right? Well, maybe. Studies have shown that large doses of certain types of vitamins can be harmful to the developing baby. If you don't think you can get all the necessary nutrients in your diet through healthy eating alone, look for a vitamin that has been specially formulated for use during pregnancy.

Get any chronic health conditions under control. If you suffer from a chronic disease or serious medical condition, you'll want to get it under control before you start trying to conceive. Certain conditions, like insulin-dependent diabetes, place your baby at increased risk of birth defects. Others, like lupus, can jeopardize your pregnancy by increasing your chances of experiencing a miscarriage or going into premature labor. You can find more information on the roles that certain maternal conditions play in miscarriage, stillbirth, and infant death by referring to Chapters 2, 3, and 4.

Check to see that your immunizations are up to date. The American College of Obstetricians and Gynecologists recommends that women who are planning a pregnancy make sure they have received a tetanus-diptheria booster shot within the past ten years and have been immunized against measles, mumps, rubella, and chicken pox, if they don't already have immunities to these diseases. They also recommend that certain women be vaccinated against hepatitis A, hepatitis B, Lyme disease, influenza, and pneumococcus. Your doctor will be able to tell you if you're a good candidate for one or more of these vaccines.

Note: While there was a lot of concern a few years ago about the rubella vaccine causing chronic joint or nerve problems in certain women, the *Journal of the American Medical Association* has spoken out in favor of continued immunization of rubella-susceptible women. When you consider the devastating effects on the fetus if rubella is contracted during pregnancy—birth defects and even death—you'll agree that the vaccine and the resulting three-month delay before you can start trying to conceive are a small price to pay for avoiding this type of tragedy.

Get tested for STDs. There's no denying it: Your sexual past can come back to haunt you at reproduction time. If there's even the slightest possibility that you could have an STD, you'll want to seek out treatment before you become pregnant. Here's why: Gonorrhea and chlamydia can impair your fertility, syphillis can cause birth defects, and herpes can be harmful (even fatal) to your baby. If you are HIV positive or have developed full-blown AIDS, your pregnancy will have to be particularly well managed to reduce the risk that you will infect your baby.

Watch out for workplace hazards. Are you or your partner exposed to hazardous substances on the job? If so, you might want to consider a job change or, at the very least, a job modification. The following types of substances should be avoided while you're trying to conceive and during pregnancy: chemicals such as paints, lacquers, woodfinishing products, industrial or household solvents, and darkroom chemicals; nuclear medicine testing procedures, X rays, and anesthesia—day-to-day hazards for many people who are employed in hospitals, laboratories, and dental offices; and lethal and teratogenic gases used in fire fighting.

Deal with your root problem now. While the jury is still out on the dangers of dyeing your hair during pregnancy, this is one risk to your baby that you can easily eliminate. Get your hair dyed before you start trying to conceive or switch to a toxin-free type of hair color. At the very least, you should avoid having your hair dyed while you're actively trying to conceive or during the first trimester of pregnancy.

The best advice that anyone can give you about preconception planning is to start acting like you're already pregnant *before* you start trying to conceive. That means making the healthiest possible choices for your future baby long before the pregnancy test becomes positive. The payoff to going this route can be enormous: Rather than spending the next nine months sweating about the glass of wine that you drank the night your baby was conceived or the fact that you got your hair dyed before you knew you were pregnant, you'll be able to feel confident that you did everything possible to get your pregnancy off to the healthiest possible start.

Will my pregnancy be managed differently this time around?

You probably have a few ideas about how you would like your next pregnancy to be managed. You might decide, for example, that you would like to have an ultrasound performed as early in the pregnancy as possible so that you can see that reassuring flicker of your baby's heartbeat on the ultrasound screen, or that you'd like to come in for more than the standard number of prenatal checkups.

It's important to convey this information to your doctor before you become pregnant, so you can be sure you'll both be working from the same game plan. That way, if it looks as if you're going to have to fight every inch of the way to get the support and reassurance you need, you'll still have plenty of time to start shopping around for another doctor.

Following is a list of questions that should help you to decide whether your current doctor is going to be able to provide you with the support and reassurance you have every right to expect (no, *demand!*) during your next pregnancy.

Questions to Ask a Potential Caregiver

- How soon will you see me once my pregnancy is confirmed?
  After that, how frequent will my prenatal visits be? Can I schedule extra prenatal visits if I'm feeling particularly anxious?

- Do you plan to perform at least one ultrasound during my first trimester to confirm that the pregnancy is proceeding as it should? At what other stage(s) of pregnancy will you send me for an ultrasound?
- What other tests will you order during my pregnancy? What are the pros and cons of each of these procedures?
- Under what circumstances, if any, would you transfer me into the care of a high-risk pregnancy specialist?
- How will I get in touch with you in the event of an emergency? Who will provide backup during those times when you are out-of-town or otherwise unavailable?
- Will you be able to take my nonemergency calls during working hours? If not, who will be available to handle my calls?
- Do you intend to inform each member of your staff about my history so that they can handle my questions and concerns in an appropriate manner?
- How likely is it that you will be present at the birth of my baby? If you're not available, who else might be present? Will I have a chance to meet this person ahead of time?
- Under what circumstances would you induce my labor early?
- How much time will you spend with me when I'm in labor?
- How would you feel if I wanted to use the services of a doula or other support person during labor?
- Will my labor be managed any differently this time around? If so, how?
- Will you perform the newborn check yourself or will a pediatrician be performing the check?

Your doctor or midwife will likely wrap up the appointment by giving you a physical examination. You can expect:

- A pelvic exam and a Pap smear (to check for symptomless infections, ovarian cysts, and other conditions that might be difficult or risky to treat during pregnancy).
- A blood test (to determine if you are anemic or carrying any sexually transmitted diseases).

- A urine test (to screen for diabetes, urinary tract infections, kidney infections, and asymptomatic infections that may pose a problem during pregnancy).
- A rubella test (to determine whether you are immune to rubella).

GENETIC COUNSELING

According to the American College of Obstetricians and Gynecologists, approximately 3 percent of babies born in the United States have some sort of major birth defect. In approximately 20 percent of these cases, the cause is genetic.

There are five major types of genetic disorders listed here. Some of these occur only when both parents carry the same defective gene; others occur when just one of the parents carries a defective gene.

The Five Major Types of Genetic Disorders

TYPE OF DISORDER	WHAT CAUSES IT	EXAMPLES OF THIS DISORDER
Dominant gene disorders (a genetic disorder that occurs when a baby inherits an abnormal gene from one or both parents)	A single abnormal gene from either parent.	Huntington's disease
Recessive gene disorder (a genetic disorder that occurs when a baby inherits an abnormal gene from both parents)	Both genes in a gene pair (in other words, the gene passed on by each parent) are abnormal.	Cystic fibrosis, sickle-cell disease, Tay-Sachs disease, Thalassemia
X-linked gene disorders or sex-linked gene disorders (genetic disorders that involve an abnormal gene on the x-chromosome; these disorders generally affect males only because they don't have	An abnormal gene on the X-chromosome.	Hemophilia, Duchenne muscular dystrophy

TYPE OF DISORDER	WHAT CAUSES IT	EXAMPLES OF THIS DISORDER
a Y chromosome to counteract or compensate for the abnormality, as females do)		
Chromosomal disorders (See Chapters 2, 3, and 4.)	Problems with the fetus' chromosomes. In most cases, they are caused by an error that occurred when the sperm or egg were being formed, but some are genetic in origin.	Down's syndrome, fragile X syndrome, Klinefelter syndrome, Turner syndrome
Multifactorial disorders (disorders that are caused by both genetic and environmental factors)	A mix of both genetic and environmental factors.	Congenital heart defects, neural tube defects

Genetic counseling is generally recommended to couples who have a family history of a particular genetic disorder or who come from certain ethnic groups in which there is a higher-than-average number of carriers of a particular genetic disorder. Tay-Sachs—a disease that causes fatal brain damage—is more common in people of Central and Eastern European Ashkenazi Jewish descent and in certain French-Canadian subpopulations. Sickle-cell anemia—a blood disorder—is more commmon in African-Americans and people of Mediterrarean, Arabian, and Asian Indian origin. Thalassemia—a blood disorder—is more common in people of Mediterranean and Indian origin.

Because it's possible to carry a gene for a particular disorder without knowing it, some parents who have experienced miscarriage, stillbirth, or infant death choose to go for genetic counseling. The following checklist may help you to decide if you are likely to benefit from genetic counseling.

As helpful as it can be, genetic counseling isn't necessarily for everyone. If you think that "knowing too much" will only boost your worry level during your next pregnancy, you might want to forgo genetic counseling. If, however, you'd like to be armed with as many facts as possible before you start trying to conceive, it could be just what the doctor ordered.

Are You a Good Candidate for Genetic Counseling?

You are likely a good candidate for genetic counseling if
- You or your partner have been diagnosed with a particular genetic disorder.
- You or your partner suspect that you may have a particular genetic disorder.
- You, your partner, your child, or another close family member has a birth defect or a condition that has not been diagnosed.
- You have given birth to a liveborn or stillborn infant with an undiagnosed birth defect or condition, or have experienced three or more miscarriages or an unexplained stillbirth.
- You had a miscarriage where tests of the placental tissue revealed a chromosome abnormality.
- You have a close family member with a disorder that you suspect is genetic.
- You are concerned that you may be a carrier for a genetic disorder that runs in your (or your partner's) ethnic group.
- You and your partner are planning a pregnancy and want to know your chances of giving birth to a baby with a genetic disorder or birth defect.

How Genetic Counseling Works

In you decide to go for genetic counseling, you will meet with a genetic counselor who will help you to understand how genetic disorders are passed along and then assess your chances of passing on any such disorders to any future children you conceive. The counselor will also make you aware of the types of tests that are available to you:

- carrier tests (performed prior to conception to assess your risk of passing on a particular genetic disorder to any future children)
- preimplantation tests (can detect genetic disorders in the fertilized embryo prior to implantation for couples who are conceiving through in vitro fertilization) and
- prenatal diagnostic tests (performed during pregnancy to determine whether the baby you are carrying is affected by a particular genetic disorder)

We'll talk about prenatal testing in Chapter 11, so our discussion in this chapter will focus on the type of testing that you'd be most interested in knowing about prior to pregnancy—carrier testing.

Carrier Testing

As the name implies, carrier testing is designed to help you to determine whether you are a carrier for a particular genetic disorder. (Remember, you don't have to exhibit any symptoms of a particular disorder in order to be a carrier.)

There have been some amazing breakthroughs in carrier testing in recent years—breakthroughs that would have been the stuff of science fiction novels until very recently. It's now possible, for example, for couples of Jewish descent to undergo an Ashkenazi DNA carrier test that will predict with 95 percent to 100 percent accuracy whether a particular person is a carrier for such diseases as Tay-Sachs, Gaucher's, Niemann-Pick–Type A, and Canavan disease, all of which are more common in people of Jewish descent. (*Note:* These diseases are classified as lipid storage diseases. Because a baby with one of these diseases lacks certain enzymes or has some defective enzymes, it isn't possible for the baby's body to metabolize substances properly. Over time, the baby accumulates buildups of these substances in critical areas of the body such as the brain and the liver, something that can cause organ damage or even the death of the baby.)

Similarly, couples of African, Hispanic, Mediterranean, Asian, and Middle Eastern descent, who are at increased risk of giving birth to a child with such potentially life-threatening blood diseases as sickle-cell disease and thalassemia, can also undergo carrier testing for these diseases.

Carrier testing may soon be part of the standard prenatal workup for would-be parents. It's now possible to detect 90 percent of carriers of cystic fibrosis (a lung disease) and a significant number of carriers for—and fetuses affected by—fragile X syndrome (a major cause of mental retardation).

While carrier testing can be a source of valuable information—some couples want to know with certainty what their odds are of having a baby who is affected by a particular disease and what their options are for diagnosing that condition prenatally—sometimes that knowledge can be emotionally costly. Learning that you are a carrier for a particular disease may devastate you. What's more, it could make it more difficult for you to obtain health insurance. (You can find a more detailed discussion of this topic—including tables that spell out the disease incidence for various populations—in our book *The Unofficial Guide to Having a Baby*.)

Now that you've settled on a caregiver, gone for your preconception checkup, and decided whether genetic testing is right for you, you're ready to move on to the "action phase" of planning a pregnancy.

⚘ 7 *Trying Again*

AS MUCH AS you might like to believe that getting pregnant is as easy as abandoning your birth control method for a month, for most couples it's not quite that easy. Given that even the most fertile couples have no more than a one-in-four chance of conceiving in any given cycle (see "The Odds of Conceiving in Any Given Cycle or Year" following), it's hardly surprising that the vast majority of couples don't win at baby roulette the first time around.

Getting pregnant is, after all, a bit of a numbers game. And, like any game of chance, the more times you play, the more chances you have to win. Still, even if you don't manage to luck out and become pregnant during your very first month of trying, there's plenty of cause for optimism over the long-run. While you may have less than a one-in-four chance of conceiving this month, if you're in your early thirties and actively trying to conceive, you have better than a three-in-four chance of being pregnant a year from now.

In the meantime, however, you're in for quite a roller-coaster ride. If you've got your heart set on conceiving again quickly, you may find that your entire emotional state hinges on what stage you are at in your menstrual cycle: As ovulation approaches, you feel cautiously optimistic that this could be your lucky cycle; when your period starts again, you feel angry and disappointed.

In this chapter, we will talk about the challenges of conceiving again after a miscarriage, stillbirth, or infant death. We will start by reviewing the facts about conception and talking about what you can do to increase your odds of conceiving quickly. Then we will discuss some of the most

The Odds of Conceiving in Any Given Cycle or Year

AGE	ODDS THAT YOU WILL CONCEIVE IN ANY GIVEN MONTH	AVERAGE NUMBER OF MONTHS IT TAKES TO CONCEIVE	PROBABILITY THAT YOU WILL BECOME PREGNANT WITHIN ONE YEAR
Early 20s	20 percent to 25 percent	4 to 5 months	93 percent to 97 percent
Late 20s	15 percent to 20 percent	5 to 6.7 months	86 percent to 93 percent
Early 30s	10 percent to 15 percent	6.7 to 10 months	72 percent to 86 percent
Late 30s	8.3 percent to 10 percent	10 to 12 months	65 percent to 72 percent

Adapted from a similar chart in *How to Get Pregnant,* by Sherman J. Silber, M.D. (New York: Warner Books, 1980). NOTE: The data reported by Silber is supported by some more recent data from the National Center for Health Statistics, which reports that a couple under the age of twenty-five has a 96 percent of conceiving within one year; a couple between the ages of twenty-five and thirty-four has an 86 percent chance of conceiving within a year; and a couple between the ages of thirty-five and forty-four has a 78 percent chance of conceiving within one year.

frequently asked questions about trying again when you have already experienced the death of a baby. Finally, we'll talk about how you and your partner may be feeling as you start trying to conceive again.

WHAT YOU CAN DO TO INCREASE YOUR ODDS OF CONCEIVING QUICKLY

If your heart is sinking at the thought of having to wait months—maybe even years—to see the home pregnancy test turn positive again, take heart. While there's no magic "on-off" switch you can hit to kick your reproductive system into overdrive, there are a few things you can do to increase your odds of conceiving quickly. Here are a few tips.

Brush Up on the Facts of Life

While you might think you have a handle on how your reproductive system works, there's a surprising amount of misinformation floating around.

One study found that many couples assume that they can become pregnant within the few days after ovulation when, in fact, actually the opposite is true: The monthly window of opportunity for conception slams shut approximately twelve hours after you ovulate.

Other studies have indicated that some couples who think they are experiencing fertility problems are simply mistiming intercourse. There's a common misconception that you ovulate two weeks after the first day of your last period when, in fact, you ovulate two weeks before your next period. It's a moot point if you have a "textbook" twenty-eight-day cycle, but it can throw your baby-making efforts off by an entire week if your cycle happens to be thirty-five days long. Even the hardiest sperm can't camp out for an additional week in a fallopian tube, hoping that some egg will come strolling by.

Because there's so much inaccurate information in circulation on the whole subject of conception, let's take a moment to quickly run through the most important facts about the female reproductive system. The first thing you need to know is that there's no such thing as a "one size fits all" menstrual cycle. While a "textbook woman" (whoever she is!) has a twenty-eight-day cycle, it's not unusual for women to have cycles that are a week longer or shorter than that. (If your cycle is shorter than twenty-one days or longer than thirty-five days, however, your cycle is definitely outside the "normal" range, and it's possible you have a fertility problem.)

Not all women can set their watches by their menstrual cycles. While some women are fortunate enough to be blessed by gloriously regular menstrual cycles, others aren't. Unfortunately, it becomes a little more challenging to predict your fertile period accurately if the length of your cycle varies a lot from month to month. Also, there are both ovulatory (cycles in which ovulation occurs) and anovulatory (cycles in which ovulation does not occur) menstrual cycles. It's not unusual for a woman to occasionally have anovulatory cycles (perhaps because illness or severe stress caused her not to ovulate), but women who regularly fail to ovulate probably have an underlying fertility problem (polycystic ovarian syndrome, for example).

An ovulatory menstrual cycle (a cycle in which ovulation occurs) consists of two distinct phases: the follicular (or proliferative) phase and the luteal (or secretory) phase. During the follicular phase, approximately twenty eggs begin to ripen inside fluid-filled sacks (called follicles) that can be found inside the ovaries. At the same time that the eggs are ripening, the level of estrogen in your body begins to rise, boosting the production of cervical mucus (the egg-white-like substance that is designed to help the sperm make its way to the egg) and causing the lining of your uterus (endometrium) to thicken so that it will be ready for the implantation of the fertilized egg, should conception occur. Toward the end of the follicular phase (right before ovulation), the high levels of estrogen trigger the pituitary gland to release a brief surge of lutenizing hormone (LH). The LH then causes the most fully developed of all the developing follicles to rupture and release its egg. (If you've ever experienced pain in the lower abdomen—the sensation the Germans call *mittelschmerz* or "pain in the middle," referring to pain at midcycle—this is what you were feeling.)

The release of the egg signals the beginning of the second half of your cycle—the luteal phase. The ruptured follicle (now known as the corpus luteum or "yellow body," because of its color) begins to produce progesterone, the hormone that your body needs in order to sustain a pregnancy. (The corpus luteum will continue to produce this hormone until the placenta assumes responsibility for manufacturing it toward the end of the first trimester of pregnancy.) The rising levels of progesterone cause the endometrial glands to prepare the uterus for the arrival of a fertilized egg. If conception occurs, the progesterone levels remain high in order to support the pregnancy; if conception doesn't occur, the corpus luteum begins to degenerate, progesterone levels begin to drop, and—twelve to fourteen days after ovulation—the uterus begins to shed the endometrial lining that it built up in anticipation of a pregnancy, beginning your menstrual period.

Know Thy Cycle

Of course, it's one thing to know how a "textbook" woman's menstrual cycle works and quite another to know exactly how your own cycle works. Since learning how to predict your most fertile days can be one of the keys to achieving a pregnancy sooner rather than later, you might want to learn how to monitor your body's three key fertility signals:

Your cervical mucus. The quality and quantity of your cervical mucus (the substance secreted by your cervix) changes dramatically over the course of your menstrual cycle. As ovulation approaches, your secretions become thin, clear, and slippery (like egg white) rather than thick and opaque. After ovulation, the secretions become thick and opaque again. (Because the function of the "egg white" mucus is to help to transport the sperm to the awaiting egg, your body needs this type of mucus during your most fertile period.) Monitoring this fertility signal is relatively easy: You simply take note of the quality and quantity of the cervical fluid that shows up on your toilet tissue each time you wipe yourself when you go to the bathroom.

The position and feel of your cervix. The position and the feel of your cervix also changes as your menstrual cycle progresses. As ovulation approaches, your cervix rises up in your vagina and becomes soft and fleshy. The os (the opening of your cervix) also dilates slightly so that it will be easier for the sperm to make their way into your uterus. Then, after ovulation, hormonal changes cause your cervix to drop down a bit again. You can monitor this particular fertility sign yourself by washing your hands throughly (to help prevent infection) and then inserting your fingers in your vagina and feeling for your cervix. (You'll want to try to do your checks at relatively the same time each day, for consistency's sake.) In addition to checking the position of your cervix (high or low), note how your cervix feels. If it feels firm, like the tip of your nose, you probably haven't ovulated yet; if it feels soft and mushy, kind of like your lips, your body is probably getting ready to ovulate. *Note:* Don't be discouraged if you have trouble monitoring this particular fertility sign. Even obstetricians have difficulty appreciating these often subtle signs when they're doing checks on their patients!

Your basal body temperature (BBT). Your basal body temperature (your temperature first thing in the morning before you get out of bed and start moving around) can help you to track your most fertile periods because there's a distinct temperature shift after ovulation occurs. This is because your body suddenly starts producing large quantities of

Basal Body Temperature (BBT) Chart

	1	2	3	4	5	6	7	8	9	10	11	12	13	14	15	16	17	18	19	20	21	22	23	24	25	26	27	28	29	30	31	32	33	34	35
Date																																			
Time																																			
Intercourse																																			
Cervical mucus/ cervical position																																			
Menstruation																																			
Cycle Day	1	2	3	4	5	6	7	8	9	10	11	12	13	14	15	16	17	18	19	20	21	22	23	24	25	26	27	28	29	30	31	32	33	34	35
99.0																																			
98.9																																			
98.8																																			
98.7																																			
98.6																																			
98.5																																			
98.4																																			

98.3	98.2	98.1	98.0	97.9	97.8	97.7	97.6	97.5	97.4	97.3	97.2	97.1	97.0	Comments (e.g. illness, insomnia taking your temperature earlier or later than usual)

progesterone, which cause your temperature to shoot up. Typically, right before she ovulates, a woman's temperature will dip slightly from her usual preovulatory temperature range of 97.0 to 97.5 degrees and then shoot up to her postovulatory temperature range of 97.6 to 97.8. (*Note:* Not everyone experiences the brief temperature dip.) You can monitor this fertility signal by taking your BBT each morning before you get out of bed and then charting your results on a temperature graph. You can either make your own chart using graph paper or photocopy the one provided on pages 116–117.

Basic Instructions for Using the Chart

- Start a new chart on the first day of each menstrual cycle (e.g., the day on which your period starts). Record the month and day across the top of the chart (e.g., "1/1," "1/2," "1/3").
- Decide what time you plan to take your temperature each morning and set your alarm clock for that time. (You'll still need to take your temperature at 6:00 A.M. on the weekend, if that's the time you get up to go to work during the week, since varying the time that you take your temperature by even an hour or two can affect the accuracy of your readings.)
- Keep your temperature chart, your thermometer, and a pencil on the night table beside your bed. A digital thermometer may be a better choice than a mercury thermometer: Digital thermometers are easier to read, don't require shaking (something that can throw off the accuracy of your temperature reading), and they give you your results in two minutes (as opposed to the five minutes required for an accurate temperature from a mercury thermometer).
- Each morning, place the thermometer in your mouth as soon as you wake up. Then, record your temperature on the chart by drawing a dot in the center of the appropriate box. (As you get more readings, you'll be able to connect the dots to get a better feel for the pattern of your temperature readings.) Be sure to note the time that you took your temperature in the appropriate box on the chart, too.
- Note the days when you have menstrual bleeding or spotting by placing checkmarks in the appropriate boxes for those days.
- Note the days when you have sexual intercourse by placing checkmarks in the appropriate boxes for those days.

- If you're also monitoring the quantity and quality of your cervical mucus and the position of your cervix, you can jot down some notes on those observations, too. You'll probably want to come up with your own form of shorthand—e.g. using "+" or "–" to indicate an increase or decrease in the amount of cervical mucus over the day before; using *s* to describe sticky cervical mucus, *c* to describe creamy cervical mucus, and *e* to describe "egg white" cervical mucus; using *h* for high and *l* for low to describe the position of your cervix; and using *f* for firm and *m* for mushy to describe the way your cervix feels. (*Note:* These are some of the abbreviations that Toni Weschler suggests in her excellent book, *Taking Charge of Your Fertility* [Harper-Collins, 1995].)

Don't assume that your basal body temperature chart will tell you when to have intercourse. You have to be having intercourse at regular intervals (daily or every other day) *before* that temperature shift shows up if you hope to conceive. The reason is obvious: Once your temperature shoots up, ovulation has already occurred, and any subsequent baby making efforts will be in vain.

Still, even if it isn't exactly the fertility world's equivalent of a crystal ball, your temperature chart can provide you with a lot of valuable information about your fertility. It can:

- Tell you whether you're actually ovulating. If your temperature doesn't rise at midcycle, it's possible that you aren't.
- Tell you whether your luteal phase (the post-ovulatory phase of your menstrual cycle) is sufficiently long to allow implantation and development of the early pregnancy tissues to occur. If there isn't a twelve-day or longer gap between ovulation and the start of your period, you may be experiencing a fertility problem known as a luteal phase defect.
- Tell you whether your progesterone levels are sufficiently high during your luteal phase. If your temperature levels aren't much higher than they were during the first phase of your menstrual cycle, it's possible that your body isn't producing adequate quantities of progesterone, something that can lead to miscarriage.
- Tell you whether you are pregnant. If your temperature remains elevated for at least eighteen days after ovulation—or at least three days

longer than your longest nonpregnant luteal phase to date—you're probably pregnant.

- Help tell you whether the "late period" that you experienced was, in fact, an early miscarriage. If your temperature remained elevated for more than eighteen days after ovulation and then began to drop, you probably experienced an early miscarriage. If you didn't have a temperature chart to refer to, you would probably have simply assumed that your period was late.

- Help you to predict—after several months of observation—when your most fertile days typically fall. Obviously, temperature charts are useful for this purpose only for women whose cycles are relatively consistent month after month.

- Save you time if you have to consult a doctor for treatment of a fertility problem. Often, one of the first things that a fertility specialist will ask you to do is to track your BBT for a couple of months. If you haven't been doing so all this time, there may be a delay in diagnosing or treating your underlying fertility problem until you manage to collect a couple of months' worth of BBT chart data.

While monitoring your fertility signals can give you a sense of moving toward your goal of becoming pregnant again, not everyone chooses to go this route. If you think that tracking your fertility to this extent is going to drive you (or your partner) crazy, you might be better off putting the thermometer away for a while and leaving things to Mother Nature. (*Note:* Some guys find that their libidos disappear when they're confronted by a woman who is frantically waving a BBT chart. The pressure to "perform" can simply be too much. The moral of the story? If you suspect that tonight might be "the big night," you might want to keep the news to yourself—at least until after Romeo has made his contribution to Project Baby!)

Make Love on the Right Days

While this may seem like a no-brainer, as any fertility specialist can tell you, it's the cause of more "fertility" problems than you might think.

Since an egg is only capable of being fertilized during the first twelve hours after its release (after that, an unfertilized egg will degenerate and die), you need to either time intercourse so that it will occur during this tiny twelve-hour window or ensure that there's an ample supply of sperm already waiting in the fallopian tubes for an egg to come by. (Unlike eggs, which have an unbelievably short "best before" date, sperm can survive for up to five days inside the female reproductive tract.)

Recent studies have shown that the most fertile period in a woman's cycle occurs during the five days leading up to and including the day of ovulation. Making love every day—or even every other day—during this time period will ensure that there's a steady supply of sperm waiting for that chance to rendezvous with an egg.

Here's some final food for thought on the timing front: A recent study at the University of Modena in Italy concluded that men's sperm counts are 25 percent higher between 5:00 P.M. and 5:30 P.M. than they are between 7:00 A.M. and 7:30 A.M. So if you're a morning person, you might want to postpone that early morning romance until later in the day!

Don't Get Too Much of a Good Thing

It can be physically and mentally exhausting to attempt to make love every single day, particularly if you initiate the daily baby-making routine too early in your cycle. What's more, it doesn't do all that much to increase your odds of conceiving quickly.

Researchers at the National Institute of Environmental Health Sciences concluded that couples who had intercourse every other day during their most fertile periods had a 22 percent chance of conceiving in any given cycle as opposed to the 25 percent chance faced by couples who had intercourse every day.

In some cases, overachieving in the bedroom can actually work against you. Daily sex is not recommended for couples in which the male partner is "subfertile" as a result of a lower-than-normal sperm count. Not only should they stick with an "every other day" regime during their partner's most fertile days, they should also consider conserving sperm by refraining from ejaculating at all during the several days leading up to this period.

Abstaining from sex in an effort to conserve sperm isn't a good strategy for most couples, however, as studies have shown that not ejaculating for more than seven days can decrease the male partner's fertility. (Any gain in sperm counts resulting from this type of "conservation measure" is more than offset by the buildup of aged sperm cells with lower fertilization potential.) What's more, if you miscalculate the timing of your most fertile period and only manage to have intercourse once during this time, you could end up drastically reducing your chances of conceiving in a particular cycle. Studies have shown that couples who have intercourse only once during their fertile period have just a 10 percent chance of conceiving.

Don't hop out of bed right away   While you don't need to stand on your head for a half hour after making love, as some folk wisdom suggests, it's a good idea to remain in a horizontal position for at least five minutes after you've finished making love. The reason is obvious: Gravity is a formidable adversary for swimming sperm!

Create a sperm-friendly vaginal environment   It's one thing to get the sperm into your body. It's quite another to make sure they can survive once they arrive. That's why it's important to try to create the most sperm-friendly vaginal environment possible. That means avoiding vaginal sprays and scented tampons (they can cause a pH imbalance in your vagina); artificial lubricants, vegetable oils, glycerin, and natural lubricants such as saliva (they kill off sperm); douching (it can cause vaginal infections and/or pelvic inflammatory disease, and may wash away the cervical mucus that would otherwise help to transport the sperm to the egg); and seeking treatments for vaginal infections that can alter the vaginal environment. (*Note:* If you really need some sort of lubrication, use egg whites that have been warmed to room temperature. Of course, you won't want to go with this particular alternative if you happen to be allergic to eggs.)

Go with the Candlelight, but Skip the Glass of Wine

While having a glass of wine might help to put you in the mood, new evidence suggests that women who are hoping to conceive in the near future should become virtual teetotalers. Researchers studied 430 Danish couples of childbearing age for seven years and discovered that women who drank between five and ten servings of alcohol per week reduced their fertility by a startling 50 percent. What's more, those who had more than ten drinks per week saw their fertility dive by two-thirds.

Here's another good reason for passing on that glass of wine: If you do manage to conceive, you'll end up sentencing yourself to nine months of sweating about the effects of that one glass of wine! Trust us, it simply isn't worth it.

Pass on the java Studies go back and forth on this particular issue, but some have indicated that excessive coffee consumption may play a role in infertility or miscarriage. (We'll talk more about this issue in Chapter 10.)

If you absolutely have to have some sort of caffeinated beverage from time to time, reach for a cup of tea instead. A recent study conducted through a Kaiser Permanente Medical Center Program in California showed that drinking half a cup of black tea (as opposed to standard orange pekoe tea) or nonherbal tea can actually double a couple's odds of conceiving in any given cycle.

Just say no to drugs Not only are many prescription and over-the-counter drugs potentially harmful to the developing baby, some can actually hinder your chances of conceiving by drying up your cervical mucus. Perennial offenders include antihistamines, antispasmodics, and cough syrup mixtures that don't contain guaifenesin (a common ingredient in cough syrups that is known to improve the quantity and quality of cervical mucus).

Forget about crash dieting Resist the temptation to try to get rid of the weight you gained during your last pregnancy overnight. Overexercising, bingeing, starving yourself, and yo-yo dieting can all interfere with ovulation. If you've got some extra pounds to lose, you should aim for a slow, gradual weight loss.

Also, don't set your weight goal unreasonably low. Underweight women experience even more fertility problems than overweight women. A recent study at the University of South Carolina revealed that 90 percent of underweight women and 76 percent of overweight women who had previously been unable to conceive managed to become pregnant once they reached their ideal weight.

Get Your Partner in on the Act

Make sure that your partner is doing his bit, too—and we don't just mean in the bedroom. He should do whatever he can to safeguard his own fertility. That means:

- Not exposing his genitals to excessive heat for long periods of time (e.g., hot tubs, hot baths, or working in jobs such as long-distance trucking that require sitting in one place for long stretches).
- Avoiding exposure to toxic chemicals and radiation, both of which can lead to permanent fertility damage.
- Not using anabolic steroids to build up muscle, since the fertility problems that typically occur when you're using steroids aren't always reversible.
- Postponing surgery to the urogenital area to avoid the buildup of scar tissue, which could interfere with the passage of sperm.
- Kicking his cigarette habit, since smoking can interfere with sperm motility.
- Not consuming large amounts of alcohol, which can lower both testosterone levels and sperm counts.
- Not using recreational drugs, such as cocaine or marijuana, or medications such as cimetidine (an antacid), certain antibiotics, and chemotherapeutic agents, all of which can reduce sperm counts.
- Avoiding certain blood-pressure drugs, which can lead to ejaculatory dysfunction.
- Avoiding the use of 6-mercaptopurine for inflammatory bowel disease, since a recent study linked its use by the male partner to higher rates of pregnancy complications and birth defects.
- Avoiding herbal medicines such as St. John's wort, ginkgo biloba, and echinacea, all of which are believed to damage sperm.
- Avoiding sports injuries, which can prevent sperm maturation, cause structural and hormonal damage to the genitals, and lead to ejaculatory problems.
- Limiting the amount of time he spends on his bike, since a recent study at the University of California indicated that men who cycle more than 160 km each week put their fertility at risk, because bike seats can cause damage to the arteries and nerves in the genital area.
- Losing weight, if he's carrying around a lot of extra pounds, since significantly overweight men tend to have unusually high levels of estrogen—something that can interfere with communication between the testes and the pituitary gland.

QUESTIONS YOU MAY HAVE ABOUT TRYING
TO CONCEIVE AGAIN

Many couples find that they have a lot of questions about trying to conceive again. Here are answers to some of the most common questions.

How do stress and grief affect a couple's fertility?

While severe stress can cause a woman's reproductive system to shut down, the female reproductive system is designed to be remarkably resilient. Just think of the number of babies who are born during wartime and in countries in which mere survival is a struggle. If you're getting your period regularly and your cycles are within the normal range (e.g., twenty-one to thirty-five days), you can assume that stress isn't interfering with your fertility. If, however, it has been a number of months since your baby died and you still haven't started menstruating again, it's possible that you are experiencing some sort of fertility problem, in which case you'll want to set up an appointment with your doctor to discuss your concerns.

Is there anything you can do to increase your odds of
conceiving a baby of a particular sex?

It's not unusual for parents who have been through miscarriage, stillbirth, or infant death to have a strong desire to conceive a baby of a particular sex. Some parents are eager to have a baby of the same sex as the baby who died, while others would prefer to give birth to a baby of the opposite sex. Those whose babies have died as a result of a genetic problem that only occurs in males or females may have a particularly strong desire to conceive a baby of the opposite sex.

Unfortunately, it's not nearly as easy to conceive a baby of a particular sex as most people believe. While one popular theory states that you can increase your chances of conceiving a baby of a particular sex by having sex on certain days (e.g., by having sex no closer than two to three days prior to ovulation if you're hoping for a girl, or by timing intercourse as close to ovulation as possible if you want a boy), this theory hasn't been able to withstand good, old-fashioned scientific scrutiny. Everyone knows someone who conceived a child of the "right" sex by following this advice, but what we don't know is how many of them would have conceived a baby of this sex anyway, whether or not they decided to time intercourse a particular way.

Even high-tech methods of sex selection haven't been proven to pan out. A 1996 article in the British newspaper *The Independent* revealed, for example, that one high-tech fertility clinic that promised to help couples achieve a baby of the sex of their choice offered 50-50 odds of success—exactly the same chances that are given by Mother Nature!

Should I buy an ovulation predictor kit?

The companies that manufacture ovulation predictor kits manage to ring up about $23 million in sales each year in the United States alone. It's not hard to figure out why the sales for this particular product are so enormous: You can expect to spend about $30 per cycle on a kit, assuming that your periods are regular. (If they're not, you'll need to purchase extra tests, something that simply adds to the cost.) Since it takes a "typical" couple approximately six months to conceive, you can expect to spend close to $200 on ovulation predictor kits if you use them each month.

Does this mean you should leave the ovulation predictor kits on the drugstore shelf and rely on your BBT chart instead? Not necessarily. There are some advantages to using them to help pinpoint your most fertile days. They allow you to predict the LH surge that typically occurs twenty-four to thirty-six hours before ovulation. (You won't be able to obtain this type of information by consulting your temperature graph.) In most cases, that can help you to ensure that there's an ample supply of sperm waiting in your fallopian tubes before ovulation occurs. Also, they can help to satisfy you that you're doing everything possible to try to conceive. You won't find yourself wondering after the fact if you might have had a happier outcome in a particular cycle if you had forked over the cash for an ovulation kit!

They aren't necessarily the crystal balls that the drug companies would have you believe they are, however. There are, in fact, two key drawbacks to ovulation predictor kits:

- They can't tell you whether a particular LH surge is "the real thing" (the one that immediately precedes ovulation) or merely a good imitation. (Some women experience a series of LH surges before the one that signals that ovulation is about to occur.)
- The fact that you're having an LH surge doesn't necessarily mean that

you're ovulating. It's possible to have the surge but then to fail to ovulate.

Only you can decide whether you want to go the ovulation predictor kit route. If you're obsessed with the idea of conceiving quickly, they might help to buy you a little peace of mind. Thirty dollars a month seems a small price to pay for that.

Should we use any particular position when we're trying to conceive?

No chapter on fertility would be complete without a discussion of sexual positions!

The best sexual positions to use when you're trying to conceive a baby are those that enable the sperm to be deposited high up in the vagina right next to the cervix. After all, you want to work with—not against—gravity!

If you're having trouble conceiving, you might want to try giving Mother Nature a bit of a helping hand. After you have intercourse using the missionary position (man on top), remain on your back and tuck a pillow under your hips so that you can make it as easy as possible for the sperm to reach the cervix. The semen will basically be running downhill when you're in this position, and pooling at the opening of your cervix. You don't have to stay in this position all day, of course. You can hop out of bed after half an hour.

Here's another important point to bear in mind: You increase your chances of conceiving if you have really good sex! Obviously, the male partner needs to ejaculate if you're going to be able to conceive, but what you might not realize is that there appears to be an evolutionary function to the female orgasm as well. A female orgasm causes the uterus to contract, something that helps sperm to be propelled up into the reproductive tract. All that aside, having an orgasm can help to reduce the stress of trying to conceive. One study showed that a typical orgasm is twenty-two times as relaxing as the average tranquilizer!

I lost one ovary due to surgery for an ovarian cyst. Does this mean that I will only ovulate once every two months?

Contrary to what most people think, ovulation is a random event, with both ovaries competing for the chance to release an egg each month.

This is good news for you if you have only one ovary: The healthy ovary will win the draw by default. Because Mother Nature equipped you with a "spare," you are no less fertile than a woman with two ovaries.

One of my fallopian tubes is permanently blocked. Does
this decrease my chances of getting pregnant?

Assuming your other tube is normal, which may not be the case since ectopic pregnancies are more likely to occur in women with damaged fallopian tubes, your chances of conceiving are excellent. Even when you ovulate from the ovary on the side where your tube is blocked, the egg can be picked up by the normal tube on the other side and pregnancy can occur. In fact, there are women who have only one ovary and only one tube, each on opposite sides, and manage to get pregnant because of this phenomenon.

How soon can I do a pregnancy test?

The company that ultimately brings to market a test that will allow pregnancy to be diagnosed at the time of conception stands to make billions! Unfortunately, until that happens, couples will have to rely on the existing technology: pregnancy tests that become accurate approximately two weeks after ovulation.

Because these tests are designed to detect the levels of human chorionic gonadotropin (hCG), it takes time for them to work. While your body begins to produce hCG about a week after conception, generally there isn't enough hCG in your urine for a pregnancy test to detect until at least twelve days after ovulation—and perhaps a little longer. A blood test, however, can detect hCG much earlier.

If you're one of those women who doesn't test positive on pregnancy tests until a good week or two after the rest of womankind, your BBT chart might be able to provide you with some clues about what's going on long before the pregnancy test turns positive. As we noted earlier in this chapter, if your temperature remains elevated for at least eighteen consecutive days (or for at least three days longer than your longest non-pregnant luteal phase to date), it's probably time to crack open the non-alcoholic champagne.

*Should I trust the results of my pregnancy test? What
are the odds that the test result could be wrong?*

The latest generation of pregnancy tests is astoundingly accurate—more than 97 percent accurate, in fact. When errors do occur, they tend to be false negatives (the test says that you aren't pregnant, but you actually are). The most common causes of inaccurate test results are using incorrectly collected or stored urine, not having the urine and the test kit at room temperature when you conduct the test, having traces of blood or protein in your urine, having an active urinary tract infection at the time that you do the test, or being premenopausal.

To ensure that you get the most accurate results possible from your pregnancy test, you should use your first morning urine (since the concentration of hCG will be highest), ensure that the test has not passed its expiration date, and follow the testing instructions to the letter (e.g., if you have to collect your urine in a container, make sure that the container is clean and soap-free). Be sure to pay particular attention to the amount of time you have to wait before you read the test results and at what point the test results are no longer valid. Some test results will change from negative to positive if you leave the test lying around long enough.

Just a few other important points on pregnancy tests:

- If you get a faint positive test result, you might want to repeat the test a few days later to ensure that your hormone levels have begun to increase.
- If you initially test positive on a pregnancy test, but retest a week later and get a negative test result, chances are you've experienced a miscarriage. In this case, you will want to get in touch with your doctor or midwife. He or she may wish to order an hCG test to confirm that your hCG level was normal—information that could prove very valuable if you decide to try for another pregnancy—and to talk to you about what might have gone wrong this time around.
- If you use a pregnancy test within a couple of weeks of having a miscarriage, it's possible that you could obtain a false positive reading simply because there's still an enough hCG in your urine to make the pregnancy test come back positive.
- Most pregnancy tests come with a toll-free phone number you can

call to get help with the test. Don't be afraid to call this number. The help-line staff can usually answer your questions quickly.

My period is late. What are the odds that I am pregnant?

While pregnancy is the most common reason for regularly menstruating women to skip a period, women can and do skip periods for other reasons: jet lag, severe illness, surgery, shock, bereavement, or other sources of stress.

To complicate things even further, some women continue to have menstrual-like bleeding even after they conceive.

Rather than relying on your period alone if you're trying to decide whether you're pregnant, watch for some of the other common signs and symptoms of pregnancy:

- A need to urinate more frequently (caused by hormonal changes that result in greater blood flow to the pelvic area).
- Fatigue (rising progesterone levels increase your metabolism and act as a natural sedative).
- A heightened sense of smell (you may find certain types of odors particularly offensive, such as cigarette smoke, coffee, or perfume).
- Food aversions and cravings (caused by hormonal changes that can affect your sense of taste).
- Morning sickness (you may experience anything from mild nausea to outright vomiting).
- Breast changes (your breasts may feel full, achy, or tender; the dark area around the nipple may begin to darken; and tiny glands on the areola may begin to enlarge).
- Periodlike cramping that isn't accompanied by any bleeding (caused by rising levels of progesterone).
- Bloating and gasiness (caused by rising levels of progesterone).

HOW YOU MAY FEEL ABOUT TRYING TO CONCEIVE

Even if you desperately want to have another baby, it can be stressful to go through the process of trying to conceive again. While you may feel happy and excited about the possibility of conceiving another child, you will likely find yourself experiencing a variety of other emotions as well.

Anxiety

It's very common to experience feelings of anxiety when you think of all that lies ahead, especially the possibility of having another baby die. Jenny remembers feeling very anxious when she decided to start conceiving again: "I felt like we were putting ourselves through unnecessary angst. All the joy of trying and planning was gone. It was replaced by worry and anxiety."

Debbie experienced similar emotions when she started trying again after her stillbirth and her miscarriage. "I wanted a baby more than anyone could imagine, but I was also so scared that I would have to go through the pain of losing a child again. I was very frightened that if I were to lose another baby, I'd end up in a lunatic asylum," she says.

Panic

Feelings of panic are often very common—even in parents who are fully committed to trying for another baby.

Kim recalls experiencing feelings of panic when she first started trying to conceive again after her daughter's stillbirth. "The first time we had unprotected sex (about ten weeks after the loss), I panicked. That's how I knew it was too soon. When we started trying for real (about five months after our loss), I felt like we were taking control, making a positive step in the right direction."

Obsession

If there's one word that bereaved mothers frequently use to describe their desire to become pregnant again, it's "obsession." It's not unusual to spend all your free time reading up on fertility and pregnancy, surfing the Internet so that you can connect with other women who have gone on to have healthy babies after having a previous baby die, and daydreaming about the day when the pregnancy test will finally come back positive again.

Marilyn is the first to admit that she became obsessed with the idea of becoming pregnant again after she experienced her first miscarriage. "Conceiving again became an all-consuming way of life for me after the first miscarriage, and all my friends and family members knew it. I think they were as eager for me to conceive again as I was, because they were probably tired of hearing about my loss and all the efforts my husband and I were making to conceive again," (e.g., tracking cycles, taking home pregnancy tests, and so on).

Sadness

Many women are unprepared for the strong feelings of sadness that can well to the surface the first time they start trying again. They sometimes don't realize that it's perfectly normal to still be grieving the baby who died even as they start looking forward to creating another life. That was certainly the case for Lori, who admits, "I cried the first time. It was such an emotional thing. I'm not sure how my husband felt. I think I remember him saying, 'We don't have to do this just yet.'"

Martha had a similar experience when she started trying to conceive after her first miscarriage. "The first night that we tried, I made the bedroom very romantic with candles and perfume and flowers. We had some wine and I wore a sexy nightgown that I'd bought for a trip we'd taken to Paris together when we were dating," she says. "So the stage was all set for conceiving a little one. However, as things advanced and began to reach a critical stage, I suddenly felt overwhelmed with sadness and started to cry, and we stopped. I'd suddenly thought about my child and that he or she wasn't with us anymore, and it was an awful, lonely feeling.

"I was also for a moment aware of the clinical way in which the child had left me (through a D&C) and realized that through that same passage my husband was now trying tenderly to create a new life with me. Maybe it was a delayed reaction to the D&C, but I felt very exposed and vulnerable—that so much was at stake and my body was entirely responsible for my children's lives and deaths. All of this happened in a flash—I hadn't thought it before or since—and I remember covering myself quickly and curling up and crying for a while. My husband held me and was very sweet and understanding. Maybe it was still too soon to start trying to conceive again. We waited another month and this didn't happen again," she says.

It's also not at all unusual for parents who have experienced the deaths of one or more babies in a multiple pregnancy to feel particularly sad when they start trying to conceive again. Even if they do manage to become pregnant again, chances are it will be with a single baby. In her book *Empty Cradle, Broken Heart*, Deborah Davis discusses how parents in this situation may feel about trying again: "There is something special about raising two or more children who were conceived and born together. You may feel as if you have blown an incredible once-in-a-lifetime opportunity, as the likelihood of conceiving another multiple pregnancy can be slim. When a subsequent pregnancy is not a multiple one, you may feel added disappointment."

HOW YOUR PARTNER MAY FEEL

Women aren't the only ones who can find it stressful to start trying to conceive again. Often, the male partner has issues of his own to deal with.

Laura recalls how pressured her husband, James, felt when they started trying to conceive again after the death of their daughter: "James felt a lot of pressure to perform, which we hadn't experienced the previous two times when we were trying to conceive. We did find ways to work out dealing with that pressure over the year of trying, but it was really hard in the beginning. And, of course, intense grief during the early months really magnified all the stress of trying to get pregnant."

Jennifer's husband, John, experienced similar emotions, particularly when intercourse had to be timed to coincide with the right stages of Jennifer's fertility treatments. "John didn't particularly care for the Clomid [a fertility drug]," she recalls. "He felt like he had to 'perform' and 'hit the mark' or else. We coped with it okay by using humor. I told him to prove to me how good he was. He had one chance. He jokes that he is a 'sharp shooter.' I became pregnant on my first cycle with Clomid. We were lucky, I guess."

Lisa and her husband, Rob, experienced a major crisis when it became apparent that he wasn't as ready to start trying to conceive again as she had thought he was.

"I knew I wanted another baby right away—even when I was laboring in the hospital, waiting for my son to be delivered," Lisa recalls. "Even though I would say to myself and others that another baby would not replace Gareth, there was a part of me that hoped that having another baby would help to ease the consuming ache and loss I felt. The only deciding factor for me was the four-month waiting time given to us by our midwives.

"My husband and I had talked about trying again many times before the end of the four-month period. He had agreed that he wanted to try again. I had reminded him before my appointment with the obstetrician that the four months was up. When nighttime came and I said in essence, 'Let's go. The doctor gave us the go ahead,' everything changed. Suddenly Rob didn't want to try again. He was afraid not only of losing another child, but of trying to 'replace' Gareth," she says.

"A primal rage and fear came out in me. Suddenly I wasn't sure how I felt about Rob. Betrayed was definitely an overwhelming feeling. He had made promises that we would try again, and now he was telling me that he wasn't sure that he would ever want to try again. It was as if I were losing another child I had not even conceived yet, but who existed so deeply and vividly in my heart and soul."

Thinking back, Lisa thinks that there were some clues that Rob wasn't dealing with his grief as directly as she was: "During the four months after Gareth's stillbirth, Rob and I grieved very differently. We would talk and cry and console, but looking back it was always a little guarded. I feverishly read book after book, trying to deal with the grief. Rob, for the most part, was quiet."

The fact that they were at different stages in the grieving process precipitated the crisis that occurred the night when Lisa had thought that they were going to start trying to conceive again. "The story of our 'wonderful' night of conception is like something out of some comedy-drama," she admits. "It started when Rob decided to go to bed and I was determined to start trying to conceive. I was ovulating, for God's sake! I stormed into the bedroom, ripped the covers off his naked body, and said with a force I had never used before, 'Get the hell out of bed! We're going to talk.'

"At that moment that night, when I knew I was ovulating and Rob said no, I thought to myself (whether correctly or not), 'I've been working on my grief for these past four months and I'm ready. Rob has ignored his grieving and now he won't try again. Now he brings these feelings up. Why didn't he tell me this before?'

"I was hurt, scared, and angry," she says. "I explained that I was not trying to replace Gareth, but that I did long to hold another one of our children in my arms—my arms that were physically aching and hurting with no physiological cause. We talked for a couple of hours and he finally decided, albeit cautiously, that we could try again. It was a night filled with tears of hurt, anger, grief, and ultimately relief and joy mixed with moments of awkward laughter and first-date jitters."

Making the decision to start trying again requires nothing short of a leap of faith. After all, this is one area of your life over which you exercise very little control and it may remind you of the "out of control" feelings that you experienced right after your baby died. While there's no denying that you put your heart on the line by trying to conceive again, couples who have been fortunate enough to end up with a healthy baby in their arms during a subsequent pregnancy will tell you that the payoff can be tremendous.

Consider what Marie, who gave birth to a healthy boy after her daughter was stillborn the previous year, has to say about finding the courage to try again: "Everything I went through during my subsequent pregnancy—the months of stress when we were trying to conceive and the months of anxiety that followed when the pregnancy test came back positive—they were all worth it. This child has been such a blessing, such a gift. I am so grateful that my husband and I found the courage to try again."

🐦8 *Do You Have a Fertility Problem?*

ONE OF THE most common fears faced by couples who have experienced the death of a baby is the thought that they may not be able to conceive again. While most couples will manage to conceive within a few months of trying, becoming pregnant again certainly isn't quite that easy for everyone. If you had difficulty conceiving prior to your loss, you could very well have difficulty conceiving again. What's more, you could be unfortunate enough to experience secondary infertility (the medical term for an infertility problem experienced by those who have not had fertility problems in the past).

In this chapter, we will talk about the challenges of coping with infertility after miscarriage, stillbirth, or infant death: how to tell if you have a fertility problem and what to do to stay sane if you're having trouble conceiving.

WHEN SHOULD WE START TO WORRY?

As a rule of thumb, you should consider the possibility that you may be experiencing a fertility problem if you've been trying to conceive for more than a year, but still haven't managed to become pregnant again. (There's a little bit of fine print that you need to know about: You can only count yourself as "trying" during a particular cycle if you're having sex two to three times a week during your most fertile period. Therefore, you can't count those cycles in which you weren't able to have intercourse at the "right" times because one of you was ill or away on a business trip.)

The American Society of Reproductive Medicine recommends that women under the age of 35 allow themselves a full year of trying before they seek treatment for their infertility, but notes that couples who suspect that they have a fertility problem or who are over the age of thirty-five seek the help of a fertility specialist before the first year of trying is up.

If you and you partner decide to seek treatment for a possible fertility problem, you can either turn to your regular obstetrician/gynecologist (assuming, of course, that he or she regularly treats couples experiencing infertility); a urologist (a doctor who specializes in the treatment of urogenital problems, including disorders of the male reproductive system); or a reproductive endocrinologist (an obsetrician/gynecologist who has completed additional training in the medical and surgical treament of reproductive disorders).

Your doctor will start out by conducting a fertility work-up that is designed to answer four basic questions:

1.   Are you ovulating regularly?
2.   Is your partner producing healthy, viable sperm?
3.   Are the egg and sperm able to unite?
4.   Is there something preventing the fertilized egg from implanting and developing properly?

Your course of treatment will be based on what is discovered during this initial work-up. (See "The Most Common Types of Fertility Problems" for a list of the causes and treatments of the most common problems.) If these traditional methods of treating infertility do not work for you, you may wish to consider treatment with assisted reproductive technologies such as in vitro fertilization. (See pages 141–142 for a list of the most common types of assisted reproductive technologies.) While these high-tech treatments are hardly commonplace—only 7 percent of infertility patients choose to go this route—they are an alternative for couples who haven't been able to achieve a pregnancy any other way. Because of the costs involved (physical, emotional, and financial), you'll definitely want to do your homework before you make the decision to go down this particular road.

Note: You can find a more detailed discussion of the causes and treatments of infertility, as well as a detailed discussion of other routes to parenthood—namely adoption and surrogacy—in our other book, *The Unofficial Guide to Having a Baby.*

The Most Common Types of Fertility Problems

TYPE OF PROBLEM	PERCENTAGE OF INFERTILITY PROBLEMS	TREATMENT
Problems with the male partner Examples: • Undescended testicles: a congenital problem that, if left uncorrected after age two, results in sterility • A varicocele: a varicose vein in the spermatic cord that can kill off sperm • Medications that can affect libido, reduce sperm production, destroy normal DNA production, and alter the hormonal balance • Sexual problems: impotence, premature ejaculation, ejaculatory dysfunction, and so on • Hypospadias: a congenital anomaly in which the opening of the urethra is found on the underside rather than the tip of the penis, causing semen to be deposited too low in the vagina • Retrograde ejaculation: a neurological problem that causes ejaculation into the bladder rather than out through the urethra • Immunological problems: when a man's antibodies attack his own sperm • Testicular failure due to a blow to the testes, exposure to the mumps, or a birth defect	35 percent	Three basic types of treatments are available for male infertility: drug and hormone therapy, surgery, and artificial insemination (introducing sperm into the female reproductive tract by a means other than sexual intercourse).

TYPE OF PROBLEM	PERCENTAGE OF INFERTILITY PROBLEMS	TREATMENT
Problems with the female partner **Tubal and pelvic problems** • Scarring of or damage to the fallopian tubes caused by an ectopic pregnancy, endometriosis, pelvic inflammatory disease, gonorrhea, chlamydia, or an intrauterine device • Congenital abnormalities of the reproductive organs • Fertility problems caused by polyps, fibroids, and other types of conditions (e.g., Asherman's syndrome, in which bands of scar tissue in a woman's uterus cement the walls of the uterus together)	35 percent	Surgery can help to correct certain types of structural problems and damage to the female reproductive system. Such surgery is not without its own risks, however, and may result in the formation of adhesions that can add to a fertility problem.
Ovulatory dysfunction (irregular ovulation accompanied by poor quality cervical mucus) Examples: • Polycystic ovarian syndrome, where the ovaries develop small cysts that interfere with ovulation and hormone production • Hyperprolactinemia, where the secretion of an excessive amount of the hormone prolactin interferes with ovulation • Deficiencies in gonadotropin-releasing hormone, the hormone responsible for triggering the	15 percent	Depending on the cause of the ovulatory disorder, treatment may include the use of orally administered ovulation-stimulating drugs such as Clomid or Serophene (clomiphene citrate), or fertility drugs such as Pergonal, Humegon, and Repronex, which are injected and frequently result in a

TYPE OF PROBLEM	PERCENTAGE OF INFERTILITY PROBLEMS	TREATMENT
release of FSH and LH from the pituitary gland • A luteal phase deficiency, when inadequate levels of progesterone prevent the fertilized egg from implanting properly • Other hormonal imbalances caused by pituitary failure, glandular disorders, premature menopause, and so on • An excess of adrenal androgens (male sex hormones) • Amenorrhea (lack of menstruation) • Anovulation (lack of ovulation) • Oligo-ovulation/menorrhea (infrequent ovulation/menstruation)		multiple pregnancy. Other drugs frequently used to treat hormonal problems include bromocriptine (Parlodel), which suppresses the pituitary gland's production of prolactin; gonadotropin-releasing hormone (GnRH), which induces ovulaton; and Lupron, a drug that is used to treat endometriosis and to enhance the response to Pergonal in selected patients.
Immunological problems, thyroid problems, and other unusual causes	5 percent	Varies depending on the underlying disorder.
Unexplained infertility	10 percent	Approximately half of couples with unexplained infertility will manage to conceive during a three-year period.

Assisted Reproductive Technologies:
The Most and Least Successful

TYPE OF PROCEDURE AND WHAT IT INVOLVES	SUCCESS RATE (PERCENTAGE OF LIVE BIRTHS)	COST
Donor eggs	46.8 percent per retrieval	$9,000 per cycle
Eggs from a female donor are fertilized with sperm from the male partner and then implanted into the female partner's uterus.		
Gamete intrafallopian transfer (GIFT)	26.8 percent to 28 percent	$6,000-$10,000 per attempt
Eggs and sperm are inserted into the fallopian tube by way of a laparoscope.		
Zygote intrafallopian transfer (ZIFT)	24 percent to 27.7 percent	$8,000-$10,000 per attempt
Eggs are fertilized outside the uterus and then transferred to the fallopian tube.		
Intracyto-plasmic sperm injection (ICSI)	24 percent	$10,000-$12,000 per attempt
A single sperm is injected into an egg, which is then transferred into the uterus.		
In vitro fertilization (IVF)	18.6 percent to 22.3 percent	$6,000-$8,000 per attempt
An egg that has been fertilized outside the womb is implanted in the woman's uterus.		
Frozen embryo transfer (FET)	15.4 percent	$500-$1,500 per cycle
Embryos left over from an IVF cycle are frozen and stored for implantation in the uterus at some future date.		

TYPE OF PROCEDURE AND WHAT IT INVOLVES	SUCCESS RATE (PERCENTAGE OF LIVE BIRTHS)	COST
Intrauterine insemination Fresh or frozen sperm (either from the woman's partner or a male donor) is injected into the uterus via a catheter.	10 percent	$300 per cycle

SOURCES: Adapted from a similar chart in *The Unofficial Guide to Having a Baby,* by Ann Douglas and John R. Sussman, M.D., as well as the following sources: *1995 Assisted Reproductive Technology Success Rates: National Summary and Fertility Clinic Reports* (Atlanta: Centers for Disease Control and Prevention, 1997); Sharon Begley, "The Baby Myth," *Newsweek,* 4 September 1995; Denise Grady, "How to Coax New Life," *Time Canada,* Fall 1996 special issue.

INFERTILITY: ANOTHER TYPE OF LOSS

Coping with the death of a baby is hard enough; it's even more difficult to have to struggle with the heartache of infertility when you start trying to become pregnant again. If you find yourself in this difficult situation, you will need to grieve, and you can expect to experience some or all of the following emotions:

Anger It's perfectly normal to feel angry about having difficulty conceiving after a loss. You may feel that you're "owed" a baby because of your loss and may find yourself feeling bitter and resentful if you have trouble becoming pregnant again. Laura remembers feeling this way when she had difficulty conceiving again after her daughter's death. "Infertility is such a blow after having a child die. It felt like someone's cruel joke. I was angry to be having problems conceiving again—particularly since I knew that it was quite possible to go through an entire pregnancy and still not bring a baby home from the hospital," she says.

Sorrow and disappointment Couples who experience difficulty conceiving after a loss frequently struggle with feelings of sorrow and disappointment. Jennifer says that her fertility problems have only added to her pain: "The disappointment adds to and becomes a part of the sorrow. The two miscarriages, the trouble conceiving—it all becomes one: a big circle of sorrow."

Depression Depression is common among parents who are struggling with infertility after loss. Lisa found herself becoming deeply depressed when she didn't manage to conceive again immediately after her first child was stillborn. "During the time we were trying to conceive, I experienced more anxiety, sadness, and hopelessness on a daily basis than I could have imagined," she says. "It was so difficult for me to imagine that we could be blessed with a child—which is what we wanted more than anything—when we encountered endless months of waiting and disappointment while trying to conceive.

"I once read that, after losing a baby, many couples are only able to accept the loss and have hope in life again after having other children. Based on my experience, I believe this is true. I feel that if we had been able to conceive sooner, I would have spent less time feeling so miserable."

Fear In addition to feeling anxious about conceiving again, many couples are afraid that their dreams of having another baby will never come true.

"I was terrified that Matty would be my only child," says Deb, whose son Matty was stillborn and who subsequently went on to experience a miscarriage. "I was obsessed with becoming pregnant again and so afraid that I wouldn't be able to conceive. I felt like there was a race going on in the world—a race to have babies—and somehow I was being left behind."

Cheryl has also experienced similar fears—but in her case, her biggest fear is that her husband won't want to continue trying for another baby: "I fear Tom will say, 'Don't worry. Let's just be happy with Matthew,' and that's not what I want to hear."

Feelings of inadequacy It's not unusual for women who are having trouble conceiving again after a loss to experience feelings of inadequacy. Often, they feel angry at their bodies for "betraying" them. Some even feel that not conceiving quickly has only added to their sense of failure.

This is exactly how Lori feels, now that she's into her fifteenth month of trying to conceive after her daughter's stillbirth: "My body betrayed me when it failed to sustain my baby. Now it's failing me again by not giving me another chance at pregnancy. I am very afraid that Katie was my one shot at motherhood and I blew it. What an awful feeling, to be so close to something you've wanted for so long, only to have it snatched away, with no reassurances that you'll ever have anything like it again. With every passing month, I feel my hope of having a baby slip further and further from my grasp."

Frustration   For couples struggling with infertility after a loss, one of the most difficult things to deal with is the reactions of other people. Most find that others aren't able to understand what they're going through unless they've been through a similar struggle themselves.

"People in general didn't seem to understand why after six months of trying to conceive I was so upset that I wasn't pregnant yet," says Laura, whose daughter Sarah died during early infancy. "I heard lots of the awful comments that I think most women who go through infertility hear, like stories about friends who 'just relaxed' and then got pregnant. I got to the point where I didn't talk about our problems conceiving with anyone other than the few people I knew who would be supportive."

Jackie has also been shocked by the insensitive comments that she's been subjected to since experiencing her ectopic pregnancy: "On the few occasions that we have brought up the subject, we have been met with comments like, 'Don't take it all so seriously,' or we are told stories about couples who went on holidays and 'magically' conceived."

Your life is out of control   It's not the least bit unusual for couples who are struggling with infertility after a loss to report feeling like they are no longer in control of their own lives.

That's how Jackie feels, now that she's into her eighteenth cycle of trying to conceive since her ectopic pregnancy. "I'm a person who likes to have things planned out and, with this, I can't plan anything," she says. "I'm basically living from month to month, hoping that this month maybe it will work out. I'm tired, irritable, weepy, and often unable to cope with things that, before we started trying to conceive, wouldn't have bothered me at all. I want to be myself again. I want my 'old life' back. I'm afraid that I am pinning my hopes on becoming pregnant, hoping that miraculously everything will become what it was before. I can only hope and wait to see.

"We have got to the stage where we are asking ourselves if we really want to become parents—if we want to go for infertility treatments. Maybe it would be better to stop and make a decision not to have children, but that is such a difficult decision to make and my husband has basically left the decision in my hands. This is a decision that I don't want to make alone and am not able to make alone: I'm afraid to make this decision and later down the road regret it or have my husband blame me. I feel that if we carry on like this for much longer, it will destroy us. I am sad that we started out with so many hopes that aren't becoming a reality," Jackie says.

Stress of coping with fertility treatments   As if the emotional roller-coaster ride of infertility weren't enough to contend with, many couples also find themselves undergoing painful, expensive, and stressful fertility treatments.

Carleen had to overcome her fear of needles and fit numerous doctors' appointments into her schedule. "I have always had a terrible fear of needles, which I had to come to grips with," she says. "The worst was when I had to let my husband give me an injection of hCG using a very long needle. By that point, I was able to give myself the shots, but that long needle was scary. It was also difficult to have to go to the doctor's almost daily at times, and the reproductive endocrinologist's office was over forty-five minutes away."

Then there were the financial concerns: "Insurance didn't cover the cost of the medications, but fortunately it covered the doctors' costs," she says.

Carleen finds it amazing that she managed to weather the stress of the fertility treatments: "Looking back, I don't know how I made it through it. It was the toughest time in my life—so tough, in fact that I had decided to make the month I conceived the final month of trying for a while. I had made plans to do some things that I would not be able to do if I was pregnant. It gave me something to look forward to in case I didn't manage to conceive."

Loneliness   It's never easy being an infertile person in a fertile world, but those feelings of loneliness and isolation can be even more acute if you've been through the heartbreak of losing a baby. In many ways, you can feel like you're caught in a "no man's land": You don't belong to the fertile or the infertile world.

Robin, who has struggled with infertility and repeated pregnancy loss, explains: "When you can or have previously been able to get pregnant, even if your pregnancies all ended in loss, you're shunned in the infertile world and the fertile world. You really belong in neither place. Technically, you're fertile because you can get pregnant. However, you aren't ready to join the fertile world because your children are never born."

HOW TO COPE WITH INFERTILITY AFTER A LOSS

You may find that fertility problems merely add to the grief associated with your earlier loss or losses. If you find yourself in the difficult situation of experiencing infertility after a loss, you will need to develop some strong coping strategies to help yourself to weather this emotionally draining time in your life.

Talk about how you are feeling.   You'll drive yourself crazy if you try to keep all your emotions bottled up inside. Talk to your partner, an understanding friend, or a counselor who specializes in infertility and pregnancy or infant loss, or join a support group for couples who are struggling with infertility after a loss. (You'll find some leads on these types of support groups in Appendix B.) Deb—whose son Matty was stillborn, and who subsequently went on to experience a miscarriage—spent a lot of time talking with her husband, her mother, and a close friend, and participating in some online support groups. Laura—who lost her second child at eight days of life during open heart surgery—went back to see the therapist who had been helping her to work through her grief-related issues and joined some E-mail support lists as well.

Make sure that you're getting the support you need and deserve from your doctor.   Jackie learned the hard way that not all doctors are cut out to deal with the emotional aspects of infertility. "I think that many doctors deal only with the physical aspects of pregnancy loss and infertility," she explains. "I can recall that on one occasion, I mentioned to my doctor that I was having a hard time dealing emotionally with my failure to conceive. He looked distinctly uncomfortable and tried to usher me out of his office by telling me that I'd be pregnant again 'soon.'"

Find outlets for your stress. Make a point of having fun on a regular basis—even if you have to force yourself at first. It's particularly important to try to have fun with your partner and to continue to nurture that part of your relationship that takes place outside of the bedroom.

Consider taking a brief time out if the stress of trying to conceive is taking its toll on your marriage and your sex life. Pamela and her partner decided to take a break when they realized that the fertility problems that they experienced after their miscarriage were taking over their entire life. "Every month that came and went without a pregnancy created more urgency and frustration. We needed to stop trying for a while and put our focus and energy on other things," she says.

Now that we've talked about the challenges of trying to conceive after a loss, let's move on and talk about how you may feel if the pregnancy test comes back positive.

9 *How You May Feel about Being Pregnant Again*

WHILE YOU WERE busy focusing all of your efforts on getting pregnant again, you might have allowed yourself to assume that all your problems would magically disappear the moment the pregnancy test came back positive.

As you've no doubt discovered by now, that's simply not the way things work. As wonderful as it can be to be pregnant again, most parents find themselves faced with a whole new set of challenges as they embark on that nine-and-a-half-month-long roller-coaster ride known as a subsequent pregnancy.

In this chapter, we will talk about how you may feel when you find out that you're pregnant again: the good, the bad, and the ugly. We'll talk about the pros and cons of sharing your news with other people right away. Finally, we'll talk about what you can do to weather the emotional highs and lows that you may face over the next nine months.

HOW YOU MAY BE FEELING

Most women who become pregnant after experiencing miscarriage, stillbirth, or infant death find themselves hit by a flood of different emotions when they first discover that they're pregnant again. Here are just a few of the emotions that you may experience during this exciting and yet scary time in your life.

Mixed feelings   Don't be surprised if you find yourself feeling a mix of emotions when the pregnancy test comes back positive. Julie, whose son Bryan was stillborn at forty-one weeks due to a tight nuchal cord, remembers feeling confused by the conflicting emotions that hit her all at once when she found out she was pregnant again. "I was both scared and excited," she recalls. "Becoming pregnant again was no longer some wonderful thought: It was reality. I think my husband was terrified, too. I remember looking at the test and then we looked at each other and he said, 'Well, here we go.'"

Jennifer, whose first child was stillborn for unknown causes, also remembers experiencing a smorgasbord of conflicting emotions when she found out that she was pregnant again. "I experienced an odd mix of emotions," she recalls. "We had been trying for some time, and so I knew I wanted to be pregnant. And yet when I found out, part of me said, 'What was I thinking?' Somehow finding out that I was, in fact, pregnant caused me to feel a fear I had never known before. Still, the hope was there, too, and I was happy to be expecting again. I guess you could say that we were excited initially and then scared as hell. The scared part was only temporary though: It only lasted the next nine months or so!"

Hesitation and detachment Many parents who become pregnant again are afraid to allow themselves to become overly excited about their pregnancies, both because they're afraid of "jinxing" themselves by getting too attached to the pregnancy and because they've learned that there's a world of difference between being pregnant and ending up with a healthy baby in your arms nine months down the road.

This was certainly the case for Jenny, who experienced three miscarriages following her first live birth, and who is now pregnant for the fifth time. "I had to emotionally detach myself—to treat each pregnancy with a 'we'll see' attitude. I knew that each time was a 'try' and not a baby," she says. "I mourn the fact that I couldn't run out and tell all my friends and family and start buying cute clothes. Even with this pregnancy—I'm nineteen weeks now—I don't have the same joy as I did with my first pregnancy. I'm not as excited. No matter how many doctors' appointments I have, I still feel I need to remain somewhat detached. That makes me feel sad and guilty, but I'm having a hard time getting over it."

Cynthia also felt a similar sense of detachment after experiencing three miscarriages in between the births of her first and second living children. "I was not excited at all during my last pregnancy. I didn't feel any excitement at all until about the last six weeks. I was scared. I held my breath for forty-and-a-half weeks and was afraid that if I allowed myself to relax and breathe, something awful would happen," she says.

Anxiety concerning the timing of the pregnancy   Sometimes the timing of a pregnancy can be a cause for much anxiety, either because the new baby's due date is very close to the due date of the baby who died, or because the parents managed to conceive again before they were ready.

Lisa experienced the latter situation. She felt tremendously anxious during her subsequent pregnancy because she became pregnant much more quickly than she had planned—about two weeks after her miscarriage. "We didn't plan to conceive for two to three months, but it happened immediately and unintentionally," she explains. "I miscarried on February 20, and conceived again on March 8 or 9. I found out about the pregnancy during a routine physical on March 31. I'd requested a pregnancy test on the off chance that I'd conceived. I was a little concerned because I'd been told to expect my period after the normal twenty-eight-day interval after the miscarriage, and I hadn't gotten it. At that point, I was about ten days late I think. The doctor was in the middle of explaining why I probably wasn't pregnant when the nurse came in with the results of the test. I could see the word 'positive' as she handed the paper over.

"My first question was 'Is this okay?' The doctor was very reassuring and reminded me that there are women who get pregnant immediately after giving birth to a full-term baby. I'd only been pregnant for six-and-a-half weeks. I wondered if I would be considered a high-risk pregnancy, but her answer was no. I was a little shocked at that, but it was also somewhat reassuring," she says.

Janann also managed to conceive more quickly than she had planned, and felt positively panicked when she first discovered that she was pregnant again after her stillbirth: "I was shocked. I hadn't felt that I was ready to try again yet. I just sat there in disbelief holding the test. I was overwhelmed and felt that I wasn't ready for this."

Guilt   Desirae, whose first child died at twenty-seven days of age due to congenital heart disease and other anomalies, experienced overwhelming feelings of guilt when she became pregnant again. "I felt guilty whenever I felt happy about the new baby," she recalls. "I didn't know how to grieve for the first baby and feel joy for the second baby at the same time."

Christi experienced similar emotions when she became pregnant again after her first child died during open heart surgery for hypoplastic left heart syndrome at three days of age. In her case, she was able to work through her guilty feelings by writing in a journal. "I kept a journal and dedicated it to my daughter, Alyssa, who died. I would tell her that being pregnant again wasn't going to take her memory away. I would never stop loving her. I explained to her that I needed another baby in order to have any sense of normalcy in my life again and to remain sane. I told myself that this baby was going to help heal me and it was in no way a form of betrayal," she says.

Confidence   Not every mother who finds out that she's pregnant again reacts with fear and guilt, however. Some women feel confident that they are going to experience a happier outcome this time around. "I was surprised about how confident I felt about the new pregnancy," recalls Janna, whose second child died when she went into premature labor as the result of an incompetent cervix. "Right from the start, I felt that this pregnancy would have a happy ending."

HOW YOUR PARTNER MAY BE FEELING

Women aren't the only ones who may find themselves feeling simultaneously euphoric and panic-struck when the pregnancy test comes back positive. Their partners can also find themselves dealing with a smorgasbord of emotions.

Mixed feelings   Michael recalls how he felt when he found out that his wife was expecting again. "I was thrilled, terrified, elated, anxious, hopeful, and hopeless when Judy confirmed she was pregnant again," he recalls. "It seemed too good to be true that we could actually be pregnant again. After the realization had set in that conception had occurred, I was filled to bursting with expectations for the pregnancy. At the same time, I now knew so much about what could go wrong during a pregnancy and was afraid to let myself admit any of those fears. The worst had already happened, and I knew I would be on edge throughout the pregnancy, expecting that the worst was about to happen again."

One woman found that her husband dealt with his anxiety by refusing to even consider the possibility that something could go wrong with her next pregnancy. "My husband didn't want me to talk about my fears; I think it made him feel helpless to see me so upset. He wanted desperately for me to believe that this baby would make it—even if he didn't believe it himself," she says.

Guarded joy   Many women who become pregnant again find that their partners' joy about the new pregnancy is extremely guarded—something that can dampen their own enthusiasm for the pregnancy. "My husband has had a hard time getting excited," says Nora, whose first child died shortly after birth. "He was the cheerleader with our son's pregnancy and we got so hurt by losing him that he's holding back. I understand that, but it still hurts a little. I feel like he's holding back about the baby. This has been challenging for us, but we're getting through it."

"My husband has gotten to the point where he doesn't get excited at all," says Holly, who has experienced a series of losses at various stages of pregnancy as well as the birth of four living children. "He takes the 'wait to see attitude': he wants to wait to see if the baby is born alive before he allows himself to feel too many emotions toward it. I'm kind of disappointed by that, but I understand completely why he does it. Sometimes I wish I could do it, too."

Lisa, whose first child was stillborn due to a placental abruption, found that her partner reacted with anger when she discovered that she was pregnant again. "I was terrified of losing another baby; my husband was terrified of losing me," she explains. "We conceived by accident. My husband was very angry. For weeks, he thought I had planned the whole thing. We talked, we fought, and we cried. There was no way I would have chosen to conceive a baby exactly one year after the baby we lost was conceived, and my husband finally realized that I was being honest and truthful about that."

Cynthia also remembers her husband experiencing a lot of anxiety about her pregnancy: "He was very scared for me—afraid of what would happen to me if I had another loss."

SHARING YOUR NEWS WITH OTHER PEOPLE

Once you've shared your news with your partner, the two of you will need to decide what to do about sharing your news with other people. If you're like most parents, you'll probably want to be selective in deciding *whom* to tell and *when*.

Whom to tell   The key factor that Laure took into consideration when deciding whom to share her news with was how that person had responded when her babies had died: "Anyone who responded in a cold or unfeeling manner to our last loss never got told about this pregnancy. They either found out by seeing my big tummy or heard about it from someone else."

When to tell   There are advantages and disadvantages to sharing your news with other people right away. On the one hand, you'll be able to share your excitement and anxiety about your pregnancy with other people, and won't have to sort through these complex emotions on your own. On the other hand, you'll be inviting those people along on a forty-week-long roller-coaster ride—and you may not have the energy or inclination to deal with their anxiety, advice, questions, and general meddling. You may want to hedge your bets a little until you feel confident that the pregnancy is well established.

Even if you know that your news will be met with rejoicing, you may not want to share your news for fear of having to subsequently share any bad news with the friends and family members who were so happy about your new pregnancy. You have to decide for yourself whether the benefits of taking such a risk (e.g., having a group of people who will share your joy about the new pregnancy and help you to weather any storms) outweighs the potential costs of having to share any subsequent bad news.

Some parents feel quite strongly that they owe it to family members and friends to share their news as soon as possible. "We told everyone immediately," recalls Janann, who has experienced both miscarriage and stillbirth. "I knew that if I were to have a miscarriage or anything else were to happen to this baby, I would need their support. Besides, I wanted them to share in our good news, not just wait to see if something bad would happen. I felt that if I were to have a miscarriage, I would have to tell them for their support, and it would be wrong for me to want help from them then if I had not allowed them to share in our joy."

The solution for some parents is to tell some family members and friends right away, but to keep everyone else in the dark until the peak risk period for a miscarriage has passed. This was the approach Roberta chose to take when she became pregnant again following her two miscarriages. "We told our parents right away, but we did not tell anyone else for three months. We wanted to get past that 'critical' period first," she says. "I did tell my boss at work sooner than that, because I knew I would have extra doctors' appointments, but we did not tell anyone else for fear of having to 'untell' them later on."

A lot of parents choose to disclose their news on a "need to know" basis. Cheryl, who experienced a series of losses before giving birth to a healthy baby, only told her supervisor at work about her pregnancy because she needed time off to have a cerclage placed. She then waited ten more weeks before she shared her news with any of her coworkers.

Some parents choose to keep their news to themselves until they have reached certain milestones in their pregnancy: the point at which their previous baby died (if their baby died before birth); their previous baby's "due date" (a particularly important milestone for many women whose babies were miscarried or stillborn); or until they receive test results that indicate that this pregnancy is likely to have a happier outcome.

Marcella, whose son Jacob died of bacterial meningitis at ten months of age, had her own reasons for waiting to share the news of her subsequent pregnancy: "We decided to share our news the day after Jacob's first anniversary. We wanted to make sure he 'had his year.'"

Sharing the News with Family Members and Friends

As much as you may want to believe that family members and friends will react to your news with excitement and joy, it's important to be prepared for a less-than-positive response from at least some of the people in your life. Some people may be so worried about the possibility that you could lose this baby, too, that they may end up saying the wrong thing.

Kathy encountered this type of situation with her mother-in-law: "She hugged me and told me not to worry because she had a 'good' feeling about this pregnancy—like that was going to help! That really hurt me because she obviously had no clue what I was going through. I wanted to ask her if she had had a 'bad' feeling about my first pregnancy, but I kept my mouth shut."

Jayne was similarly disappointed by the responses she received when she announced that she was pregnant again: "Family members were very supportive. However, we did miss out on the excited reactions. As we told people, we could feel the tension in the air. We both found this quite sad: We wanted to be treated like any other expecting couple, but that was no longer possible."

Janna also received a lukewarm reaction when she shared her news: "We were surprised at the reactions people had. Most were more apprehensive than happy."

Pandora found that a lot of people questioned her decision to have another baby, given the heartbreak that she'd experienced when her daughter died as a result of SIDS: "While some people admired my courage, others wondered why I would put myself through potential heartbreak again."

Telling Your Other Children

If you have living children, you will need to decide when to let them know about the pregnancy. Many parents postpone telling their children about the pregnancy until after the peak risk period for miscarriage has passed.

That was what Laura and her husband decided to do when it came to sharing the news of their pregnancy with their five-year-old daughter. "We decided we'd try to spare her some of the stress of the pregnancy since we knew she would worry about whether this baby would die and figured that waiting until twelve weeks to tell her was reasonable. Our not telling friends about the pregnancy was partly a result of our not telling our daughter. We felt that if we told friends, it would greatly increase the likelihood that she might overhear us talking about it, which we didn't want to happen," she says.

Regardless of when you decide to share your news with your children, however, you should be prepared to answer some tough questions. Many children ask their parents point blank if this baby will die, too!

While you'll want to do your best to be reassuring to your child if she asks questions like this—to let her know that you're doing everything possible to ensure that the new baby arrives safe and sound—you won't be doing your child any favors by promising her that the new baby will be okay. No one can offer her that kind of guarantee—not even you.

Sharing Your News at Work

As much as you might like to keep your news from your coworkers for at least the first couple of months, you may or may not be able to keep your pregnancy a secret that long. If, for example, you need a lot of time off work to go to doctors' appointments or you end up dashing to the bathroom at regular intervals, it won't take your coworkers very long to figure out what's going on.

Rather than waiting for the rumor mill to go into overdrive, you might decide to announce your pregnancy at work sooner rather than later. The first person you should share your news with, of course, is your boss. (The last thing you want is for her to hear the news from someone else.)

Career experts caution that you should handle this particular announcement carefully. While you'll want to reassure your boss that you'll do your best to ensure that it's "business as usual" during your pregnancy, you shouldn't make promises that you can't keep. If anything, you should err on the side of caution by being upfront about any special accommodations that you may need during your pregnancy, particularly if yours is likely to be a high-risk pregnancy.

No matter how sensitively you handle your announcement, you should be prepared for a lukewarm reaction. As happy as your boss may be for you, she's likely to be concerned about how your pregnancy is going to affect your ability to do your job and what she'll need to do to replace you when it's time for you to go out on maternity leave.

It's one thing to have a boss who's lukewarm; it's quite another to have one who's outright hostile. No matter how upset your boss may be about what your pregnancy may mean to the company, she has no right to fire you, deny you certain types of health benefits, or otherwise discriminate against you because you're pregnant. If you think that you've been a victim of pregnancy discrimination, you should contact the U.S. Equal Employment Opportunity Commission at 1-800-669-4000; if you live in Canada, contact the employment standards branch of the ministry of labor for your particular province or territory. They can advise you of your rights as a pregnant employee and tell you how to proceed if you feel that you've been a victim of pregnancy discrimination.

HOW TO STAY SANE

It isn't easy making it through a subsequent pregnancy. At times, you may wonder how you'll ever manage to make it through the entire nine months with your sanity relatively intact. While there's no magic cure for what ails you other than giving birth to a healthy baby, there's plenty you can do to try to minimize the amount of stress that you experience between now and then. Here are a few tips.

- *Line up as much support as possible.* You wouldn't dream of venturing out on a tightrope without ensuring that there were appropriate safety nets in place. Given that you're about to embark on the ultimate of tightrope walks—another pregnancy—it only makes sense to ensure that you've put your own support system in place. That means hooking up with other women who have been through or who are currently going through the same experience, as well as others who will be able to help you to cope with the stress of a subsequent pregnancy. You might consider joining an online or face-to-face support group for women who have experienced pregnancy after miscarriage, stillbirth, or infant death, or seeing a counselor who specializes in helping women to cope with the stress of a subsequent pregnancy.
- *Take each day at a time.* If you focus on the fact that there are nine long months ahead of you, you'll drive yourself crazy. That's why you may find it helpful to try to focus on a series of "mini-milestones" instead. Cheryl—whose first two babies died prior to birth—tried this during her last pregnancy. "I wouldn't allow myself to think about or make any plans beyond a certain time," she recalls. "I broke down my pregnancy into a series of milestones and then focused on making it to each of them: the ultrasound at six weeks, the cerclage at twelve weeks, Thanksgiving (when I was sixteen weeks), Christmas (when I was twenty weeks), then Valentine's Day, St. Patrick's Day, and so on. It may sound silly, but for the most part it worked for me."
- *Realize that worrying is part of the turf.* Rather than resenting the fact that you feel worried all the time, realize that this is simply your body's way of looking out for your baby and that, given what you've been through, you'll probably always worry about him or her to some degree. Desirae remembers how she finally came to terms with the amount of worry she was experiencing: "It dawned on me one day

that there will always be something to worry about. I recognized that someday my baby will be thirty-five and driving home in a storm and I will be worrying."

- *Don't expect your new pregnancy to wipe away the grief you feel about the baby who died.* That simply isn't possible. "The ache for the child you lost may intensify," stresses Lisa, whose third child was stillborn. "My arms literally physically ached to hold him. I think I felt that some of the pain would be alleviated with another pregnancy, but just the opposite was true in some ways."

- *Remind yourself that you've got what it takes to weather any storms that may lie ahead.* "I discovered that many of the skills I learned in order to cope with my loss helped me through my subsequent pregnancy," says Kim, who went on to give birth to a healthy baby after experiencing both a miscarriage and a stillbirth. "Just like in the early days of the loss when you just needed to focus on getting through that day or hour, you need to use a similar coping strategy to get through the pregnancy as well."

- *Make sure that you've got a supportive caregiver.* You need someone who will take your concerns seriously and who will do her best to reassure you during those times when panic sets in.

- *Don't be afraid to create memories of this pregnancy.* "Gather as many mementos of this baby's life as you can," suggests Mim, who recently gave birth to a healthy baby after her previous baby was stillborn. "Keep the pregnancy test, a copy of any reports your doctor receives, any ultrasound photos, cards of congratulations, any poems you see that grab your attention, and so on. If the worst should happen, at least you'll have some tangible mementos—some 'proof'—that you were pregnant again."

Christi agrees, noting that she made a point of creating some special memorabilia during her last pregnancy. "I felt that if I lost my subsequent baby, I would want some sort of memento from my pregnancy and a reminder of the baby, so I bought something special for her early in pregnancy and I made her a few things: a baby blanket, a stuffed animal, a pillow, and other small things. I just needed to keep myself thinking that there really was a baby in there and I would share all these things with her someday. It gave me something to look forward to," she says.

- *Keep reminding yourself that history won't necessarily repeat itself.* The fact that you've had one or more babies die doesn't necessarily mean that you're destined to repeat the same nightmare this time around.
- *Realize that the stress won't last forever.* "It's a long journey, and it's very scary," admits Cindy, who has given birth to two healthy babies since her first child was stillborn. "But when that baby is born, you will feel a sense of completion and joy. A new baby will not replace the baby you lost, but it sure helps to have those empty arms filled."

Now that we've talked about the emotions that you may be experiencing as you embark on a subsequent pregnancy, let's move on and talk about an equally important subject: what you can do to get your pregnancy off to the healthiest possible start.

$\mathscr{\mathcal{F}}10$ *Making the Healthiest Possible Choices for Your Baby*

WHILE LEADING A healthy lifestyle during pregnancy doesn't provide you with any guarantee that you'll end up with a healthy baby in your arms, it can certainly help to put the odds in your favor.

In this chapter, we will focus on the importance of leading a healthy lifestyle during pregnancy. We'll talk about the importance of scheduling your first prenatal checkup sooner rather than later. Then we'll consider what the latest research has to say about nutrition and weight gain during pregnancy, prenatal fitness, avoiding harmful substances during pregnancy, sexuality during pregnancy, and working during pregnancy.

WHEN TO SEE YOUR HEALTH CARE PROVIDER

A generation ago, it wasn't unusual for pregnant women to be starting their second trimester before they scheduled their first prenatal visit. For one thing, they often didn't even suspect that they were pregnant until they missed their second menstrual period. And even if they did call their doctor's office to try to set up an appointment right away, they were frequently told that the doctor wouldn't see them until the start of the second trimester, when the peak risk period for miscarriage had passed.

For the most part, that attitude has gone the way of the dinosaur. These days, doctors and midwives generally like to schedule their patients' first prenatal visits within a week or two of the first missed period, or as soon as possible after a pregnancy has been confirmed via a home pregnancy test.

If you have a history of miscarriage, stillbirth, or infant death, or have experienced a number of complications in previous pregnancies, your caregiver may want to see you even earlier than this, both so that she can diagnose any potential problems and commence treatment right away, and so that she can provide you with as much reassurance as possible.

How You May Feel During Your First Prenatal Visit

Don't be surprised if you find yourself experiencing a variety of emotions during your prenatal checkup, particularly if this is the first time that you've been back to your doctor's or midwife's office since your baby died. You may experience flashbacks and a flood of painful memories about your previous experiences. You may find that you have an irrational fear that the pregnancy test was wrong and that you're not really pregnant. You may feel anxious that history will repeat itself and you will lose another baby. And you may feel frustrated—even angry—that your caregiver can't offer you any guarantees that you'll experience a happy ending this time around.

The best way to cope with these feelings is to accept the fact that they're perfectly normal for someone who's been through the heartache of having a baby die. Talk to your caregiver about how you're feeling: You may find that he or she is feeling equally frustrated about not being able to offer you any guarantees.

What to Expect During Your Prenatal Checkup

In addition to answering any questions you may still have about the circumstances surrounding your baby's death and discussing your feelings about your new pregnancy, your caregiver will likely perform a series of physical tests and examinations at your initial prenatal visit.

You can expect your caregiver to:

- Confirm your pregnancy with a urine test, blood test, and/or physical examination.
- Estimate your due date by considering the date of your last menstrual period (see Due Date Chart on page 161) and then modifying that estimate based on such factors as your cycle length, any pregnancy

Your Estimated Date Of Delivery

January	1	2	3	4	5	6	7	8	9	10	11	12	13	14
October	8	9	10	11	12	13	14	15	16	17	18	19	20	21

February	1	2	3	4	5	6	7	8	9	10	11	12	13	14
November	8	9	10	11	12	13	14	15	16	17	18	19	20	21

March	1	2	3	4	5	6	7	8	9	10	11	12	13	14
December	6	7	8	9	10	11	12	13	14	15	16	17	18	19

April	1	2	3	4	5	6	7	8	9	10	11	12	13	14
January	6	7	8	9	10	11	12	13	14	15	16	17	18	19

May	1	2	3	4	5	6	7	8	9	10	11	12	13	14
February	5	6	7	8	9	10	11	12	13	14	15	16	17	18

June	1	2	3	4	5	6	7	8	9	10	11	12	13	14
March	8	9	10	11	12	13	14	15	16	17	18	19	20	21

July	1	2	3	4	5	6	7	8	9	10	11	12	13	14
April	7	8	9	10	11	12	13	14	15	16	17	18	19	20

August	1	2	3	4	5	6	7	8	9	10	11	12	13	14
May	8	9	10	11	12	13	14	15	16	17	18	19	20	21

September	1	2	3	4	5	6	7	8	9	10	11	12	13	14
June	8	9	10	11	12	13	14	15	16	17	18	19	20	21

October	1	2	3	4	5	6	7	8	9	10	11	12	13	14
July	8	9	10	11	12	13	14	15	16	17	18	19	20	21

November	1	2	3	4	5	6	7	8	9	10	11	12	13	14
August	8	9	10	11	12	13	14	15	16	17	18	19	20	21

December	1	2	3	4	5	6	7	8	9	10	11	12	13	14
September	7	8	9	10	11	12	13	14	15	16	17	18	19	20

```
15  16  17  18  19  20  21  22  23  24  25  26  27  28  29  30  31
22  23  24  25  26  27  28  29  30  31   1   2   3   4   5   6   7

15  16  17  18  19  20  21  22  23  24  25  26  27  28
22  23  24  25  26  27  28  29  30   1   2   3   4   5

15  16  17  18  19  20  21  22  23  24  25  26  27  28  29  30  31
20  21  22  23  24  25  26  27  28  29  30  31   1   2   3   4   5

15  16  17  18  19  20  21  22  23  24  25  26  27  28  29  30
20  21  22  23  24  25  26  27  28  29  30  31   1   2   3   4

15  16  17  18  19  20  21  22  23  24  25  26  27  28  29  30  31
19  20  21  22  23  24  25  26  27  28   1   2   3   4   5   6   7

15  16  17  18  19  20  21  22  23  24  25  26  27  28  29  30
22  23  24  25  26  27  28  29  30  31   1   2   3   4   5   6

15  16  17  18  19  20  21  22  23  24  25  26  27  28  29  30  31
21  22  23  24  25  26  27  28  29  30   1   2   3   4   5   6   7

15  16  17  18  19  20  21  22  23  24  25  26  27  28  29  30  31
22  23  24  25  26  27  28  29  30  31   1   2   3   4   5   6   7

15  16  17  18  19  20  21  22  23  24  25  26  27  28  29  30
22  23  24  25  26  27  28  29  30   1   2   3   4   5   6   7

15  16  17  18  19  20  21  22  23  24  25  26  27  28  29  30  31
22  23  24  25  26  27  28  29  30  31   1   2   3   4   5   6   7

15  16  17  18  19  20  21  22  23  24  25  26  27  28  29  30
22  23  24  25  26  27  28  29  30  31   1   2   3   4   5   6

15  16  17  18  19  20  21  22  23  24  25  26  27  28  29  30  31
21  22  23  24  25  26  27  28  29  30   1   2   3   4   5   6   7
```

symptoms you are experiencing, changes that she can detect to your cervix and uterus, and any information you are able to provide about your possible date of conception (e.g., whether you were able to pinpoint the most likely date of conception by tracking your basal body temperature, using ovulation predictor kits, and so on).

- Review your medical and reproductive history and conduct a general physical examination to ensure that you are in overall good health (e.g., check your heart, lungs, breasts, abdomen, and so on).
- Give you a blood test to check for anemia, hepatitis B, HIV, syphilis, antibodies to rubella, and—should your medical history warrant it—certain genetic diseases.
- Take a vaginal culture to see if you have any vaginal infections that may require treatment.
- Do a Pap smear to check for cancerous or precancerous cells on your cervix.
- Weigh you so that your weight gain during pregnancy can be monitored.
- Check your blood pressure.

Don't forget to raise the issue of the timing of your next prenatal checkup with your caregiver. While a "typical" pregnant woman would expect to see her caregiver only once every four weeks during the early months of pregnancy, you may wish to ask your doctor or midwife if it's possible for you to come in more frequently, if you feel the need for more frequent reassurance. You may or may not ever take them up on that offer, but it's nice to know that your concerns will be taken seriously if you pick up the phone and make that call.

NUTRITION DURING PREGNANCY

It takes an additional 80,000 calories over the course of your pregnancy— or an extra three hundred calories per day—to "grow" a baby. What you eat during pregnancy is every bit as important as how much you eat, however. Rather than simply adding three hundred calories worth of junk food to your diet, you'll want to ensure that you're upping your intake of healthy foods. This is not to say that you should never treat yourself to a donut or indulge your corn chip habit, of course. Despite what some pregnancy book authors would have you believe, pregnancy is not supposed to be a nine-month-long exercise in deprivation!

The Foods Your Body Needs During Pregnancy

The American College of Obstetricians and Gynecologists recommends that pregnant women consume the following types and quantities of food servings each day:

FOOD GROUP	NUMBER OF SERVINGS PER DAY	WHAT CONSTITUTES A TYPICAL SERVING
Bread, cereal, rice, and pasta	9	one slice of bread; one cup of ready-to-eat cereal, rice, or pasta; or five to six small crackers
Vegetables	4	one cup of raw, leafy vegetables; one-half cup of cooked or chopped raw vegetables; or three-quarters of a cup of vegetable juice
Fruit	3	one medium apple, banana, or orange; one-half cup of chopped, cooked, or canned fruit; one cup of berries; or one-half to three-quarters of a cup of fruit juice
Milk, yogurt, and cheese	3 to 4	one cup of milk or yogurt; one-and-a-half ounces of natural cheese; or two ounces of processed cheese
Meat, poultry, fish, dry beans, eggs, and nuts group	2 to 3	two to three ounces of cooked lean meat, poultry, or fish (about the size of the palm of your hand or a deck of cards); one-half cup of cooked dry beans; one egg; two tablespoons of peanut butter; or one-third cup of nuts

The Ten Nutrients Your Body Needs Most During Pregnancy

All nutrients are not created equal—at least not when it comes to pregnancy. Certain nutrients have a particularly important role to play in ensuring the health of both you and your developing baby.

An Important Note about Special Diets

If you are on a special diet, you may want to meet with a dietitian to talk about what types of dietary modifications, if any, may be required during pregnancy.

If, for example, you are a vegetarian or vegan and do not eat meat, you may need to take steps to ensure that you are getting adequate quantities of vitamins B_{12}, B_2, and D; calcium; iron; and zinc. In addition to maximizing your iron absorption by combining iron-rich foods (e.g., eggs and fish or vegetables such as spinach) with foods that are rich in vitamin C and that can help with the absorption of iron (e.g., citrus fruits, strawberries, and tomatoes), you may want to ask your doctor to recommend a vitamin B_{12} supplement and to check your hemoglobin regularly to ensure that you aren't becoming anemic.

Similarly, if you are lactose intolerant (you have difficulty digesting the sugar in milk), you may have trouble getting an adequate amount of calcium in your diet while you're pregnant. You will want to try to get your calcium from as many nonmilk sources as possible (e.g., tofu, calcium-fortified bread or juice, dark-green leafy vegetables, sardines, and salmon); to eat yogurt that contains acidophilus or active cultures (these active cultures can actually help you to digest lactose); to experiment with smaller portion sizes (to see if your body can process small amounts of lactose); and to try drinking milk at mealtimes rather than on its own, since this has been shown to eliminate lactose intolerance problems in some people. You might also want to try some of the growing number of lactose-free dairy products that are available on the grocery store shelves.

A dietitian can help you to identify any possible nutritional challenges and to come up with practical ways to ensure that both you and your baby get the nutrients you need during pregnancy.

The Ten Nutrients Your Body Needs Most During Pregnancy

NUTRIENT	WHERE TO FIND IT	WHAT IT DOES
Protein	Meat, eggs, beans	Helps to produce the extra blood your body needs during pregnancy, provides extra stores of energy for labor and delivery, and acts as the main "building block" for your baby's cells.
Carbohydrates	Bread, cereal, rice, potatoes, pasta	Provides energy to you and your baby.
Calcium	Milk, cheese, yogurt, sardines, spinach	Helps your baby to develop strong bones and teeth.
Iron	Lean red meat, spinach, whole-grain breads, and cereals	Helps to create the red blood cells that deliver oxygen to your baby; helps to prevent fatigue.
Vitamin A	Carrots, dark, leafy greens, sweet potatoes	Plays an important role in the formation of healthy skin, good eyesight, and strong bones.
Vitamin C	Citrus fruit, broccoli, tomatoes	Promotes healthy gums, teeth, and bones. Helps your body to absorb iron.
Vitamin B_6	Beef liver, pork, ham, whole-grain cereals, bananas	Helps with the formation of red blood cells; helps the body to use protein, fat, and carbohydrates.
Vitamin B_{12}	Liver, meat, fish, poultry, milk	Maintains the central nervous system and assists with the formation of red blood cells.
Folic acid	Green, leafy vegetables, dark yellow fruits and vegetables, liver, legumes and nuts	Helps the body to produce blood and protein, helps certain enzymes to function.
Fat	Meat, dairy products, nuts, peanut butter, margarine, dressings, vegetable oils	Provides energy.

SOURCE: The American College of Obstetricians and Gynecologists

The Role of Vitamin Supplements During Pregnancy

While the American College of Obstetricians and Gynecologists does not formally endorse the use of vitamin supplements during pregnancy (other than, of course, folic acid, which it recommends even before conception), most doctors and midwives recommend that pregnant women take some sort of prenatal multivitamin supplement, since it is almost impossible for them to meet their bodies' demands for iron and folic acid through diet alone.

Don't just reach for your usual bottle of vitamins, however. Before you take any type of vitamin supplement, you need to make sure it's one that's safe to take during pregnancy. Believe it or not, you can get too much of a good thing. Some studies have pointed to a link between excessive quantities of vitamin A and certain types of birth defects. The American College of Obstetricians and Gynecologists recommends that pregnant women consume less than 5,000 international units (IU) of vitamin A during pregnancy—roughly the amount that is found in most prenatal vitamins, but far less than what you might normally expect to find in a standard multivitamin, some of which have been found to contain as much as five times the recommended amount. Also, some studies have demonstrated that high doses of calcium can cause complications for women with kidney disease and/or a history of kidney stones. (*Note:* While it was once believed that boosting a pregnant woman's intake of calcium could help to reduce the risk of preeclampsia, a recent study conducted by the National Institute of Child Health and Human Development indicated that calcium supplementation was not an effective means of preventing preeclampsia after all.)

Enough doom and gloom. Let's wrap up this section by looking at a good news story on the vitamin front: Nutritionists believe that zinc has a lot to offer pregnant women and their babies. A study at the University of Alabama at Birmingham revealed that women who took 25 mg of zinc along with their standard prenatal vitamins delivered bigger and healthier babies than their non–zinc-consuming counterparts.

A Note about Caffeine and Artificial Sweeteners

While caffeine and artificial sweeteners aren't foods per se, they certainly play a major role in the diets of most North Americans. Here's what you need to know about the effects of each of these substances during pregnancy.

Caffeine While there's still a fair bit of controversy surrounding the issue of caffeine intake during pregnancy—some researchers feel that a pregnant woman can safely enjoy a cup or two of her favorite caffeinated beverage each day, while others say that caffeine should be avoided entirely during pregnancy—many women decide to err on the side of caution during pregnancy. After all, you have enough things to worry about when you're pregnant without adding another item to the list!

Even if the scary research linking caffeine use to miscarriage and SIDS doesn't hold up over the long run, there are still some very good reasons for avoiding caffeine during pregnancy: it acts as a diuretic, removing both fluid and calcium from your body; it can prevent your body from absorbing iron; it can heighten mood swings; and it can cause insomnia. So unless you relish the thought of being wide awake at 3:00 A.M., wondering if drinking that cup of coffee was really such a great idea after all, you might want to kick your caffeine habit—at least for now.

Artificial sweeteners Despite all the scary rumors you've no doubt heard about the use of artificial sweeteners during pregnancy, there really isn't a lot of evidence to show that artificial sweeteners are dangerous to a pregnant woman or her baby. All three of the artificial sweeteners currently on the market today—aspartame, saccharin, and acesulfame K—are believed to be safe during pregnancy. (There's just one exception: Pregnant women who have phenylketonuria or PKU cannot consume products containing aspartame.) That said, it's probably a good idea to limit the quantity of artificial sweeteners you consume during pregnancy, if only because you'll leave yourself with one less thing to worry about.

YOUR PREGNANCY "GAIN PLAN"

You already know how important it is to eat properly during pregnancy. What you might not know, however, is exactly how much weight you should plan to gain over the next nine months.

According to the Institute of Medicine of the National Academy of Sciences, just as there's no such thing as a "typical" pregnant woman, there's no such thing as a "one size fits all" pregnancy weight-gain recommendation. A woman who is underweight when she conceives needs to gain substantially more weight than a woman who is obese when she becomes pregnant.

Weight Gain During Pregnancy

PREPREGNANCY WEIGHT	HOW MUCH WEIGHT YOU SHOULD GAIN
Underweight women	28 to 40 lbs.
Normal weight women	25 to 35 lbs.
Overweight women	15 to 25 lbs.
Obese women	15 lbs. or more

SOURCE: *The Institute of Medicine of the National Academy of Sciences*

Of course, women who are carrying more than one baby will need to gain even more than these recommended amounts. In fact, in their book *When You're Expecting Twins, Triplets, or Quads,* (Harper Perennial, 1999), Barbara Luke, R.D., and Tamara Eberlein recommend that pregnant women aim for a weight gain of forty to fifty pounds if they are carrying twins; fifty to sixty pounds if they are carrying triplets; and sixty-five to eighty pounds if they are carrying quadruplets. (*Note:* Not all doctors go along with the idea that women need to gain a certain amount of weight during a multiple pregnancy. Some feel that it's more important for the pregnant woman to focus on ensuring that she is consuming an adequate quantity of nutrients than to become overly concerned about the number on the scale.)

Wondering where the pounds go when you gain weight during pregnancy? According to the American College of Obstetricians and Gynecologists, your body distributes a 30-lb. pregnancy weight gain as follows:

- Baby: 7.5 lbs.
- Breasts: 2 lbs.
- Maternal stores of fat, protein, and other nutrients: 7 lbs.
- Placenta: 1.5 lbs.

- Uterus: 2 lbs.
- Amniotic fluid: 2 lbs.
- Blood: 4 lbs.
- Body fluids: 4 lbs.

Why It's Important Not to Gain Too Much or Too Little Weight

While you don't want to drive yourself crazy by carefully scrutinizing each and every bite of food that goes into your mouth, it's a good idea to try to keep your weight gain within in the healthy range. Here's why:

- Gaining *too much* weight can contribute to a range of pregnancy-related problems, such as back pain, high blood pressure, and diabetes, and may—according to a study at the Duke University Medical Center in Dallas—increase your odds of requiring a cesarean delivery.
- Gaining *too little* weight puts you at increased risk of giving birth to a low-birthweight baby.

Just as important as how much weight you gain overall, however, is when you gain that weight. Rather than packing on twenty-five pounds during your first trimester and then trying to limit your weight gain during the remainder of your pregnancy, you should aim for a slow, steady weight gain throughout your pregnancy. The American College of Obstetricians and Gynecologists recommends a weight gain of three to five pounds during the first trimester and a pound or two a week during the second and third trimesters.

Just one additional point before we wrap up our discussion of weight gain during pregnancy: It's a rare woman indeed who is able to follow the ACOG schedule for weight gain to the letter. You may find that you don't gain any weight at all during the first part of your pregnancy, but that you make up for lost time later on. Or you may find that no matter how much food you eat, you can't seem to gain any weight at all. Try not to obsess about the amount of weight you are—or aren't—gaining. Instead, try to focus on ensuring that your body is receiving a steady intake of the nutrients it needs to sustain your pregnancy.

PRENATAL FITNESS

Don't assume that you have to put your workout program on hold just because the pregnancy test has come back positive. Most pregnant women are able to remain physically active throughout their pregnancies. What's more, those who do tend to go through pregnancy and delivery a lot more easily than their less physically active counterparts.

There are, of course, certain reasons for skipping your workouts for a while. Your doctor or midwife will likely advise you *not* to exercise (or to reduce the intensity of your workouts) if:

- You are underweight.
- You have been diagnosed with pregnancy-induced high blood pressure or a preexisting medical condition such as heart disease or diabetes, which might make prenatal exercise inadvisable.
- You are having problems with persistent bleeding during the second or third trimester of pregnancy.
- You have experienced preterm rupture of the membranes (PROM) or preterm labor in either your current pregnancy or a previous pregnancy.
- Your baby is not growing as quickly as he or she should be.
- Your cervix is weak.
- You have a history of second-trimester miscarriage.
- You are carrying multiples.

The Benefits of Being Physically Active
During Pregnancy

Remaining active during pregnancy offers a number of benefits: your energy level increases; it's easier to keep your weight gain within the target range; you feel more relaxed and positive (a tremendous benefit to women who are going through what can at best be described as a stressful pregnancy!); your blood glucose levels remain more stable (something that can help to reduce your chances of developing gestational diabetes); you can get a better night's sleep; you're less likely to suffer from backache, leg cramps, and constipation; you can help to prepare your body for the challenges of labor; and you reduce the amount of time it will take your body to recover after the delivery.

Sold on the idea of starting a prenatal fitness program? Here are a few more things you need to know about before you hit the gym:

- Not all exercises are suitable for pregnant women. While you'll want to make sure that your workout includes the four most important prenatal exercises (squatting, pelvic tilting or rocking, abdominal curl-ups, and pelvic floor exercises), you'll want to ensure that it doesn't include any exercises that could leave you susceptible to injury (e.g., deep knee bends, full sit-ups, double-leg raises, and straight-leg toe touches). *Note:* Be sure to avoid weight-bearing exercises such as running and high-impact aerobics if you're experiencing sciatica (pain starting in the buttock and radiating down the outer thigh and into the calf), since these types of exercise may further stress your joints and increase the amount of pain you are experiencing.
- It's not a good idea to exercise flat on your back after the fourth month of pregnancy. Exercising in this position can leave you feeling lightheaded or nauseated. (The weight of your pregnant uterus on your inferior vena cava—the vein that is responsible for returning blood from the lower body to the heart—can disrupt your blood flow, causing dizziness.)
- You should aim for a moderate rather than a strenuous workout. The American College of Obstetricians and Gynecologists (ACOG) recommends that you limit the duration of strenuous activity to no more than fifteen to thirty minutes at a time. You should also plan to start your workout with a five-minute warm-up and to end it with a cool-down. (*Note:* You don't have to worry about getting your heart rate up in the training zone. While ACOG used to advise pregnant women to keep their heart rate below 140 beats per minute, they've since scrapped that recommendation as a result of information garnered from newer research. So while you shouldn't overdo things, it's now considered okay to give your body a good workout.)
- Never exercise to the point of exhaustion, and stop exercising immediately if you experience vaginal bleeding or uterine contractions, or if your membranes rupture.
- Be careful. Pregnant women are more likely to be injured while they're working out than nonpregnant women. Not only is your center of balance thrown off by your growing uterus—something that can

make it easier for you to stumble or fall—but also high levels of progesterone in your body cause the connective tissue in the body to relax, something that makes it easier for you to become injured if you happen to overstretch a muscle or ligament. As a rule of thumb, you should avoid jerky or bouncy movements and overflexing or overextending your joints when you exercise, as these are the types of movements that are most likely to result in injury.

- Keep in mind that it can be dangerous for you to become overheated or dehydrated when you're exercising. Dehydration can trigger premature labor, and allowing your body's core temperature to rise too high (above 38 degrees C or 101 degrees F) could harm your developing baby—two good reasons to skip your workout if it's hot and humid outside, or if you've got a fever.

- Pregnancy is no time to embark on a "get fit quick" scheme. In general, you should focus on maintaining your current fitness level rather on than trying to become super fit overnight.

DRUG USE DURING PREGNANCY

According to the U.S. Department of Health and Human Services, U.S. women take an average of four prescription or over-the-counter drugs during pregnancy. These include medications needed to control preexisting medical conditions (e.g., asthma medications), antibiotics for infections that develop during pregnancy (e.g., treatments for urinary tract infections), medications needed to treat pregnancy-related complications (e.g., high blood pressure), and over-the-counter products (e.g., headache tablets) that are used to treat everyday aches and pains.

While some drugs are considered safe to take during pregnancy, others pose considerable risks to the developing baby. Depending on the baby's developmental stage, the potency of the drug, and the dosage taken, a drug may alter the mother's biochemistry (something that indirectly affects the baby as well); interfere with the functioning of the placenta, possibly disrupting the flow of oxygen and nutrients to the baby; cause a variety of birth defects; and/or be toxic to the developing baby.

Wondering whether or not a particular over-the-counter drug or prescription drug is safe to take during pregnancy? You'll find detailed information about the FDA ratings for hundreds of over-the-counter and prescription drugs as well as detailed information about the possible effects of these drugs on the developing baby by visiting the official *Trying Again* web site: www.having-a-baby.com/tryingagain.htm.

OTHER TYPES OF HAZARDS

Drugs aren't the only hazardous substances that you'll want to avoid during pregnancy, of course. Here's a list of some of the other types of substances that could prove harmful to your developing baby:

- *Cigarette smoke.* Even though a number of studies have linked smoking during pregnancy to a range of undesirable outcomes—including miscarriage, stillbirth, preterm birth, low birthweight, and SIDS—in 1995, 14 percent of pregnant women in the United States continued to smoke during pregnancy. While it's unlikely that you would choose to smoke during pregnancy, given your history, it's important to remember that you don't have to be the one lighting up the cigarette to expose your baby to tobacco smoke. Bottom line: If your partner hasn't already kicked his nicotine habit, he now has a compelling reason to do so.
- *Alcohol.* While doctors used to tell their patients that an occasional drink of alcohol during pregnancy wouldn't harm the developing baby, most are now reconsidering this "wisdom." Since studies have been unable to pinpoint a safe level of alcohol consumption during pregnancy, you're best to avoid consuming any alcohol at all while you're pregnant.
- *Radiation.* Abdominal X rays, CAT scans, and diagnostic procedures involving radioactive dyes should be avoided during pregnancy. If other types of X rays are performed (e.g., X rays to areas of the body other than the abdomen), appropriate radiation shields must be used.
- *Toxins.* Your baby's body can't process toxins as efficiently as your body can. It takes longer for these types of substances to leave your baby's system. That's one of the reasons why it's important to avoid exposing yourself to cleaning products with strong odors (e.g., chlorine- and ammonia-based products), paints, solvents, lawn-care products, and other powerful chemicals during pregnancy.
- *Infectious diseases.* While it's hard to avoid picking up at least one garden-variety head cold during pregnancy, you'll want to avoid exposing yourself to anything more serious. As noted back in Chapters 2, 3,

and 4, high fevers and certain types of infectious disease, including sexually transmitted diseases, can be harmful to the developing fetus. Here's some detailed information on some of the infectious diseases you'll want to avoid during pregnancy.

Infectious Diseases and Their Effects on the Developing Baby

TYPE OF INFECTIOUS DISEASE	EFFECTS ON THE DEVELOPING BABY
Chickenpox and shingles (problem for the 10 percent to 15 percent of pregnant women who aren't immune to the virus that causes these diseases)	prematurity, skin lesions, neurologic anomalies, eye anomalies, skeletal abnormalities, gastrointestinal and genitourinary anomalies, limb deformities, low birthweight, meningoencephalitis, miscarriage, or stillbirth
Cytomegalovirus (CMV) (also see Chapter 3)	miscarriage, mental retardation, psychomotor retardation, developmental abnormalities, progressive hearing impairment, respiratory illness, jaundice, intrauterine growth restriction, failure to thrive, or eye infections
Listeriosis	miscarriage, stillbirth, premature labor, serious illness in newborn
Measles	prematurity or fetal loss
Mumps	increased risk of adult onset diabetes
Rubella	severe birth defects, death of baby
Toxoplasmosis (more dangerous during the first half of pregnancy)	hydrocephalus, eye problems, psychomotor retardation, convulsions, microphthalmia, or intracerebral calcification (calcium deposits in the brain)

NOTE: See Chapter 3 for information on other infectious diseases

SEXUAL ACTIVITY DURING PREGNANCY

It's not unusual for parents who have had a baby die to worry that they might increase their chances of experiencing a miscarriage or of triggering premature labor or another obstetrical emergency, if they continue to be sexually active during pregnancy.

While sexual intercourse is generally considered to be safe for most pregnant couples, there are a few exceptions. Your doctor or midwife may recommend that you abstain from sexual intercourse, nipple stimulation (which can cause the uterus to contract), and/or having orgasms altogether if:

- You have a history of recurrent pregnancy loss.
- You have a history of premature labor or are showing signs of going into premature labor this time around.
- You have been diagnosed with placenta previa (the placenta is blocking all or part of the cervix) or a placental abruption (the placenta is prematurely separating from the uterine wall).
- You are carrying more than one baby.
- You or your partner has an untreated sexually transmitted disease.
- Your membranes have ruptured.

In some cases, you may wish to abstain from sex even if your caregiver gives you the green light. One woman who became pregnant again found the spotting she experienced after intercourse during the first few months of pregnancy caused her a tremendous amount of anxiety. Even though her caregiver had tried to reassure her that the spotting she was experiencing was perfectly harmless and the result of the cervix getting bumped by her husband's penis during intercourse, she chose to abstain from sex rather than subject herself to any unnecessary anxiety. By the start of the second trimester, her cervix was no longer as apt to bleed during intercourse, so she and her husband were able to resume sexual relations again.

If you and your partner abstain from sex during your pregnancy, you will need to work hard to keep the channels of communication open. Sex plays an important role in the relationships of most married couples and it can be stressful to have to give up this part of your relationship "cold turkey." Most couples find that it helps to keep a sense of humor and to have fun planning for the time when the green light goes on in the bedroom once again.

WORKING DURING PREGNANCY

While it's generally considered safe for a woman to work during pregnancy, your doctor might advise you to ask to be assigned to other types
of work, to change jobs, or quit working entirely if:

- Your job is highly strenuous or physically demanding.
- Your job involves a lot of repetitive work that could increase your
  chances of developing carpal tunnel syndrome (repetitive stress syn-
  drome)—a condition to which pregnant women are especially suscep-
  tible.
- You have to do a lot of bending, stooping, stair- or ladder-climbing, or
  heavy-lifting on the job.
- You are exposed to infectious diseases, chemicals, or toxic substances
  on the job.
- You have to stand for more than three hours per day at work.
- You work in an especially hot, cold, or noisy environment.
- You work long hours or rotating shifts.

Assuming that you do decide to continue to work, you'll want to do
whatever you can to ensure that you stay comfortable and healthy from
nine-to-five. Here are a few tips:

- *Watch the amount of time that you spend on your feet.* Standing for more
  than three hours at a time may affect blood flow to your baby, reducing the amount of oxygen and nutrients your baby receives. If your
  job requires a lot of standing, you should try to avoid standing for
  more than three hours, plan to take several short breaks during the
  day, and rest once in a while by sitting down and putting your feet up
  on a stool.
- *Get up and move around.* Sitting for more than three hours without a
  break can cause fluid retention in your legs and feet, reduced blood
  flow to your baby, muscle strain (particularly in your lower back), and
  tension in your neck and shoulder areas. You can minimize these
  problems by using a cushion to reduce the stress on your lower back
  while you are sitting down, keeping a footstool handy so that you can
  change the position of your feet from time to time, and getting up
  and moving around on a regular basis.

- *Leave the lifting to someone else.* Lifting and carrying heavy items may increase your chances of experiencing a variety of pregnancy-related complications, including back strain and uterine prolapse. As a rule of thumb, you shouldn't attempt to lift as much during pregnancy as you can normally lift when you're not pregnant. (*Note:* If you find that you do have to lift heavy objects, be sure to bend your knees and keep your back straight as you squat and to alternate strenuous, routine, or repetitive lifting and carrying with less strenuous tasks.)
- *Put your feet up whenever possible.* Placing your feet on a stool or an open filing cabinet drawer can help to reduce some of the strain on your lower back.
- *Dress for comfort, not style.* You'll have plenty of opportunity to dress for success after your baby arrives. For now, focus on comfort. Wear loose, comfortable clothing, and dress in layers so that you can take off a layer or two if you start to feel overheated.
- *Put your best foot forward.* Leave the high-heeled shoes in the back of your closet for now. You'll be far less likely to take a tumble or wrench your ankle if you're buzzing around the office in low-heeled shoes.
- *Eat, drink, and be merry.* Stop for lunch no matter how crazy it is at the office. Keep a glass of water on your desk so that you can remember to keep yourself well hydrated. And try to minimize the amount of stress you have to deal with on a day-to-day basis. Remember: your pregnancy is causing you more than enough stress as it is. Don't let office politics cause your stress level to go off the Richter scale!
- *Get the rest you need.* Take a power nap during your lunch hour, if you can swing it, and make a point to hit the couch for a while when you arrive home at the end of the day.
- If it's likely that you'll have to head out of town on business at least once during your pregnancy, be sure to ask your caregiver for a copy of your prenatal record. That way, if you have to make a pit stop at the nearest emergency ward, the doctor on call will have the information he needs to provide you and your baby with the best possible medical care.

Now that we've talked about what you can do to give your baby the healthiest possible start in life, it's time to zero in on another important topic: prenatal testing.

✎ 11 *The Prenatal Testing*
Merry-Go-Round

THERE'S NO DENYING it: There have been some amazing break-throughs in the area of prenatal testing during the past thirty years. It's now possible for doctors to diagnose a growing number of health problems and congenital anomalies in utero.

Unfortunately, as many parents have discovered for themselves, this knowledge doesn't come without a price. Sometimes what you learn from one prenatal test can catapult you into having a series of other tests performed—tests that you may not have ever intended to have before you decided to step onboard the prenatal testing merry-go-round.

In this chapter, we will focus on the complex issue of prenatal testing. We'll start out by considering who is—and isn't—a good candidate for prenatal testing, as well as the pros and cons of prenatal testing. Next, we'll zero in on the various types of prenatal tests that are available: what each type of test involves and what information it can provide. We'll wrap up the chapter by talking about the most difficult aspect of prenatal testing: the anguish that many parents experience in making the decision about whether to terminate a pregnancy.

TO TEST OR NOT TO TEST?

It's an issue that many parents who have had a baby die struggle with at some point during their subsequent pregnancies: whether to go for prenatal testing. Some parents decide they want to be armed with as much information as possible during their subsequent pregnancies. Others decide they don't want to subject themselves to any unnecessary stress during what is already likely to be a highly stressful pregnancy.

The Pros of Prenatal Testing

Prenatal testing can help you to determine whether there's a problem with your baby before he or she is born. This may enable you to:

- Seek treatment for your baby's condition before birth (e.g., blood transfusions may be given to a baby with Rh incompatibility problems).
- Make appropriate choices for the delivery (e.g., schedule a cesarean delivery to minimize any birth-related injuries that a baby with spina bifida might sustain during a vaginal delivery, or avoid an emergency cesarean for fetal distress if you know ahead of time that your baby will be born with a fatal birth defect and will live, at most, for a few hours after birth).
- Prepare to give birth to a baby who has special needs (e.g., choose to give birth in a hospital with state-of-the-art neonatal care facilities or emotionally prepare yourself for the challenges of caring for a mentally retarded infant) or a baby who will be stillborn.
- Decide to terminate the pregnancy.

The Cons of Prenatal Testing

- Only certain types of problems can be detected through prenatal testing. Scientists have yet to invent a test that can guarantee that you'll end up with a healthy baby.
- Prenatal tests aren't 100 percent accurate. There is a small margin of error in even the most sophisticated diagnostic test, and screening tests are notorious for having high rates of false positives (an issue we'll discuss in greater detail elsewhere in this chapter).
- Diagnostic tests simply answer the question "Is my child affected?" not "How severely is my child affected?" Without this information, it can sometimes be hard for you to gauge what quality of life your child could expect to enjoy.
- Once you hop on board the prenatal testing merry-go-round, it can be pretty hard to get off. If, for example, you obtain a positive (abnormal) result on one of the less invasive prenatal screening tests (e.g.,

the alpha-fetoprotein test—a simple blood test), you might decide to go for one of the much more invasive diagnostic tests (e.g., amniocentesis—a test that involves inserting a needle into the amniotic sac and removing a small sample of amniotic fluid, and that carries a risk of miscarriage). In the end, you may find yourself faced with a decision you'd rather not have to make.

Making the Decision

Caryl made the decision to terminate her first pregnancy at twenty-one weeks when it was discovered that her baby would not be able to survive beyond birth, because he didn't have any kidneys. She decided to go for prenatal testing during each of her three subsequent pregnancies. "I recommend having the AFP test," she explains. "I didn't have it with my first pregnancy. If I had, I would have known much sooner that our son had a fatal birth defect. It was much harder on me physically since we didn't find out about his problems until we were twenty-one weeks along."

Carla, whose first child was stillborn at thirty-eight weeks, also wanted to arm herself with as much knowledge as possible during her subsequent pregnancy. "We did not want any surprises with this baby including [finding out] the sex of the baby," she explains. "We had to have some control over this pregnancy, and knowledge is power. The more you know, the better."

Julie felt the same way when she became pregnant again after losing her first child through stillbirth: "On delivery day, I wanted no surprises. If my baby was to have a defect, I wanted to know ahead of time."

Not all women who become pregnant again share Julie's viewpoint. Cynthia, who experienced three miscarriages in between the births of her first and second living children, decided to forgo prenatal testing because she was reluctant to add to her stress level during her pregnancy by subjecting herself to a lot of unnecessary tests. "Sometimes, too much knowledge and information is a scary thing," she explains. "I will always treasure the experience of my first pregnancy because that was a truly blissful pregnancy. I was so naïve and innocent and really had no idea at all of the complications or problems that could arise. It was a truly wonderful pregnancy, something I would never experience again."

Cynthia also knew that she was not prepared to terminate her pregnancy if she discovered that her baby had a problem. "My husband would have preferred me to have the testing done because he was of the opinion that he could not handle a baby who had some type of severe malformation or disease. The conversation was pretty brief. Basically, I told him that he'd be surprised how you can rise to the occasion if you have to, but the bottom line was that after all I had been through, there was no way I would ever terminate the life of my child. The child we get is the child we get," she says.

Jenn, who has experienced four miscarriages as well as the birth of two living children, decided to decline prenatal testing during her last pregnancy, even though her doctor wasn't particularly supportive of her decision. "I decided not to have any type of prenatal tests done other than the blood tests to monitor my hCG levels," she recalls. "By the time I was three months' pregnant during my subsequent pregnancy, I was already on part-time bedrest from partial placenta previa, had experienced several episodes of hemorrhaging, and my stress level was through the roof. I could not imagine the pressure and anxiety of getting a test done when there could be false positives and false negatives. No way! My obstetrician was not very happy about that and always seemed to make me feel guilty for not doing the AFP test. It was like he 'needed' to know. Not me: I didn't."

Laura, whose second child died at nine days of age during open heart surgery, decided to decline the AFP test during her third pregnancy because she and her partner knew that they weren't prepared to go for amniocentesis if they happened to get a bad result on the AFP test. "Because we were very sure that we did not want to do an amniocentesis, we decided against doing the AFP/triple screen test. A good result from that test was not going to be particularly reassuring and a bad result was going to make us feel like we needed the amnio, which we really did not want," she says. "My rule of thumb now on deciding about prenatal testing is to try to figure out whether the test will increase or decrease my stress. With something like the amnio that has risk associated with it, I weigh whether I'm willing to take the risk and whether there's enough benefit to taking the test. I also think about what actions I would take based on the test results. With the AFP, which has no risks associated with the test itself, I look at whether a good result would reduce my stress and how much a bad result would increase my stress—and whether it would propel me to do additional tests I didn't want."

Nancy decided against prenatal testing, both because she knew that no prenatal test could detect the metabolic disorder that had led to her first child's death, and because she wasn't prepared to take any prenatal test that might put her baby at risk. "We simply couldn't tolerate any additional risks 'just in case' there was a problem," she explains. "Had there been no problems with the baby but I miscarried *because* of a test—I don't think we could have handled that very well."

Lori, whose first baby died as a result of severe intrauterine growth restriction, offers these cautionary words to parents who are trying to decide what to do about prenatal testing: "Prenatal testing is a slippery slope. Once you start down that slope, it's hard to stop or go back. Get lots of information and think very carefully about what you think is best for you and your baby. If you decide to have testing done, think carefully about what you might want to do—or not do—should the results not be the ones you had hoped for. Don't forget that the tests aren't 100 percent accurate and that they can only test for certain things. No test can guarantee you that your baby will be 100 percent healthy."

ARE YOU A GOOD CANDIDATE FOR PRENATAL TESTING?

Wondering if you're a good candidate for prenatal testing? The following guidelines may help you to make up your mind. Just be sure to bear in mind that there's no right or wrong answer to this question; only you and your partner can decide what's right for the two of you.

Who's a good candidate for prenatal testing?   Prenatal testing is generally recommended for parents who: have a family history of genetic disease or who know that they are carriers of a particular disease; have been exposed to a serious infection, such as rubella or toxoplasmosis, during pregnancy; have been exposed to a substance that is known to cause birth defects; have had one or more unsuccessful pregnancies or who have previously given birth to a birth defect; and is anxious to know with some degree of certainty whether their baby has a detectable anomaly.

Who's not?   Prenatal testing is generally not recommended for parents who: have concerns about the accuracy of certain types of prenatal tests (an issue we'll discuss later on in this chapter); feel that taking the test will only add to—rather than decrease—their anxiety level; wouldn't consider terminating their pregnancy under any circumstances; and are afraid to undergo certain types of prenatal testing (e.g., amniocentesis) for fear of the discomfort of the procedure or inadvertently miscarrying or otherwise harming a normal, healthy baby.

The age argument revisited   Despite what you might have heard, age alone is not a strong enough reason to opt for prenatal testing. While your risk of giving birth to a baby with a chromosomal anomaly does increase with age (see "The Risk of Giving Birth to a Liveborn Child with Down's Syndrome or Another Chromosomal Anomaly" on page 59), this increase is gradual, rather than sudden.

Some doctors try to make the case that prenatal testing is justified only when the risk of miscarriage as a result of the test is less than the risk of giving birth to a child with a birth defect—something that typically happens, statistically speaking, when a woman reaches age thirty-five. What this across-the-board rule fails to take into account, however, is the fact that not all women of a particular age share the same feelings about giving birth to a child with a severe—even fatal—birth defect, and that this kind of reasoning is of the "apples and oranges" sort.

A twenty-year-old woman might decide, for example, that she's unprepared to care for a child who has a serious birth defect and that she's willing to accept the risk of miscarriage that is associated with amniocentesis (one in 250 tests) even though her odds of giving birth to a baby with a chromosomal anomaly are roughly half that: one in 526 cases. And a forty-year-old woman who has experienced repeated miscarriages might decide that she's not willing to risk the one in 250 chance of experiencing a miscarriage as a result of complications resulting from the amniocentesis, even though her chances of giving birth to a baby with a chromosomal anomaly are considerably higher than that: one in sixty-six.

As you can see, there's no such thing as a "one size fits all" policy when it comes to prenatal testing. Only you and your partner can weigh the pros and cons and decide whether prenatal testing is right for you. Bottom line: Don't let your caregiver or other people in your life try to pressure you into taking any prenatal tests that you don't particularly want, simply because you've reached the "magic" age of thirty-five.

The Two Basic Types of Prenatal Tests

There are two types of prenatal tests: screening and diagnostic. It's important to understand the difference between the two types of tests so that you can make informed decisions about prenatal testing.

Screening Tests

Screening tests are designed to screen a large number of pregnant women in order to identify those who have a higher-than-average chance of giving birth to a child with a serious or life-threatening health problem. Screening tests are not supposed to determine whether there is a problem: that's the job of diagnostic tests. Screening tests are simply supposed to alert a pregnant woman and her caregiver to the possibility that there *could* be a problem.

Screening tests are often criticized, because of their high rates of false positives (cases in which a pregnant woman is identified as being at risk of giving birth to a baby with a particular problem when, in fact, her baby is perfectly healthy). What many people don't know is that there's an art to designing a screening test: You have to compromise between maximizing the rate of detection and minimizing the rate of false positives. If you make the testing criteria too rigid, in an effort to reduce the number of false positives, you end up with an unacceptable number of false negatives (cases in which problems are missed).

Diagnostic Tests

Diagnostic tests are designed to determine whether a particular baby is affected by a particular problem or problems. Unfortunately, no single diagnostic test is capable of detecting every possible problem in a developing baby. What's more, as hard as it may be to believe in this era of high-tech medicine, a significant number of conditions still can't be detected prior to birth by *any* available test.

SPECIFIC PRENATAL TESTS

Now that we've considered the difference between screening tests and diagnostic tests, let's talk about some specific types of prenatal tests. We'll start out by talking about four of the most commonly used types of prenatal tests—the alpha-fetoprotein test, ultrasound, amniocentesis, and chorionic villus sampling—and then we'll look at two less commonly used tests—percutaneous umbilical blood sampling (PUBS) and transabdominal embryo fetoscopy.

Alpha-fetoprotein (AFP) Test (or the Triple- and Quad-Screen Test)

Type of test: Screening.

When it is performed: Between the fifteenth and eighteenth weeks of pregnancy.

How it is performed: A sample of blood is taken from the pregnant woman's arm and then sent to the laboratory for analysis. High levels of alpha-fetoprotein (a substance produced by the fetal liver) in the woman's blood may indicate that she is carrying a child with a neural tube defect, while low levels may indicate that she's carrying a child with Down's syndrome. The test is frequently combined with tests of human chorionic gonadotropin (hCG) and unconjugated estriol (a form of estrogen that is produced by the placenta). In this case, it is called the triple-screen test or referred to simply as maternal serum screening (MSS). If it's combined with testing for inhibin-A (a chemical produced by the ovaries and the placenta that, when done as a screening test along with AFP, estriol, and hCG, can be used to more accurately pinpoint the risk of Down's syndrome), it's known as the quad-screen test.

How long it takes to get the results: Anywhere from a couple of days to a week.

What it can tell you: The test results indicate the likelihood that you are carrying a baby who is affected by Down's syndrome, a neural tube defect, or certain other types of anomalies (severe kidney or liver disease, esophageal or intestinal blockages, other types of chromosomal anomalies, urinary obstructions, and osteogenesis imperfecta—the medical term for fragile bones). Since women with elevated levels of AFP that are not associated with any identifiable birth defect are at increased risk for preterm labor, intrauterine growth restriction, and stillbirth, women with these types of elevated levels will be watched particularly closely for problems during their third trimester.

Accuracy: The AFP test can detect 82.1 percent of cases of open neural tube defects and 73.7 percent of cases of Down's syndrome in women under the age of thirty-five, according to a study conducted at the University of Connecticut. The test can also pick up evidence of certain other types of problems. It does, however, have a false positive rate of 95 percent. (In other words, only one in twenty women who receives a positive result on the test is actually carrying a baby with a problem.)

Note: The AFP test is designed for pregnant women under the age of thirty-five—women who might want to know whether they are at risk of giving birth to a baby with Down's syndrome or a neural tube defect, but who would not normally be considered candidates for amniocentesis and other more invasive types of prenatal testing. It cannot provide women over the age of thirty-five with sufficient reassurance to enable them to opt out of amniocentesis or chorionic villus sampling, simply because their AFP results are good. There hasn't been enough data collected on women in this age bracket to allow for such conclusions to be drawn.

Risks: The AFP test doesn't pose any direct risks to the developing baby, but a false positive on the test could lead to more invasive types of prenatal tests (e.g., amniocentesis) that may carry a risk of miscarriage. An ultrasound to look for markers for any particular problem and/or to detect a multiple pregnancy (something that can throw off the AFP results) is typically the next step for a women who receives a positive test result on her AFP test.

Ultrasound (Sonogram)

Type of test: screening or diagnostic

When it is performed: An ultrasound can be performed at any stage of pregnancy. Early on, it may be used to detect a fetal heartbeat. Later on in pregnancy, it may be used to detect fetal anomalies and/or to monitor fetal growth. It is often done routinely in perfectly normal pregnancies without any particular risk factors to screen for fetal anomalies, intrauterine growth restriction, multiple gestation, placenta previa, and incorrect pregnancy dating.

How it is performed: High-frequency sound waves are bounced off the fetus to create a corresponding image on a computer screen. Either a transducer is rubbed across the pregnant woman's abdomen or an ultrasonic probe is inserted into her vagina (a procedure that is more commonly used early in pregnancy, when it might be difficult to detect the fetal heartbeat via the woman's abdomen). Because having a full bladder helps to push the uterus out of the pelvic cavity and into full view of the ultrasound equipment, women who are having an abdominal ultrasound performed before the twentieth week of pregnancy are sometimes asked to drink thirty-two ounces of liquid prior to the test.

How long it takes to get the results: If your doctor is performing the ultrasound, you will likely be given the results immediately. If an ultrasound technician is performing the test, you may have to wait to see your doctor before you receive the test results.

What it can tell you: An ultrasound can help to confirm your due date; check for the presence of an intrauterine device; check for multiples; monitor the growth and development of your baby; detect certain types of fetal anomalies; locate the fetus, the umbilical cord, and the placenta during amniocentesis and chorionic villus sampling; measure the amount of amniotic fluid; determine the cause of any abnormal bleeding; assess the condition of the placenta; determine the condition of the cervix; check for evidence of miscarriage, an ectopic pregnancy, a molar pregnancy, or fetal demise; determine the baby's sex; determine whether a cesarean section will be required, based on the baby's size and position, the position of the placenta, and other factors; and reassure the mother that the pregnancy is progressing normally.

Accuracy: Accurate when performed by a skilled technician using optimal equipment. Accuracy varies depending on the type of abnormality being screened for.

Risk factors: While no specific risk factors have been identified, ultrasound is still a relatively new technology. That's why the American

College of Obstetricians and Gynecologists does not recommend that it be used routinely during pregnancy.

Amniocentesis

Type of test: diagnostic

When it is performed: Amniocentesis is typically performed at fifteen weeks of pregnancy, although some doctors will perform it at twelve to fourteen weeks (in which case it is referred to as early amniocentesis).

How it is performed: A fine needle is inserted through a pregnant woman's abdomen and into the amniotic sac. A small amount (less than an ounce) of amniotic fluid is withdrawn for analysis. Ultrasound is used to pinpoint the location of the pocket of amniotic fluid and to reduce the risk of injury to the fetus and the placenta. *Note:* The procedure can be done with or without local anesthetic.

How long it takes to get the results: ten to fourteen days.

What it can tell you: Amniocentesis is used to detect chromosomal defects, neural tube defects, certain genetic and skeletal diseases, fetal infections, central-nervous-system diseases, blood diseases, and chemical problems or deficiencies. It can also be used to determine the sex of the baby (important if a couple is known to be a carrier for a sex-linked disease such as hemophilia), assess the lung maturity of the baby (important if a mother is threatening to go into premature labor or experiencing pregnancy-related complications that may necessitate an early delivery), and measure the bilirubin count of the amniotic fluid (something that can indicate whether a baby with Rh disease may need a blood transfusion prior to birth).

Accuracy: Rates vary depending on what's being tested, but generally highly accurate.

Risk factors: Approximately one in two hundred to five hundred women who have amniocentesis will miscarry or go into premature labor as a result of the procedure. Those having early amniocentesis face a greater risk of miscarriage than women who have amniocentesis during their second trimester. In rare cases, injury to the fetus, placenta, or umbilical cord may result.

Chorionic Villus Sampling

Type of test: diagnostic

When it is performed: CVS is performed at ten to twelve weeks of gestation.

How it is performed: A catheter is passed through the cervix or a needle is inserted through the abdomen to obtain a sample of chorionic villus tissue (the tissue that will eventually become the placenta).

How long it takes to get the results: Anywhere from a few days to a few weeks.

What it can tell you: CVS can tell you if your baby is affected by Down's syndrome, sickle-cell disease, thalassemia, cystic fibrosis, hemophilia, Huntington's disease, or muscular dystrophy. Unlike amniocentesis, chorionic villus sampling cannot be used to detect neural tube defects.

Accuracy: CVS is less accurate than amniocentesis, due to the possibility that the sample may become contaminated with maternal cells.

Risk factors: CVS is not as risky as early amniocentesis, but it is riskier than conventional amniocentesis. The rate of miscarriage following CVS is approximately 1 percent. Approximately 30 percent of women who go for CVS experience some type of bleeding. While there was concern a few years ago about the possibility that CVS was linked to limb reduction abnormalities in babies whose mothers underwent the procedure during pregnancy, no one has been able to prove such a relationship.

Percutaneous Umbilical Blood Sampling (PUBS)

Type of test: diagnostic

When it is performed: PUBS is performed after sixteen weeks of gestation.

How it is performed: A sample of fetal blood is taken, using an amniocentesis-style needle that is inserted through the maternal abdominal wall and into the baby's umbilical cord (near the point where the umbilical cord meets the placenta). Ultrasound is used to guide the procedure. The sample of fetal blood is analyzed for blood disorders and infections. *Note:* PUBS is a rare procedure that is generally limited to cases in which additional fetal cells are required to clarify genetic results from CVS or amniocentesis, or when fetal anemia is suspected.

How long it takes to get the results: Varies according to the type of test being performed. While you'll have the results for a test for anemia in a matter of minutes, test results requiring a culture (e.g., a test for a particular type of infection) could take much longer to obtain.

What it can tell you: PUBS can be used to detect Rh incompatibility problems, blood disorders, infections, and chromosomal problems.

Accuracy: Highly accurate.

Risk factors: Approximately 1/50 to 1/100 babies die as a result of complications resulting from the procedure.

Transabdominal Embryo Fetoscopy

Type of test: diagnostic

When it is performed: Transabdominal embryo fetoscopy is performed after ten weeks of gestation.

How it is performed: An ultrafine scope is passed through the woman's abdomen and into the uterus.

How long it takes to get the results: Visual results are immediate, but biopsies may take several days.

What it can tell you: Transabdominal embryo fetoscopy can be used to observe the fetus, placenta, and amniotic fluid, and to remove small amounts of fetal or placental tissue as well as blood samples from the umbilical cord. It is generally reserved for parents who have previously given birth to a baby with a condition that cannot be detected through any other form of prenatal testing.

Accuracy: Highly accurate, if the structures of interest are successfully visualized.

Risk factors: Transabdominal embryo fetoscopy has a miscarriage rate of 3 percent to 5 percent.

WHAT TO DO IF THE TEST BRINGS BAD NEWS

Every couple going for prenatal testing needs to consider what to do if the test brings bad news. While some parents will decide to carry their pregnancy to term, regardless of what is wrong with the baby, others will make the difficult and painful decision to terminate their pregnancy as soon as possible.

If you find yourself faced with heartbreaking news and you're trying to decide whether to carry your pregnancy to term, you need to consider the following:

- Are you prepared to raise a child who will be born with a severe disability or to give birth to a baby who will either be stillborn or die shortly after birth?
- If your child were to survive past birth, how much would the child suffer physically and emotionally? Are the baby's disabilities treatable? What are the odds of success for various types of treatments and what quality of life could your child expect to enjoy after these treatments?
- Would the baby be able to live at home with you and your partner or would the baby have to remain in a hospital?
- Is your marriage strong enough to survive the emotional and financial stress of caring for a severely disabled child?
- Are you opposed to abortion under all circumstances or just certain circumstances? Does your partner share your views on abortion?
- Would you like to cherish the remaining time you have left with your baby by carrying your pregnancy to term and then letting nature take its course, or would you find it excruciatingly painful to continue

your pregnancy, knowing that you would be giving birth to a baby with a severe disability or fatal birth defect?

• Are you concerned that your child may be subjected to painful and costly medical interventions if he survives beyond the delivery?

There are no easy answers to these questions. If you find yourself wondering after the fact if you made the right decision, you may find it comforting to consider these words of wisdom from Deborah L. Davis, Ph.D., author of *Empty Cradle, Broken Heart:* "It is important to remember that whether you had two minutes or two years [to make your decision], emotional turmoil would accompany whatever decision you made. After all, you had to make an impossible choice between 'terrible' and 'horrible.'"

Gabriela agrees that the decision to terminate a pregnancy is an awful one, but notes that she and her husband were able to make peace with their decision to terminate their first pregnancy when it was determined that their son Ethan had major birth defects that would have allowed him to live for, at most, a few hours outside the womb. "We could not see ourselves carrying the baby to term knowing that his brain was outside the skull. What should have been a belly full of life would have been the opposite. Even though we were able to reach our decision instantaneously, it was a horrible and difficult decision. Still, we have never second-guessed ourselves. Seeing our child and the extent of his problems made us understand that he would never have had the life we wanted him to have: a healthy life with running, playing, learning, and so on," she says.

Karen and her husband were also able to come to terms with their decision to terminate their pregnancy when it was revealed that their daughter would have been born with Down's syndrome. "It is hard, but my husband and I remind ourselves that we made the decision to terminate the pregnancy once we found out our baby girl had Down's because we loved her, not because we hated her," she says. "It was the worst decision anyone could ever have to make, but it was the right one for us."

✒12 *The Worry Zone*

SOME WOMEN ARE fortunate enough to be able to sail through the entire nine months of pregnancy, seemingly oblivious to all the things that can go wrong between conception and birth. Unfortunately, women who have had a baby die are no longer able to enjoy that luxury. They have learned the hard way that pregnancy doesn't always result in the birth of a living child and that babies can and do die after birth.

In this chapter, we will look at some of the most common pregnancy-related worries experienced by couples with a history of miscarriage, still-birth, and infant death. (*Note:* You'll also find a detailed discussion of the types of worries associated with a high-risk pregnancy in Chapter 13.)

FIRST TRIMESTER CONCERNS

The pregnancy test has just come back positive, but you've already started to worry. Here are a few of the concerns that may be keeping you up at night.

Will this baby die, too?

As much as you may hate to even consider the possibility that you could end up experiencing the death of another baby, it's only natural to wonder if you will be forced to say good-bye to this baby, too.

Jeannie, whose first child was stillborn, was so afraid that something might go wrong that she tried to avoid becoming attached to the new pregnancy. "Sometimes when I would worry, I would almost prepare myself for the worst. I would try to imagine how I would cope again if I lost the subsequent pregnancy. Also, I would try not to get too excited about my pregnancy. I thought to myself that if I didn't get too excited and I were to lose the baby, then somehow I would be able to cope better," she says.

Unfortunately, your fear about the possibility of experiencing another death is one worry that's not likely to be resolved until you end up with a healthy baby in your arms. You'll find it easier to get through the upcoming months if you have someone to talk to about your fears—perhaps your partner, a trusted friend, a member of a pregnancy loss support group, a counselor, or your doctor or midwife. It doesn't matter whom you talk to about your fears, as long as you find someone who will take your concerns seriously without offering false reassurances that everything will be fine.

Will my baby be healthy?

In addition to wondering if the baby will be born alive, many parents worry about the baby's health. This was certainly a major concern for Michael, whose daughter Robyn died as a result of twin-to-twin transfusion syndrome. "Throughout [each of Judy's subsequent pregnancies], there was never a moment that I was not filled with anxiety, wondering whether the baby would be okay," he recalls. "I was also filled with anxiety, wondering whether I was having these thoughts to prepare me because the baby was not okay—and I was filled with anxiety that by having these thoughts, I was somehow jinxing the pregnancy. It was a terrible mind game."

Once again, this is one of those worries that's likely to stick around until a pediatrician gives your baby a clean bill of health. In the meantime, however, you might want to talk to your caregiver about your concerns, to see if there are any tests (e.g., ultrasounds) that might help to reassure you about your baby's well-being.

Will the morning sickness I'm experiencing hurt my baby?

It's one of those thoughts that tends to catch up with you as you're dashing for the bathroom for the umpteenth time in a row: Is your baby getting the nutrients he or she needs despite all the morning sickness that you're experiencing?

If your baby was only able to draw upon the food that you consumed on a day-to-day basis, there might be cause for concern. Fortunately, your baby is able to obtain nourishment from all of the nutrients that your body stored up in anticipation of just such a "famine." This is one of the reasons why women's bodies are designed to store more fat than men's bodies. It's Mother Nature's way of ensuring that a temporary shortage of food—anything from a famine to a nasty bout of morning sickness—won't jeopardize your pregnancy.

While it's easy to conclude that there must be something wrong with your pregnancy because you're feeling so ill, actually, the opposite is true: Studies have shown that women with little or no morning sickness are two to three times as likely to miscarry as women who are experiencing a lot of morning sickness.

While the passage of time is the best cure for morning sickness, there are a few things you can do to minimize the amount of nausea you're experiencing in the meantime:

- Eat something before you get out of bed in the morning. You're more likely to feel nauseated when your stomach is empty.
- Keep crackers in your purse and in your desk at work so that you don't make the mistake of allowing yourself to get too hungry.
- Don't force yourself to eat foods that don't appeal to you right now, just because they're healthy. It's better to live on crackers alone than to find yourself running to the bathroom after forcing down a couple of forkfuls of brussels sprouts.
- Avoid foods that are likely to leave you feeling queasy—basically anything fried, greasy, high in fat, or gassy. Try to choose foods that are a little more stomach-friendly.
- Watch how much you're eating. Eating too much or too little at a single sitting will only intensify your nausea.
- Chew gum or suck on mints or hard candy. They will help to settle your stomach.
- Sniff or suck on slices of lemon. (Believe it or not, a lot of women swear by this particular morning sickness cure!)
- Avoid cigarette smoke and other strong odors.
- Avoid pants with belts and tight-fitting clothing.
- Pick up a set of antinausea wristbands at your local maternity store. They apply constant pressure to the acupuncture pressure point on

the wrists that control nausea and can help to reduce the severity of your morning sickness.

This is not to say, of course, that there's never cause for concern. In rare cases—one in every three hundred pregnancies—a pregnant woman will develop a more serious condition known as hyperemesis gravidarum (Latin for "excessive vomiting in pregnancy"), which occurs when heavy vomiting causes the body's electrolyte balance to go out of whack. The symptoms of hyperemesis gravidarum include heavy vomiting (e.g., an inability to keep any food or drink down for more than twenty-four hours); reduced frequency of urination (due to dehydration); dryness of the mouth, eyes, and skin; extreme fatigue, weakness, or faintness; and confusion. The condition is usually treated with IV fluids and antinausea medications.

Fortunately, for most women morning sickness is more of a nasty inconvenience than an out-and-out health concern.

*Does the cramping that I've been experiencing mean
that I'm experiencing a miscarriage?*

It's not unusual to experience periodlike cramping (but without any bleeding) around the time that your first missed period was due. This abdominal cramping is caused by the hormonal changes of early pregnancy. Unless the cramping is accompanied by heavy bleeding (one of the key signs of a miscarriage) or is sharp and limited to one side of your abdomen (one of the key signs of an ectopic pregnancy), there's generally no cause for concern.

*I just experienced some spotting. Am I about
to miscarry?*

Any type of bleeding from the vagina during pregnancy—light or otherwise—can be downright scary. As a rule of thumb, however, light spotting (very light bleeding that can be caused by cervical bleeding or the sloughing of uterine tissue) is generally less worrisome than heavy bleeding that is accompanied by cramping. Still, you should let your caregiver know about any bleeding you experience during pregnancy. He or she may want you to come in for a physical examination, a blood test, and/or an ultrasound to try to determine what's going on.

When to Call the Doctor or Midwife

You should call your doctor or midwife immediately if you experience one or more of the following symptoms:

- Heavy vaginal bleeding or clotting or the passage of tissue from the vagina.
- Lighter vaginal bleeding that lasts for more than one day.
- Any amount of vaginal bleeding that is accompanied by pain, fever, or chills.
- Severe abdominal or shoulder pain.
- A severe or persistent headache (especially one that is accompanied by dizziness, faintness, or visual disturbances).
- Dehydration.
- A fever of more than 101° F.
- Painful urination.
- A watery discharge from the vagina.
- Sudden swelling of the face, hands, or feet.
- Premature labor symptoms (see pages 204–205 for a list of these symptoms).
- A significant decrease in fetal movement after the twenty-fourth week of pregnancy.

Spotting can occur for a couple of different reasons during early pregnancy. It can happen about seven days after conception when the fertilized egg attaches to the uterine wall (in which case it is known as "implantation bleeding"), and it can happen if the cervix (which is especially tender, due to hormonal changes) happens to get bumped during intercourse or an internal examination.

Because vaginal bleeding can also be a sign of a possible miscarriage, you'll want to report any spotting to your doctor as soon as possible. Try not to panic until you find out exactly what's going on, since in many cases light spotting is completely harmless.

My pregnancy symptoms have disappeared. Could I
have experienced a "missed" miscarriage?

You've spent weeks rushing to the bathroom each morning, overwhelmed by waves of nausea. Or, your breasts have been so sore you can't touch them without wincing. Suddenly, the morning sickness or breast pain have disappeared. Instead of feeling overjoyed, you feel panicked: You're worried that the sudden disappearance of your symptoms may mean that you have experienced a missed miscarriage (a miscarriage in which the developing baby dies but is not expelled from the uterus immediately).

Before you hit the panic button and conclude that the absence of pregnancy symptoms means that you've miscarried, be sure to consider how far along you are in your pregnancy. It's normal, after all, for morning sickness and other symptoms of early pregnancy to disappear at the start of your second trimester.

My vaginal secretions have changed. Could I have a
vaginal infection?

While it's important to be on the lookout for bona fide vaginal infections—there is, after all, a link between bacterial vaginosis and premature labor—it's important to keep in mind that the hormonal changes of pregnancy affect a woman's vaginal secretions. It's normal to experience an increase in the amount of leukorrhea (the odorless white mucousy discharge that your body produces) during pregnancy, but you should be concerned if your vaginal discharge is greenish-yellow, foul-smelling, or watery. These types of discharges may indicate that you may have an infection that requires treatment or that your membranes may have ruptured prematurely. *Note:* It is important to report *any* increased discharge that occurs after you have had an amniocentesis.

I fell down a couple of stairs today. Will my baby be
all right?

As scary as it can be to take a tumble or find yourself experiencing a fender-bender during pregnancy, in most cases your baby is unharmed by these types of minor accidents. This is because your body is designed to protect your developing baby. Your uterus is made up of a thick, strong wall of muscle that helps to keep your baby safe, and within the uterus,

your baby floats around in amniotic fluid that helps to cushion the baby
further. At the same time, your uterus (in the first trimester) is protected
by the thickness of your pelvic bone. Imagine how hard it would be to
break an egg that is floating around inside a jar full of water simply by
shaking that jar. That should help to reassure you that your baby is well-
protected inside the fortress of your uterus.

Still, there are times when a fall can be harmful to the developing
baby. As a rule of thumb, you should notify your doctor or midwife of
any fall you experience after twenty-four weeks of pregnancy, noting any
pain or bleeding that you may be experiencing. Your caregiver may then
ask you to come in for a checkup so that the baby's heartrate can be monitored.

*Do I have a greater chance of giving birth to a baby
with a chromosomal problem because I'm older this
time around?*

While your chances of giving birth to a baby with a chromosomal
problem do increase as you age, they increase gradually rather than dramatically. The risk of giving birth to a baby with a chromosomal anomaly goes from one in 192 at age thirty-five to one in 66 at age forty, for
example. These figures look scarier than they are until you sit down and
do the math: Your risk of giving birth to a baby with a chromosomal
problem has jumped from 0.5 percent to 1.5 percent. In other words,
you've only experienced a 1 percent increase in risk over a five-year period, and you still enjoy a better than 98 percent chance of conceiving a
chromosomally normal child.

Of course, there's always the possibility that the chromosomal problem could be genetic rather than random in origin, in which case you
would face a higher-than-average chance of experiencing a recurrence.

*I find my prenatal checkups very reassuring, but I start
worrying again almost right away. Is this normal?*

It's perfectly normal to feel anxious about your baby's well-being
when you have previously experienced a miscarriage, stillbirth, or infant
death. While you may feel momentarily reassured when you get a clean
bill of health from your doctor or midwife during your prenatal checkup,
this feeling tends to wear off fairly quickly.

Many women who have experienced pregnancy loss find the first half of pregnancy to be particularly nerve-wracking. Not only is the risk of pregnancy loss highest during the first trimester (approximately one in four women will miscarry during this time period), but it's also too soon to detect fetal movement. This makes it difficult to tell on a day-to-day basis whether your baby is still alive.

Jayne, who has a long history of pregnancy and infant loss, remembers how emotionally challenging it was to get through the first trimester of pregnancy: "My biggest concern was that the baby's heart would stop beating and I wouldn't know it. I hated the fact that I couldn't tell whether the baby was okay. Every time I went to the toilet, I was so frightened that I would see blood, and every so often I would think that I was bleeding and rush to the toilet."

While it's unlikely that your anxiety level will decrease significantly until after your baby arrives safe and sound, you can expect to feel slightly less anxious once your baby's movements become more vigorous. There's nothing more reassuring, after all, than feeling your baby's movements from hour to hour and day to day.

*I'm worried about how pregnancy is affecting my
other children.*

It's only natural to want to shield any children you may have from any anxiety resulting from your subsequent pregnancy. Unfortunately, that's not always possible. If your child was old enough to remember when your other baby died, he or she may wonder if this baby will die, too.

Laura recalls how her five-year-old daughter, Elizabeth, reacted when she found out that her parents were expecting another baby: "Elizabeth expressed concern that something could go wrong. I remember her saying to our baby-sitter, 'I hope we don't have to have a funeral this time.'"

As much as you might like to offer your children some sort of a guarantee that there will be a happy ending this time around, you're simply not able to do that. Instead, you have to settle for the next best thing: letting your children know that you're doing everything possible to ensure that the new baby arrives safely, and that you're also hoping for a happy ending.

If your child has a lot of questions or concerns about your pregnancy, you might want to invite her to your next prenatal checkup. That way, she will have the opportunity to hear the baby's heartbeat on the doppler and to ask the doctor or midwife any questions about the pregnancy.

SECOND TRIMESTER WORRIES

Here are just a few of the things you may find yourself worrying about as you enter your second trimester of pregnancy:

*I've been doing a lot of reading on pregnancy and
infant loss. I'm terrified about all the things that
can go wrong.*

The only downside to doing a lot of research into the causes of miscarriage, stillbirth, and infant death is that it can make you a little paranoid. Instead of just worrying about how your previous baby died, you now have a whole raft of other things to worry about as well.

This has certainly been the case for Kathy, who joined some pregnancy loss support groups and who is now pregnant again after losing her first baby thorough miscarriage. "I think the support groups have been wonderful and I don't know how I would have gotten through this without them, but because of the people in the groups, I've learned a lot about other bad things that can happen. I am worried that there will be a knot in the cord or my baby will get an infection from group B strep, or something horrible will happen. It's likely that I would have read about these things or come up with the worries myself, but knowing people who lost babies in these ways makes it seem like more of a possibility," she says.

The best way to cope with this particular fear is to keep reminding yourself that the majority of pregnancies do result in the births of healthy babies, and that while tragedies can and do occur, they tend to be the exception rather than the rule.

*Will I be able to recognize the symptoms
of premature labor?*

It's also very common for a woman who has experienced the death of a baby to worry that her next baby will be born prematurely (between the twentieth and thirty-seventh weeks of pregnancy), even if she has never experienced premature labor during any of her previous pregnancies.

Nancy experienced these types of emotions when she conceived again after her daughter Kali was stillborn. She didn't feel that she could trust her body to tell her if there was a problem. "I worried a lot about preterm labor. I was plagued early and often with Braxton-Hicks contractions and they scared me this time around. I was so concerned I wouldn't know if something was wrong," she says. "Heck, I hadn't known something was wrong with Kali. So how would I know this time around?"

While preterm labor is fairly common—it happens in 10 percent of pregnancies—it is more common in women who have a history of preterm labor. While a woman who has never delivered a baby prematurely faces just a 5 percent risk of going into labor before term, a woman who has given birth to a premature baby in the past has a 15 percent chance of doing so again; a woman who has given birth to two premature babies in a row has a 32 percent risk of having a third premature birth.

Your best strategy for avoiding a preterm birth is to familiarize yourself with the symptoms of preterm labor. (See "The Signs of Preterm Labor" following.) If you're having a hard time distinguishing between Braxton-Hicks contractions (the so-called "practice" contractions that occur before your body actually goes into labor for real) and preterm labor contractions ("real" labor contractions that are kicking in too soon), call your doctor or midwife. Sometimes the only way to tell true and false labor apart is by having an internal examination. Don't feel foolish if you're convinced that you're experiencing preterm labor but it turns out that you're not. It's better to be safe than sorry where preterm labor is concerned.

The Signs of Preterm Labor

If you experience one or more of the following symptoms, you could be going into labor prematurely:

- *Uterine contractions* (tightening) that may or may not be painful. You should be particularly concerned if these contractions are regular, if you experience more than four contractions over the course of an hour, and if the contractions don't go away when you lie down on your side and drink a large glass of water or juice.
- *Vaginal bleeding or discharge.* Be sure to tell your caregiver if you notice a change in the quantity or quality of the discharge; if the discharge is pink- or brown-tinged, and if it is more mucousy or watery than normal.

- *Vaginal pressure or pressure in the pelvic area* that may radiate to the thighs. You may feel as if the baby is "falling out."
- *Menstrual-like cramping* in the lower abdomen that may cause continuous or intermittent discomfort.
- A *dull backache* that radiates to the side or the front of your body, and that is not relieved by any changes in position.
- *Stomach or intestinal cramping and gas pains* that may be accompanied by diarrhea, nausea, or feelings of indigestion.
- *A general feeling of unwellness.*

I'm eighteen weeks pregnant, but I haven't felt my baby move yet. Does this mean there's something wrong with my baby?

Most women feel their baby's first movements and flutters sometime between the eighteenth and twenty-second weeks of pregnancy (or between sixteen and twenty weeks after conception). These first fetal movements can easily be confused with intestinal bubbles and gas. Initially, these fetal movements feel like little flutters or twitches, rather than kicks or pushes, but over time, they become stronger.

The baby's movements also tend to be rather infrequent at first. The number of movements recorded in a twenty-four-hour period increases steadily until the seventh month of pregnancy, when crowded conditions in the womb put a damper on your baby's usual gymnastics routine.

Not all babies are highly active in the womb, however. The number of kicks that a baby makes in the womb at twenty weeks of pregnancy can vary from fifty kicks to one thousand kicks a day, with most babies kicking about 250 times a day.

You are most likely to be able to detect your baby's movements when you're resting. Some studies have shown that babies are rocked to sleep by their mothers' movements during the day, and are at their most active between 8:00 P.M. and 8:00 A.M.

Given your history, don't be surprised if you experience at least one episode in which you're totally convinced that something awful has happened to your baby. Janann remembers experiencing just such a scare: "I sat through a movie two weeks before I had him and he wasn't moving.

I pushed and prodded and got so worried that I was just about ready to ask my girlfriend to drive me to the ER when finally he moved. I couldn't even remember what had happened during the first part of the movie."

I just failed the one-hour glucose screening test. Does
this mean that I have gestational diabetes?

As the name implies, the glucose screening test is simply designed to *screen* for diabetes (in other words, to indicate whether you are at increased risk of having gestational diabetes). It is not designed to state definitively whether you've got it; in fact, there's an 85 percent chance that you don't!

The only way you can find out for sure whether you have gestational diabetes is by taking the three-hour glucose tolerance test. This involves fasting for at least eight hours before the test and then having your blood sugar measured before and then at regular intervals after you consume a beverage with an extremely high concentration of glucose.

If you are diagnosed with gestational diabetes, take heart. The majority of women are able to control this disease by following a special diet of between 2,000 and 2,400 calories per day. Only a small percentage of these women have to resort to using insulin, and the number of women who experience stillbirth or infant death as a result of gestational diabetes is very small indeed.

I feel a shooting pain in my lower abdomen each time I
roll over in bed. Should I be concerned?

The sometimes excruciating painful sensation that you're describing is round ligament pain. It's caused by the sudden stretching of the ligaments and muscles that support the expanding uterus and tends to be at its worst during the first half of the second trimester, when the uterus is large enough to exert pressure on the ligaments, but not large enough to rest some of its weight on the nearby pelvic bones. You can help to minimize this painful and sometimes scary sensation by supporting your belly and moving slowly and carefully when you are changing position. Soaking in a warm bath can also help to ease some of the resulting discomfort.

My rings feel tight on my fingers by the end of the day.
Does this mean that I'm developing preeclampsia?

Most women experience at least a small amount of swelling during their pregnancies—and for good reason. Not only do the increased quantities of progesterone in your body help you to retain fluid, but also your uterus puts pressure on the veins that carry blood back from your lower extremities, something that can encourage fluids to pool in your feet and ankles.

If you notice that you are experiencing a lot of swelling, however, you'll want to mention your concerns to your caregiver. She'll likely want to monitor your blood pressure and to check your urine for protein to make sure you're not developing preeclampsia.

Assuming that you're dealing with run-of-the-mill swelling rather than preeclampsia (a potentially life-threatening condition that is characterized by swelling and high blood pressure), your caregiver will likely encourage you to help your body to get rid of the excess fluids by

- Lying on your side or—at the very least—sitting with your feet up.
- Soaking in a warm—not hot—bath (to reduce the amount of swelling that you're experiencing).
- Upping your intake of fluids.
- Limiting (but not cutting out entirely) your salt intake.

I don't know what to say when someone asks me if this
is my first pregnancy.

This is the $10,000 question for women who have had a previous baby die. On the one hand, you don't want to feel like you're being disloyal to the baby who died by pretending that she never existed. On the other hand, it can be awkward to get into your whole reproductive history with a grocery clerk!

You will probably want to do many couples decide to do: Pick and choose whom you share your story with, telling those people who are most likely to respond with compassion and understanding, and forgetting about explaining your story to anyone else.

I can't decide whether or not to find out my baby's sex.

Some couples feel quite strongly that they want to know the baby's sex as soon as possible. In some cases, they feel like there were too many surprises during their last pregnancy, and consequently they are eager to find out as much as possible about the baby they are expecting now, including his or her sex. In other cases, they are eager to find out the baby's sex sooner rather than later, because they have their hearts set on having a baby of a particular sex, and they'd rather deal with any disappointment about having a baby of the "wrong" sex prior to, rather than after, the birth.

Some parents feel very guilty about wanting a baby of a particular sex. "After all," they tell themselves, "shouldn't we just be grateful to end up with a healthy baby, regardless of the baby's sex?"

Unfortunately, it's not quite that simple for everyone. As Deborah Davis points out in her book *Empty Cradle, Broken Heart,* some parents hope for a baby of the opposite sex, while others feel quite strongly that they want to give birth to a baby of the same sex of the baby who died. Davis notes that it is particularly common for a woman to be disappointed when her only daughter dies and she subsequently gives birth to a son: "This may have to do with the mother's 'loss of self' being less repaired when a son instead of a daughter is born. Or it may be the fear that she has forever lost her chance to have the special relationship that mothers and daughters often have."

No matter which way you decide to go with this issue—finding out now versus finding out later—it's important to let your caregiver know your preference. That way, she won't accidentally spill the beans by divulging your baby's sex during an ultrasound if you're hoping to keep your baby's sex a secret until after the birth.

My partner and I seem to be growing apart just at the time when I need his support most. Is this normal?

It's not unusual for couples to go through a difficult time following the death of a baby. Men and women often grieve quite differently and find it hard to relate to one another for a while. These problems can be intensified if they find themselves simultaneously faced with the stress of coping with a subsequent pregnancy.

It's important to keep the lines of communication open between you and your partner, particularly if you've been advised to avoid sex during pregnancy (or if you've made that decision on your own because you're simply too scared to make love). Because sexual intimacy plays an important role in the lives of most married couples, you may have to work to find other ways to relate to one another during what could very well end up being one of the most stressful times in your life. (*Note:* Don't be tempted to cheat on the "no sex" rule if your doctors told you to put on the brakes. Patricia and her partner did and immediately regretted it: "I freaked out about it and practically lived in the bathroom for days. After that incident, we didn't lay a hand on one another.")

THIRD TRIMESTER WORRIES

As you move into the final trimester of pregnancy, you may find that your worries increasingly focus on the upcoming birth:

I don't think I'm doing a very good job of bonding with this baby.

You've no doubt read about all the scary studies that show that a pregnant woman's emotional state can influence the personality of her child. One study showed that women who were anxious during their pregnancies tended to give birth to anxious babies. Another showed that women who felt no attachment to their babies before birth tended to give birth to children with emotional problems.

You may be particularly concerned about these studies if you're having a hard time allowing yourself to bond with your baby—something that many women go through when they become pregnant again. Jenn, for example, freely admits to spending more time preparing for her son Jaden's death than his birth because she was convinced that she'd never actually get to take him home. "I wrote out several obituaries," she recalls. "I looked at advertisements for grave sites. It seems awful, I know, but my pregnancy was very hard and there were so many things that went wrong. I was even told that there was doubt that my pregnancy would continue. I was afraid to bond with the baby, afraid that I would be too attached if I lost him."

What Jenn didn't realize at the time, however, was that it's almost impossible to prevent yourself from becoming attached to your baby, no matter how hard you try. "If something did go wrong, you would quickly realize just how invested you actually are in this baby," explains Davis. "Even though it is scary, allow yourself to have hopes and dreams for this baby, and dare to feel devoted. But if you absolutely find that you can't, at least rest assured that, after your baby arrives and is safely in your arms, you will have plenty of time to acquire the full depth and joy of maternal love."

Davis also stresses that no single episode can disrupt the powerful bond that typically emerges over time between mother and child: "Bonding is a process, not a single event. It happens over time."

Last night, I was talking to my new baby and I
accidentally used the name of the baby who died.

Most women with living children make this mistake on a regular basis: mixing up the names of their various children. Don't be overly hard on yourself for making the same mistake. It is not a sign that there is something wrong with you. Even though your deceased child is not living with you, he or she still dwells in your heart. It's hardly surprising, then, that his or her name naturally springs to mind.

My best friend wants to throw me a baby shower, but
I'm afraid to let her for fear of "jinxing" the pregnancy.

It's hard to get into the mood to celebrate the birth of your baby when you're still not convinced that you're actually going to be able to take a baby home this time around. If you feel that having a shower thrown for you before your baby arrives would only heighten your anxiety, ask your friend to postpone the shower until after your baby has been born, when you're more likely to be in a more celebratory mood.

The same goes for shopping for baby before his arrival. If you're too afraid of "jinxing" your pregnancy to go shopping now, remember that acquiring baby things doesn't have the power to harm your baby. How you handle this situation is entirely up to you: If purchasing a few items brings you a sense of hope, then do it; if it fills you with fear and anxiety, then postpone that shopping trip until after your baby has arrived.

I'm trying to decide whether to mention the baby who
died in the new baby's birth announcement.

A lot of couples find it very comforting to mention the baby who died in the birth announcement that welcomes the new baby. It's their way of acknowledging the fact that the baby who died is still very much a part of their lives. Other couples prefer to focus on the happy event—the arrival of their new son or daughter—rather than dwell on the baby who died. Only you can decide which approach will work best for you and your partner.

My friends are all so excited about the upcoming birth
that I'm afraid they'll forget about the baby who died.

This is a very common fear faced by couples who have lost a baby. Unfortunately, it's often quite justified. Friends and family members have a tendency to assume that your pregnancy signifies a willingness to "move on" with your life and, more often than not, they assume that means that you'll no longer spend as much time thinking about the baby who died. The best way to handle this particular problem is to tackle it head on: Let your friends and family members know that the baby who died will always be an important part of your life, no matter how many other children you end up having.

I'm petrified that this baby will die at the same point
that my previous baby died.

A lot of couples who are pregnant again find it hard to relax until they get past certain significant milestones: the point at which their previous baby died, that baby's due date, or the anniversary of their child's birth or death.

Janann found it particularly difficult to get past the twenty-nine-week mark of her subsequent pregnancy—the point at which her previous baby had been stillborn: "My son died at twenty-nine weeks, so that was a hard week. I had a nonstress test on the day that I turned twenty-nine weeks in my subsequent pregnancy. I burst into tears when they couldn't find the baby's heartbeat right away.'

There's no easy way to handle these milestones other than reminding yourself that your losses happened in a different time and involved a different baby, and that history doesn't necessarily have to repeat itself. Also, take the opportunity that these milestones present to work through more of your feelings of grief.

*I'm worried that I may not be able to handle the
emotional aspects of labor, given my history.*

Labor can be challenging enough to deal with at the best of times. It
can be all the harder to deal with if you've previously given birth to a
baby who was stillborn or who died following birth. You may be afraid
that these memories will come flooding back during labor, making it difficult for you to focus on coping with your labor contractions.

You might want to discuss this possibility with your caregiver and
come up with a game plan for proceeding if you run into difficulty during labor. You might decide, for example, that you will abandon your
plans for a medication-free birth if you find it too difficult to focus on
your grief and the pain of labor at the same time. When you actually go
into labor, you may be surprised to discover, as many women do, that
you're too busy coping with the contractions to give much thought to
your grief. Still, it's better to have prepared for this possibility than to find
yourself caught off guard in the heat of labor.

*The fetal movement counting and the nonstress tests are
driving me crazy!*

It's ironic: The nonstress tests and fetal movement counts that are
frequently ordered to reassure a pregnant woman that her pregnancy is
progressing well often have the opposite effect. Some women find that
going for nonstress tests and counting fetal movements leaves them feeling more, rather than less, anxious.

Nancy, who has given birth to two healthy boys since her daughter
was stillborn, found the nonstress tests made her extremely anxious. "I
was having nonstress tests every week and they brought on great anxiety. Whenever Cody would move and they'd lose his heartbeat, I would
freak out. Here I was having a test to calm my fears and the opposite was
happening. I suppose I couldn't shake that memory of when the nurses
couldn't find Kali's heartbeat," she says.

Kim also admits to being obsessed with keeping track of her baby's
movements. "Without a doubt, my biggest fear towards the end of my
pregnancy was that I wouldn't be paying attention to the baby's kicks,
they would be slowing down, I wouldn't catch the problem in time, and
we would lose her to another cord accident," she says. "During the whole
trimester, I found myself trying to keep track of when I felt movement so

that if anyone asked me that dreaded question—'When was the last time you felt movement?'—I'd have an answer I was sure of. It's my one big regret with Molly [Kim's stillborn daughter], that I couldn't answer that question with confidence, since I'd been confusing contractions with kicks."

Despite the fact that it is frequently recommended by doctors, the jury is still out on the benefits of fetal movement counting. Some doctors feel that it can help to alert a pregnant woman to a possible problem with her baby, while others feel that there isn't enough evidence to show an improvement in outcomes for babies whose mothers do fetal movement counting. Consider what Joyce Barrett, M.D., and Teresa Pitman have to say about fetal movement counting in their book, *Pregnancy and Birth: The Best Evidence* (Key Porter Books, 1999): "When the research studies [on fetal movement counting] were completed, they found that counting the baby's movements did not improve the outcomes. Even worse, when the mother reported that her baby was moving less frequently, she was likely to undergo further testing, be admitted to hospital, and have labor induced. Each of these procedures has complications and costs, and there were no overall benefits to the babies."

I just tested positive for group B strep. What will this mean to me and my baby during labor?

As you may recall from our discussion back in Chapter 4, group B strep is carried by between 20 percent and 40 percent of pregnant women. Approximately 2 percent of the babies of affected women will end up developing group B strep disease—a serious condition with a 6 percent mortality rate.

Once you've been identified as a group B strep carrier, you will likely be treated with antibiotics when you go into labor. In the vast majority of cases, this treatment will prevent your baby from developing this potentially fatal disease.

Note: Your caregiver may routinely prescribe antibiotics for group B strep to women who go into labor prematurely, whose membranes have been ruptured for more than eighteen hours before delivery, or who have previously had a baby infected with group B strep.

*I am going crazy with worry. Can't the doctor just
deliver my baby a few weeks early?*

As anxious as you and your caregiver both are to have your baby arrive safely, there's a lot more involved in making the decision to induce labor early than just making the appropriate arrangements over at Labor and Delivery. Your doctor will need to determine whether your baby is sufficiently mature to be delivered early, because if he's not, he could face greater risks by being delivered prematurely than by remaining in the womb a little longer.

Your doctor may decide to send you for one or more of the following types of tests to assess how your baby is doing:

- *Nonstress test:* a fetal monitor is strapped to your abdomen so that your baby's heartbeat can be monitored.
- *Contraction stress test:* a fetal monitor is strapped to your abdomen so that your baby's heartbeat can be monitored while your nipples are stimulated manually or by using a breast pump.
- *Oxytocin challenge test:* a fetal monitor is strapped to your abdomen so that your baby's heartbeat can be monitored while an IV drip of Pitocin—a synthetic form of oxytocin—is used to stimulate contractions.
- *Biophysical profile:* a detailed ultrasound used to assess your baby's well-being by taking into account such factors as breathing activity, body movements, muscle tone, and amniotic fluid volume.

Your doctor will make her decision about whether to induce you early based on what is discovered from these tests. It's highly unusual for a doctor to induce a patient before thirty-seven weeks of pregnancy unless there is a pressing medical reason to deliver the baby early (e.g., preeclampsia, placental insufficiency, and so on). Even at thirty-seven to thirty-eight weeks, in the absence of an amniocentesis to confirm otherwise, the baby's lungs may not be fully mature.

*I'm worried that this baby be will be born on the
anniversary of my baby's death.*

It is entirely possible to manage to conceive at a time that renders your due date on or near a significant anniversary. If there is a chance that your next baby could be born on or around the anniversary of your baby's death, due date, or funeral date, you may have strong feelings—positive or negative.

Michael and Judy were very concerned that their new baby might be born on the anniversary of their daughter Robyn's funeral. (Because Robyn and her twin sister, Carolyn, were born on the same day Robyn died, Michael and Judy had chosen to mark Robyn's birth and death on the day of her funeral rather on the birthday that she shared with Carolyn.) "We were very anxious that our [new] child might arrive on that day and take it away from Robyn." In the end, their fears weren't realized: Baby Gregory managed to delay his arrival until the day after the anniversary of his sister's funeral.

Sarah had similar concerns about the timing of her subsequent baby's arrival. She was initially devastated when she learned that she was going to give birth on the first anniversary of her son's stillbirth. "We had an amnio the day before his birthday to check our new baby's lung maturity. During the amnio, our daughter passed meconium. The doctor let us go home, but after reviewing the video several times she left a message on our machine saying that I needed to check into the hospital that night. That would mean that he would be born on our stillborn son's birthday," she says.

"When I was finally checked in at the hospital, I broke down, telling the nurse the situation. The nurse went to the doctor to ask if we couldn't just monitor for a day and have our daughter after our son's birthday. The doctor said that she couldn't in good conscience—especially knowing our loss—leave our new baby in utero, at risk, waiting for the birthday to pass. I understood completely, but it was a difficult thing to accept."

Up until now, we've focused on the emotional challenges faced by all couples doing through pregnancy after miscarriage, stillbirth, or infant death. Let's move on to talk about the unique challenges faced by couples who are experiencing pregnancies that are medically high risk.

✑13 *Coping with a High-Risk Pregnancy*

IT'S STRESSFUL ENOUGH trying to cope with a "low-risk" pregnancy when you've previously experienced miscarriage, stillbirth, or infant death. It can be frightening—even terrifying—to have your pregnancy classified as "high risk." It is, after all, a very scary term. What many expectant couples fail to realize, however, is that the term "high risk" is applied fairly liberally. Basically, it is used to describe any pregnancy in which a woman faces a higher-than-average risk of experiencing complications during pregnancy or birth, or of giving birth to a baby in less than perfect health. In other words, the "high risk" label merely indicates that you face a statistically greater chance of running into problems than the so-called Ms. Perfect Pregnancies of the world!

In this chapter, we will talk about the reasons why your pregnancy may be classified as high risk and what you can do to stay sane during what could well be the most stressful nine months of your life!

WHAT THE TERM "HIGH RISK" MEANS TO YOU AND YOUR BABY

Your pregnancy is likely to be classified as high risk if:

- You have a chronic medical condition that may affect your pregnancy. (see a list of such conditions on pages 33–38 and 218–224.)
- You have a history of pregnancy-related complications. (See Chapter 3 and page 225.)

- You have a history of miscarriage and/or stillbirth. (See Chapters 2 and 3 for a summary of the most common causes.)
- You have experienced the death of a liveborn infant, have given birth to a child with a genetic disorder, and/or you are a carrier for a genetic disorder.
- You are over the age of thirty-five and consequently face an increased risk of giving birth to a baby with a chromosomal anomaly.
- You are carrying more than one baby. (The rate of complications for a woman who is pregnant with twins is eight times that of a woman carrying a single baby, and the rate of stillbirth in twins is four times as high as in singletons. See pages 228–230.)
- You have a history of gynecological problems, such as pelvic inflammatory disease, endometriosis, or large, symptomatic fibroids.
- You have a sexually transmitted disease that could be transmitted to your child during pregnancy or birth.
- You conceived as a result of assisted reproductive technologies (something that may increase your odds of having a multiple birth).
- Your mother took an antimiscarriage drug called diethylstilbestrol (DES) while she was pregnant with you, something that increases your chances of experiencing a miscarriage. (See Chapter 2.)

COPING WITH THE STRESS OF A HIGH-RISK PREGNANCY

It's not easy to cope with the stress of a high-risk pregnancy at the best of times. It's all the more difficult when you've previously experienced the death of a baby. You may find yourself feeling angry and sad because you're not having the "perfect pregnancy" you had hoped for; resentful of all the pregnant women you know who seem to glide through pregnancy effortlessly; helpless because you may have to rely on other people to take care of you rather than vice versa; guilty if you believe (rightly or wrongly) that you might have done something to put your pregnancy at risk; and afraid that you'll have to live through your worst nightmare again by losing another baby.

Coping with Bed Rest

The stress of coping with a high-risk pregnancy is only compounded if you end up on bed rest—something that Jenn discovered during her

Conditions That Can Result in Complications or
Place a Pregnancy at Risk

CHRONIC CONDITIONS	EFFECTS DURING PREGNANCY
ADRENAL GLAND DISORDERS	
Cushing's syndrome (too much cortisone)	You face an increased risk of premature delivery and stillbirth.
Addison's disease (inadequate adrenal production)	You may experience life-threatening infections and other health complications during pregnancy.
AUTOIMMUNE DISORDERS	
Lupus	You face a 25 percent chance of experiencing a miscarriage or a stillbirth, a 25 percent chance of going into preterm labor, a 20 percent chance of developing preeclampsia, and a 3 percent chance of giving birth to a baby with neonatal lupus (a form of lupus that lasts for the first six months of life, and that can leave a baby with a permanent heart abnormality). If you have moderate-to-severe involvement of the central nervous system, your lungs, heart, kidneys, or other internal organs, you will likely be advised to avoid pregnancy.
Scleroderma (a progressive connective tissue disorder that can cause lung, heart, kidney, and other organ damage, and that is characterized by joint inflammation and decreased mobility)	You have a 40 percent chance of having your condition worsen during pregnancy. You are at increased risk of preterm labor and stillbirth.
Myasthenia gravis (causes the skeletal muscles to weaken and that contributes to fatigue)	You have a 40 percent chance of having your condition worsen during pregnancy. You face a 25 percent risk of giving birth to a preterm baby and a 10 percent to 20 percent chance that your baby will be born with a temporary form of the disease.

BLOOD DISORDERS

Anemia	You may experience such health problems as fatigue; weakness; shortness of breath; dizziness; tingling in the hands and feet; a lack of balance and coordination; irritability; depression; heart palpitations; a loss of color in the skin, gums, and fingernails; jaundice of the skin and eyes; and (in severe cases) heart failure.
Sickle-cell anemia	You face a 25 percent chance of experiencing a miscarriage, an 8 percent to 10 percent chance of experiencing a stillbirth, and a 15 percent chance of experiencing a neonatal death. You have a 33 percent chance of developing high blood pressure problems and toxemia. You may experience urinary tract infections, pneumonia, and lung tissue damage, and you may pass along the disease to your unborn child if your partner also happens to carry a gene for the disease. Sickle-cell crises are more likely to occur during pregnancy.
Thalassemia	You may experience severe anemia and congestive heart failure that requires transfusions during pregnancy. If you have beta-thalassemia (a less severe form of thalassemia) you may require blood transfusions during your pregnancy, and you run the risk of passing the disease along to your baby if your partner also happens to carry a gene for thalassemia.
Thrombocytopenia (a blood platelet deficiency)	You face an increased risk of requiring a cesarean section. (Babies who are born vaginally to mothers with severe forms of this condition may have decreased platelet counts and problems with hemorraging—especially around the brain.)
Von Willebrand's disease (an inherited bleeding disorder)	You may need to be treated with intravenous clotting factors to prevent severe blood loss during the delivery.

BRAIN DISORDERS

(cerebro-vascular disease)	If you have a history of strokes, hemorrhages, or blood clots, pregnancy may not be a good option for you. Women with an arteriovenous malformation, for example, have a 33 percent chance of dying during pregnancy.

CHRONIC CONDITIONS	EFFECTS DURING PREGNANCY
CANCER (malignant diseases)	You should avoid becoming pregnant until you are reasonably sure that the disease won't recur while you are pregnant. Women who have recurrences during pregnancy are often advised to terminate their pregnancies so that they can obtain the medical treatment that they need, thereby increasing their odds for long-term survival.
DIABETES Diabetes mellitus	You can reduce your risk of experiencing such problems as miscarriage, stillbirth, or fetal death, and of giving birth to a baby with heart, kidney, or spinal defects, if you get your blood sugar levels down to 70 to 140 milligrams/deciliter in the months prior to pregnancy and an average of 80 to 87 milligrams/deciliter during pregnancy. You can assess your risk of giving birth to a baby with birth defects by taking a glycosylated hemoglobin (hemoglobin A_{1c}) test when you are two to three months pregnant. If your results are in the normal range, you don't face any higher risk of giving birth to a baby with birth defects than any other pregnant woman.
GASTROINTESTINAL DISORDERS Peptic ulcers (chronic sores that protrude through the lining of the gastrointestinal tract and that can penetrate the muscle tissue of the duodenum, stomach, or esophagus)	You have a 12 percent chance of having your symptoms become more severe while you are pregnant.
Ulcerative colitis (an inflammatory disease of the colon and rectum)	If your disease is active at the time when you become pregnant, there is a small chance that emergency surgery may be required at some point during your pregnancy—a procedure that poses a risk of premature delivery and/or a cesarean section.
Crohn's disease (inflammatory bowel disease)	If it is active at the time when you conceive, you face a 50% chance of miscarrying.

HEART DISEASE

Rheumatic heart disease (an autoimmune response to an infection such as untreated strep throat that can result in damage to the heart valve)

You will require intensive monitoring throughout your pregnancy and multiple cardiac drugs during labor. Also, the rate of maternal mortality during pregnancy is high.

Serious congenital heart problem (e.g., Eisenmenger's syndrome—a rare congenital form of heart disease—and primary pulmonary hypertension)

You could be putting your life at risk by becoming pregnant. Fortunately, the majority of women with congenital heart problems have relatively minor conditions (e.g., a mitral valve prolapse) that don't pose any significant risks to themselves or their babies. (**Note:** Some caregivers will prescribe antibiotics during labor to women with mitral valve prolapse in order to prevent potential complications.)

HIGH BLOOD PRESSURE
(hypertension)

If you have severe chronic hypertension (your blood pressure is over 160/105 or your condition is complicated by either kidney or heart disease), you have a 50 percent chance of developing preeclampsia or needing a cesarean section, and a 10 percent chance of experiencing a placental abruption. You also face a higher-than-average risk of experiencing problems if you're over forty, you have had problems with your blood pressure for more than fifteen years, you have experienced blood-clot related problems, you developed severe preeclampsia early on in a previous pregnancy, or you experienced a placental abruption during a previous pregnancy

KIDNEY DISEASE
Severe kidney disease

You face a higher-than-average risk of developing pyelonephritis (an acute kidney infection that can result in permanent damage), experiencing a premature delivery, and/or having a baby with intrauterine growth restriction.

Both chronic kidney disease and high blood pressure

You have a 50 percent chance of developing severe hypertension during pregnancy.

On dialysis treatments before you became pregnant

You will require them more frequently during your pregnancy.

Kidney transplant

You will need to continue to take your anti-rejection medications. You should also plan to wait two to five years after your transplant before attempting a pregnancy.

CHRONIC CONDITIONS	EFFECTS DURING PREGNANCY
LIVER DISORDERS	
Hepatitis B	Approximately 10 percent to 20 percent of women who are carriers of the hepatitis B virus, and who don't receive any preventative treatment, transmit the virus to their babies. Women who become infected with hepatitis B in the third trimester pass it on to their babies 90 percent of the time. Following the Centers for Disease Control recommendations for the screening, vaccination, and treatment of at-risk mothers and newborns can, however, reduce the transmission rate by 85 percent to 95 percent.
Hepatitis C	Approximately 7 percent of women carrying the hepatitis C virus transmit the virus to their babies. There is no known method of preventing the virus from being transmitted from mother to baby.
LUNG DISEASE	
Asthma	Most preexisting lung diseases (e.g., tuberculosis and sarcoidosis) don't require any special monitoring during pregnancy, but asthma does. While 25 percent of asthmatic women will experience an improvement in symptoms and 50 percent will find that their condition stabilizes during pregnancy, 25 percent will experience a worsening of symptoms. What's more, 1 percent of pregnant women will develop asthma as a complication of pregnancy. If you're asthmatic and become pregnant, you will want to avoid the types of substances that tend to trigger your asthma; try your best to avoid picking up colds, flus, and respiratory infections, and possibly consider having a flu shot; continue to take your allergy shots and to use your asthma medications (with your doctor's approval); and treat asthma attacks immediately to avoid depriving your baby of oxygen.

NEUROLOGICAL DISORDERS

Epilepsy or another type of seizure disorder	You face one in thirty odds of giving birth to a baby with a seizure disorder. What's more, many of the drugs used to treat these types of problems have been linked to such problems in the developing baby as facial, skull, and limb deformities; fatal hemorrhages in newborns; unusual childhood cancers; cleft palate or lip; congenital heart disease; spina bifida; intrauterine growth restriction; and fetal death. Studies have shown that you can reduce these risks by taking your epilepsy medications as directed. Women who do so have an 85 percent to 90 percent chance of giving birth to a healthy baby.
Multiple sclerosis	You have a small chance (1 percent to 5 percent) of passing the disease on to your baby. If you have a lack of sensation in your lower body, you will need to be monitored closely during the final weeks of pregnancy in case you aren't able to detect the onset of labor. You may also require a forceps- or vacuum-assisted delivery or a cesarean, since multiple sclerosis can affect your ability to push.

PARATHYROID DISORDERS

Hyperparathyroidism (too much parathyroid)	You face an increased risk of experiencing a stillbirth or neonatal death or of giving birth to a baby with tetany (severe muscle spasms and paralysis caused by inadequate levels of calcium).
Hypoparathyroidism (too little parathyroid)	Your doctor will likely prescribe calcium and vitamin D supplements to help reduce the chances that your baby will develop a bone-weakening disorder.
PHENYLKETONURIA (PKU)	You face a higher-than-average chance of experiencing a miscarriage and you are more likely to give birth to a baby with microcephaly, heart defects, mental retardation, intrauterine growth restriction, and low birthweight. Your best bet for a happy outcome is to follow a special diet prior to and during pregnancy.

CHRONIC CONDITIONS	EFFECTS DURING PREGNANCY
PITUITARY DISORDERS	
Pituitary tumors, diabetes insipidus (a rare condition caused by a deficiency in an antidiuretic hormone manufactured by the pituitary gland), or pituitary insufficiency	You may require special monitoring or treatment during your pregnancy.
SEXUALLY TRANSMITTED DISEASES AND OTHER INFECTIONS	
Herpes	You will need to seek treatment to avoid passing this disease on to your baby. Herpes can be fatal to the developing baby.
Syphilis	You will need to seek treatment, because syphilis can lead to birth defects.
Gonorrhea or chlamydia (in the past or currently)	You are at increased risk of experiencing an ectopic pregnancy.
HIV-positive	You are at risk of passing along this condition to your baby. You can reduce the chances of passing on HIV to your baby from 20 percent to 32 percent, to 1 percent by ensuring that your baby is treated with AZT prior to birth.
Hepatitis B	You are at risk of passing along this disease to your baby. You can reduce the chances of this occurring by ensuring that your baby receives the hepatitis B vaccine and immune globulin within twelve hours of birth and then again at one month and six months of age.
Bacterial vaginosis (a vaginal infection that is sometimes associated with a thin, milky discharge and fishy odor)	You are at increased risk of experiencing preterm labor, premature rupture of membranes, and/or a preterm delivery.
THYROID DISORDERS	
Overactive thyroid (hyperthyroidism)	You are at risk of developing thyroid storm—a severe form of the disorder that is associated with an increased risk of premature delivery and low birthweight.
Underactive thyroid (hypothyroidism)	You don't face any particular risks during pregnancy as long as you take your thyroid hormone medication.

PREGNANCY-RELATED CONDITIONS AND COMPLICATIONS	EFFECTS DURING PREGNANCY
AMNIOTIC FLUID PROBLEMS	
Polyhydramnios (too much amniotic fluid)	You may be carrying a baby with Rh-incompatibility problems or diabetes, or you may be carrying more than one baby. If it is believed that your baby is at risk, some of the additional fluid may be removed through amniocentesis.
Oligohydramnios (too little amniotic fluid)	You may be carrying a baby who has missing or malfunctioning kidneys, or you may be leaking amniotic fluid due to a premature rupture of the membranes. This condition is generally treated by delivering the baby as soon as possible.
Chorioamnionitis (infection of the amniotic fluid and fetal membranes)	You will be at increased risk of having your membranes rupture prematurely or of going into premature labor. If this condition develops, you will be treated either with antibiotics or by having your labor induced early. This condition occurs in one in one hundred pregnancies, and can be difficult to diagnose, because there are no symptoms at first other than a rapid heartbeat and a fever of more than 100.4° F.
OTHER CONDITIONS	
Hyperemesis gravidarum (severe morning sickness)	You may need to be hospitalized so that intravenous drugs and fluids can be administered. This condition occurs in one in three hundred pregnancies and is more common in first-time mothers, women carrying multiples, and mothers who have experienced this condition in a previous pregnancy. It can lead to malnutrition and dehydration, which can, in turn, lead to intrauterine growth restriction and/or preterm labor.

PREGNANCY-RELATED CONDITIONS AND COMPLICATIONS	EFFECTS DURING PREGNANCY
Gestational diabetes	You are at increased risk of giving birth to a stillborn or an excessively large baby who may have difficulties adjusting its glucose and calcium levels outside the womb, and your diabetes may continue after the delivery or recur later in life. The condition is controlled through diet and (if necessary) insulin injections and can, in severe cases, require hospitalization. Women face a higher-than-average risk of developing gestational diabetes if they: have experienced gestational diabetes in a previous pregnancy; have a family history of diabetes; have previously given birth to a baby larger than nine pounds; have experienced unexplained pregnancy losses; are overweight; have high blood pressure; and have recurrent yeast infections.
Intrauterine growth restriction (IUGR) (also known as intrauterine growth retardation)	If your baby is showing signs of intrauterine growth restriction (e.g., is "small for dates" or consistently measuring below the nintieth percentile of weight for its gestational age), you may be put on bedrest and/or hospitalized, or labor may be induced. Labor is induced in cases when it is thought that the baby's outcome would be better in the nursery environment rather than in the uterus. IUGR can lead to stillbirth or the birth of a low-birthweight baby with a range of health problems, and is more likely to occur in women who: have chronic health problems; are leading an unhealthy lifestyle; have high blood pressure; are carrying multiples; are having their first or fifth (or later) pregnancy; and are carrying a fetus with chromosomal abnormalities.
Jaundice (intrahepatic chloestasis)	You may be at increased risk of experiencing either a premature delivery or a stillbirth.

PREGNANCY-RELATED CONDITIONS AND COMPLICATIONS	EFFECTS DURING PREGNANCY
PLACENTAL PROBLEMS	
Placental abruption	If you show signs that your placenta is beginning to separate from the wall of the uterus (e.g., heavy vaginal bleeding, premature labor contractions, uterine tenderness, and lower back pain), your may be treated with either bedrest and careful monitoring (if it appears that the abruption is only partial) or an emergency cesarean (if it appears that a full abruption is inevitable, something that could put both your life and the baby's life at risk). Placental abruptions occur in one in 150 pregnancies.
Placental insufficiency	Can be caused by restricted blood flow due to a clot, a partial abruption, a placenta that is too small or underdeveloped, a postdate pregnancy, or maternal diabetes. In some cases, it is better to deliver the baby prematurely than to allow it to rely on the placenta any longer.
Placenta previa	You may experience bleeding whenever you cough, strain, or have sexual intercourse. Placenta previa occurs in one in two hundred pregnancies, and is more common in women who have had several children. Bedrest, monitoring, hospitalization, and/or a cesarean delivery may be required. If a placental abruption is diagnosed early in pregnancy, the condition may correct itself before you go into labor.
Preeclampsia	You will require treatment ranging from bedrest (for mild cases) to immediately delivery (in cases where both the mother's and baby's life are at risk). The condition is characterized by swelling of the hands and feet; sudden weight gain; high blood pressure (140/90 or higher); increased protein in the urine; headaches; and nausea, vomiting, and abdominal pain during the second or third trimester of pregnancy. It is most likely to occur in first-time mothers, women who are carrying multiples, and women with chronic high blood pressure, diabetes, kidney disease, or a family history of preeclampsia. When seizures are present, this condition is known as eclampsia.

PREGNANCY-RELATED CONDITIONS AND COMPLICATIONS	EFFECTS DURING PREGNANCY
Premature labor	Some women face a higher-than-average risk of going into labor prematurely, including those who: have had abdominal surgery during their current pregnancy; who have an abnormal uterine structure; have fibroids; are experiencing a great deal of physical or emotional stress; have high blood pressure; have developed a high fever or kidney infection during pregnancy; are under sixteen or over thirty-five years of age; have mothers who took DES during their pregnancies; have been diagnosed with placenta previa or polyhydramnios; haven't gained enough weight; have previously experienced a preterm labor or delivery; have been experiencing unexplained vaginal bleeding; and smoke. If you go into premature labor, your treatment plan will depend on how important it is to stop labor from progressing (e.g., how premature your baby would be). Bed rest, intravenous fluids, and/or drugs can be used to slow or stop labor, but these methods are generally only effective if your cervix has dilated by less than three centimeters and has not yet begun to thin.

Problems That Can Occur During a Multiple Pregnancy and at the Time of Delivery

TYPE OF PROBLEM	WHAT CAN HAPPEN
Anemia	Women who are carrying twins are two-and-a-half times as likely to develop anemia as women who are carrying singletons.
Birth defects	Twice as likely to occur in multiples than in singletons; birth defects are far more common in identical twins than in fraternal twins.

Growth discordance	Occurs when one of the multiples grows more slowly or more quickly than the others, either because of crowded conditions in the uterus or because of placental problems, such as twin-to-twin transfusion syndrome. In some cases, it is better to deliver the babies prematurely than to allow them to remain in the uterus.
Intrauterine growth restriction (IUGR)	Far more common in multiple pregnancies than in singleton pregnancies; can necessitate a premature delivery. If a large number of fetuses have been conceived, some parents may consider selective reduction (selectively aborting one or more fetuses) as a way to reduce the risk to the remaining babies.
Low birthweight	Approximately half of twins weigh in at less than 5.5 lbs. when they are born, both because of crowded conditions in the uterus and the need to share nutrients with another baby. Identical twins tend to weigh less than fraternal twins.
Miscarriage	Identical twins are more likely to be miscarried than fraternal twins.
Monoamniotic twins (identical twins who share the same amniotic sac)	There is a 50 percent mortality rate with such twins, due to the high risk that the babies will be born conjoined (e.g., "Siamese twins") or that they will become tangled in one another's umbilical cords.
Neonatal death	Twins are three to five times as likely to die during the first twenty-eight days of life than singletons, largely due to prematurity. The risk of SIDS is twice as high in twins as in singletons.
Postpartum hemorrhage	The uterus has been severely stretched during pregnancy and therefore may have more difficulty contracting after the delivery. Women who give birth to multiples are more likely to experience a postpartum hemorrhage than women who deliver a single baby.
Preeclampsia	Women who are carrying more than one baby are twice as likely to develop preeclampsia as women who are carrying one baby.
Pregnancy-induced hypertension (high blood pressure)	Two-and-a-half times as likely to occur when a woman is carrying multiples as when she is carrying one baby. There is no cure for pregnancy-induced hypertension other than giving birth, so it is often necessary to deliver the babies prematurely.

TYPE OF PROBLEM	WHAT CAN HAPPEN
Presentation problems (problems with the position the babies assume at the time of birth)	Leads to a higher rate of cesarean section in multiple pregnancies than in singleton pregnancies.
Preterm birth	Women who are carrying multiples tend to deliver earlier than women who are carrying a single baby. The mean pregnancy length is thirty-seven to thirty-eight weeks for twins and thirty-four weeks for triplets.
Stillbirth	The risk increases as the number of babies increases. Twins are twice as likely and triplets are four to six times as likely to be stillborn as singletons.
Twin-to-twin transfusion syndrome (TTTS)	Occurs when there is an unequal sharing of nutrients from a shared placenta in an identical twin pregnancy. The "donor" twin (who is deprived of blood flow and nutrients) tends to be smaller and anemic, while the "recipient" twin (who gets more than his or her share of blood flow and nutrients) may experience jaundice, respiratory problems, and even heart failure due to excessive blood flow.

last pregnancy. She remembers the whirlwind of worries that ran through her head while she awaited the safe arrival of her son. "During the third trimester, I started to worry about delivering a premature baby and the problems the baby might have. I was on a terbutaline pump to stop my constant contractions as well as a home uterine monitor. I had polyhydramnios and was very big, measuring almost six weeks ahead at times because of the fluid and the fact that the baby was so big," she says.

"I was uncomfortable, stuck in bed all the time, and starting to get mentally exhausted. I worried about my three-year-old and the effect that my pregnancy was having on him. He did not understand why mommy could not come out to play. He became very angry at times. Physically, my body was in bad shape. My muscle tone was bad and I worried if I would be able to get through labor. I know that sounds crazy, but I labored for thirty-six hours with my first baby and was, to say the least, exhausted by the time he was born. I didn't even have the strength to hold him. Now I wondered how my weakened body was going to go through this labor," she says.

Bed rest do's and don'ts As hard as it may be to believe if you've never experienced it, bed rest can be physically exhausting. You feel sore and achy from spending so much time in the same position and you tire more easily than you usually do. Over time, the Achilles tendon in your legs can begin to tighten, something that may even make it painful for you to walk. You can help to counter some of these physical ailments by asking your doctor to recommend some exercises to do in bed (e.g., pelvic tilts; Kegels; gluteal sets; leg, ankle, and heel raises; knee extensions; arm raises; shoulder shrugs; and wrist and neck circles).

Note: While you're talking to your doctor, be sure to find out exactly what you can and can't do while you're on bed rest. One veteran bed-rester suggests that you set up camp in your backyard if the weather is nice, but this will work only if you've got your doctor's okay to sprawl on a chaise lounge!

Questions to Ask Your Doctor about Bed Rest

Here are some questions that you should ask your doctor if you're put on bed rest:

- How long am I likely to be on bed rest?
- What is the likelihood that I will end up being hospitalized? Under what circumstances might that happen?
- Am I allowed to lounge on the sofa or do I actually have to be lying on my side in bed?
- Am I allowed to sit up in bed or do I have to lie on my left side all the time to maximize blood flow to the baby?
- What fetal monitoring, if any, will be involved? Kick counts? An electronic fetal monitor?
- Am I allowed to get out of bed to walk to the bathroom or do I need to stay in bed and use a bedpan? Do I need to take precautions to avoid straining due to constipation?
- Am I allowed to walk up and down stairs?
- Am I allowed to have a shower or do I have to limit myself to a sponge bath?

- Am I allowed to work while I'm lying down?
- Am I allowed to lift anything? If so, what are the restrictions?
- Am I allowed to exercise? If so, what are the restrictions?
- Am I allowed to have intercourse? Am I allowed to engage in other activities that could bring me to orgasm? What about nipple stimulation?
- Am I allowed to drive a car or be a passenger in a car?

Staying sane   Here are some other tips that will help you to get through this stressful time in your life:

- *Get online.* There are plenty of online support groups for women on bed rest. You can either use one of the Internet search engines to track down mailing lists and bulletin boards devoted to bed rest or get in touch with Sidelines or Sidelines Canada to inquire about sources of online support. (*Note:* If you're not the online type, call Sidelines or Sidelines Canada anyway. They can hook you up with a telephone support buddy who will help to keep you sane until delivery day. See Appendix B for contact information for both organizations.)
- *Keep everything that you need close at hand.* You may want a phone; a telephone book; a radio; the remote control for the TV or stereo; a box of tissues; a cooler that's amply stocked with cold beverages, healthy snacks, and your lunch; a tape player and books on tape; photo albums to work on; a journal to write in; and plenty of reading material.
- *Find creative ways to pass the time.* "I used markers and a ruler and drew weekly calendars," recalls Patricia, who was on bed rest during her last pregnancy. "I wrote down little notes about the pregnancy. This really helped me to stay sane. It served as a countdown to my goal of thirty-six weeks and as a diary of the pregnancy. Plus the drawing and decorating of the calendars kept my hands busy. I used the calendars for everything: kick counts, contraction counts, and even to note the day, time, and channel of a particular TV show I wanted to watch. It was a wonderful creative outlet."
- *Don't go into hermit mode.* Invite a friend over for lunch a couple of

times a week so that you'll have something to look forward to on the days when you're feeling cut off from the rest of the world.

- Hire a doula or childbirth educator to give you and your partner private childbirth education classes. (*Note:* You'll want to make sure that the person that you hire is qualified to work with couples who are experiencing a high-risk pregnancy and who have previously experienced the death of a baby.)

- Find out if your HMO will cover the costs of a personal care attendant while you're on bed rest. If they say no initially, ask your doctor to write a letter on your behalf. Sometimes that can help to get the company in your court.

- *Keep the lines of communication open.* Try not to be overly critical if the way your partner runs the household while you're on bed rest isn't quite the way you'd like it to be run. This is a stressful time for both of you. "It was a lot of work, as I had to maintain my job plus do all the parenting and housework," recalls Rob, whose wife, Jodi, was on bed rest during their last pregnancy. "It was hard to stay focused on what we were trying to achieve through this bed rest. The idea of a healthy, term baby got lost in the chaos. There was even resentment at times."

- *If you have living children,* reassure them that life will get back to normal eventually. They may feel angry, resentful, and afraid about what's going on.

- *Be prepared for a less-than-enthusiastic response* to your bed rest announcement from your employer. While most employers eventually come around and are at least moderately supportive, some initially react in a highly negative manner. Sara found that her employer was more interested in finding out when she could come back to work than in inquiring about the health of her and her baby.

- *Keep things in perspective.* "It's important to have patience and hope," says Molly, who was put on bed rest during her last pregnancy. "Nothing is as bad as losing a baby you are carrying, so even though bed rest can be grueling, boring, and annoying, it's worth it if it makes your pregnancy last."

Up until now, we've been focusing on the concerns that you may experience as your pregnancy progresses. Now let's consider how you may be feeling about the coming birth.

🐦14 *Preparing for the Birth of Your Next Baby*

AS YOUR DUE date approaches, you will likely find yourself becoming increasingly preoccupied with thoughts of the upcoming birth. If your previous losses occurred early on in pregnancy, you may actually start to believe that you could end up with a living baby in your arms in just a few weeks' time. If, on the other hand, your previous losses occurred toward the end of pregnancy or shortly after the birth, you may still be too afraid to allow yourself to consider that happy possibility yet.

In this chapter, we will consider some of the things that you may be thinking about at this stage of pregnancy: attending prenatal classes, going for a hospital tour, writing a birth plan, hiring a doula, having labor induced, going past your due date, coping with the challenges of labor, and welcoming your new baby. We'll conclude this chapter by touching on a topic no parent wants to think about: the possibility that you could experience the death of another baby.

SHOULD YOU SIGN UP FOR PRENATAL CLASSES?

While trekking off to prenatal classes with a pillow tucked under one arm is part of the pregnancy landscape for most expectant couples, many bereaved parents choose to sit these classes out. The reason is obvious: It's hard to relate to a group of women whose biggest fears are getting stretch marks or having a cesarean section when all you're really concerned about is ending up with a healthy baby in your arms.

Jennifer, whose first pregnancy ended in stillbirth, chose not to go back to prenatal classes during her second pregnancy, because she didn't feel that these classes had much to offer her and her partner at that point in their lives: "We didn't feel like the classes would pertain to us. Those classes always talk about the standard fears of [labor and delivery]. Our worries were much different."

She was also concerned about feeling out of place. "They always have you introduce yourself and talk about how many children you have," she explains. "We didn't want to have to talk about how our precious baby girl was stillborn and then have the entire class be afraid to interact with us. We'd found in the past that people who are pregnant didn't want to interact with us in case our 'bad luck' rubbed off on them or something. We felt alone enough in our subsequent pregnancy and didn't need the constant reminder of just how isolated we really were."

On the other hand, Grace, who experienced a stillbirth and three miscarriages between the births of her first and second living children—decide to attend prenatal classes, because doing so made her feel a little more "normal" during a pregnancy that may be anything but. "I was very determined to enjoy my pregnancy," she explains.

If you decide to take group prenatal classes, you may want to speak with the instructor ahead of time to let her know about your history and to find out how comfortable she is in dealing with couples who have experienced the death of a baby. Here are some questions you might want to ask her:

- Have you had couples in your classes who have experienced the death of a baby?
- Do you routinely discuss miscarriage, stillbirth, and infant death in your classes? How comfortable would you be if we were to share details of our history with other members of the class when you touch on these topics?
- How many couples will be in the class? How many of these couples will be first-time parents? Have any of the other couples experienced the death of a baby?

Don't rule out the possibility of having private prenatal classes instead of attending group classes, if that makes you feel more comfortable. It's not difficult to arrange for a childbirth educator to offer private childbirth preparation classes in your own home.

Laure decided to go this route because she knew that she would have a hard time participating in standard prenatal classes, due to her history, but yet felt strongly that she wanted to take some sort of prenatal classes before the birth of her baby. "I took Bradley classes this time around and took them privately because I knew I could not be with a bunch of 'normal' pregnant moms," she recalls. "I didn't want to listen to them talk about how perfect things were going to be. I had lived through four nightmares and knew what could go wrong. Taking the classes privately allowed me to address my fears."

Note: Many organizations that provide support to grieving parents are beginning to offer "subsequent pregnancy" classes to couples who decide to try again. Be sure to find out if these types of classes are offered in your community.

SHOULD YOU GO ON A HOSPITAL TOUR?

Another issue you'll have to think about at this stage of pregnancy is whether you'd like to go on a hospital tour. If your baby died at the hospital where you will be giving birth this time around, you might want to take a tour ahead of time so that you can work through some of your emotions prior to the onset of labor.

Nancy and her husband decided to pay just such a return visit to the birthing center where their daughter had been stillborn. Nancy explains: "I had contacted the nursing staff there and asked if we could come to visit the birth center and spend time there so we could prepare to deal with the many emotions we knew we'd encounter there when Cody was born. Many of the nurses remembered us and were extremely supportive. One nurse escorted us and even though I'd requested to be in different rooms this time around, she let us spend time in the room where I delivered and the one I recovered in when Kali died. All the nurses made sure we knew that they would do everything in their power to help us have a wonderful birth experience this time around."

Cindy, whose first child was stillborn, also got in touch with the hospital to make arrangements for her subsequent delivery. She wanted to deliver her next baby in the same room where her previous baby had been stillborn. She found that the staff were extremely caring and supportive. "They understood why I needed to be in the same room and went out of their way to do everything that they could to meet all of my emotional and physical needs."

As helpful as it can be for some couples, returning to the hospital ahead of time isn't necessarily the best option for everyone. Janann chose not to take a hospital tour because she felt that it would be too painful to return to the hospital where her baby had been stillborn and her mother had died. She decided instead to deal with her emotions at the time of the delivery.

If you do decide to visit the hospital or birthing center ahead of time, you should call ahead to set up an appointment. That way, you can be sure that a staff member will be available to answer any questions or address any concerns that you might have about your upcoming delivery. You might also consider bringing along your partner or a friend who can offer some emotional support to you when you return to the place where your baby died. It could bring back a lot of powerful memories for you.

WRITING A BIRTH PLAN

Something else you should be thinking about at this stage of pregnancy is whether you'd like to write a birth plan.

While any couple can benefit from writing a birth plan, couples who have experienced the death of a baby often find them to be particularly useful. After all, your birth plan is able to speak for you at a time when you may be too physically or emotionally caught up in the birth to tell the labor and delivery staff or birthing staff much about your history or to make your opinions and wishes known.

Here are some of the types of issues that you might wish to address in the birth plan that you write in preparation for your baby's arrival:

- Your goals and expectations for the birth.
- Where you intend to give birth (if you have strong feelings about giving birth in a particular room in the birthing unit, this is the perfect place to make your wishes known).
- The most relevant details about your history (e.g., the fact that your previous baby died at this particular hospital two years ago).

- Whom you've invited to attend your baby's birth (e.g., your partner, your children, a family member, a friend, a doula, and/or another labor support person) and what each person's role will be.
- The type of atmosphere you are hoping to create (e.g., a quiet, darkened room).
- Whether you are likely to react strongly to any standard tests or procedures that may invoke memories of the death of your other baby (e.g., are you likely to panic if the nurse has difficulty picking up your baby's heartbeat right away?).
- Where you intend to do the bulk of your laboring (at home, in the hospital's Jacuzzi, while walking around the ward).
- How you feel about such labor procedures as episiotomies, inductions, fetal monitoring, and internal examinations.
- What your preferences are with regard to pain relief during labor (see the following table for a summary of the key types of medicinal and nonmedicinal pain relief available during labor).
- Whether you are willing to have medical students or residents participate in your baby's birth.
- What birthing equipment you intend to use (e.g., a birthing stool, a squatting bar, or a birthing tub).
- Whether you would like to have the newborn examination performed in your presence (if at all possible) in order to avoid being separated from your baby.
- How long you intend to remain in the hospital after the birth of your baby.
- How you would like the hospital staff to support you and your partner if your next baby dies.

Pain Relief Options During Labor

The following are the major types of medicinal and non-medicinal pain relief options available to laboring women

NON-MEDICINAL PAIN RELIEF OPTIONS

| Acupuncture | Needles are inserted in your limbs or ears to help to block the corresponding pain impulses |

Self-hypnosis	Techniques can be used to promote relaxation during labor.
Laboring in water	Helps to counteract the effects of gravity, something that can help to make labor less painful. It also helps to relax you.
Relaxation breathing and positive visualization	Can help to relax you during labor.
Transcutaneous electronic nerve stimulation (TENS)	Stimulates the nerves in your lower back in order to block the transmission of pain impulses to the brain.
Other techniques	The use of music, massage, position change, heat or cold application, counter-pressure, reassuring touch from a caring person, and adequate hydration.

MEDICINAL PAIN RELIEF OPTIONS

Caudal block	Anesthetic is injected into the spinal area around the sacrum (a bony structure at the lowest part of the spine), numbing the perineum (the area of skin and underlying fat and muscle tissue that lies between the vaginal opening and the anus). A caudal block is a good choice when short-term relief is needed (e.g., for a forceps delivery or vacuum extraction), but less popular today than it used to be. Can inhibit labor.
Epidural	An anesthetic and/or narcotic is injected into the space between the covering of the spinal cord and the bony vertebrae of your spine, numbing you from the waist down. Provides full relief in 85 percent of women, partial relief in 12 percent of women, and no relief in 3 percent of women. The continuous low-dose epidural allows women to remain mobile during labor. Side effects include low blood pressure, difficulty in urinating, and severe postpartum headaches. Not considered to be a good option for women with certain neurological disorders or whose labor hasn't progressed beyond the 3 to 4 cm point at the time the epidural is administered. Can diminish the ability to push, necessitating a forceps delivery.
Inhalable analgesics (e.g., nitrous oxide)	Numbs the pain center in the brain. You administer the gas to yourself as you need it. Unfortunately, nitrous oxide isn't widely available and can cause drowsiness and nausea. Some studies have shown that women using nitrous oxide can aspirate (inhale the contents of their stomachs).

NON-MEDICINAL PAIN RELIEF OPTIONS

Injectible narcotics such as Demerol, and other narcotics and narcoticlike medications, such as Nubain and Stadol	Provides pain relief within fifteen minutes. Pain relief lasts for up to two hours. Unfortunately, the doses given to pregnant women often fail to provide adequate pain relief and may cause such undesirable side effects as drowsiness, nausea, vomiting, respiratory depression, and low blood pressure, and can result in breathing difficulties in the newborn if injected within a few hours of the delivery.
Local anesthetic	Injected into the tissues of the perineum so that an episiotomy can be performed or sutures can be placed after the delivery. Some studies have indicated that injections of local anesthetic can weaken the perineal tissue and increase the likelihood of tearing in the event that an episiotomy is not performed.
Paracervical block	Local anesthetic is inserted into the tissues around the cervix. The pain relief lasts only forty-five to sixty minutes, and the paracervical block can slow the baby's heartbeat.
Pudendal block	Local anesthetic is injected into the nerves of the vaginal area and perineum. A pudendal block is sometimes used when an episiotomy is being performed. Unfortunately, it doesn't reduce uterine pain and can't be used if baby's head is too far down the birth canal.
Spinal	A spinal is injected into the spinal fluid in the lower back, numbing you from the waist down within about four minutes. It is usually used for cesarean deliveries. It is not recommended for women with severe preeclampsia. Can cause low blood pressure, severe postdelivery headache, temporary bladder dysfunction, nausea, and (rarely) convulsions or infections.

When they wrote their birth plan, Miriam and her partner spelled out their expectations for the birth of their subsequent baby in great detail. They specified what type of emotional support Miriam would be looking for during the delivery: "As the labor progresses, Miriam would appreciate it if you would keep her informed of her progress and whether the baby is coping okay or becoming distressed. We don't mind Jasmine's [their stillborn baby] name being mentioned. . . . In fact, it would be appreciated if the staff ask us how we are coping and give us the opportunity to express our feelings about this baby's birth and also about Jasmine's birth and death."

Dawnette, whose first pregnancy ended in miscarriage, also chose to write a detailed birth plan. She included a section on how she wanted the situation to be handled in the event that her baby was stillborn or died shortly after birth. "I had no reason to believe that my baby wouldn't live after birth, but somehow feared this outcome anyway," she recalls. "I had a section in my birth plan just in case of my baby's death that specified that I wanted to hold and see my baby."

While the majority of couples who have experienced the death of a baby go on to give birth in hospitals and birthing centers, some couples feel more comfortable giving birth at home. If you decide to go this route, you can also benefit from writing a birth plan. Not only will it help to make your midwife aware of your hopes and plans for the birth, but it will also help to reassure you and your partner that you've made all the necessary preparations to welcome your next baby at home.

HIRING A DOULA

Think you and your partner will need a lot of support to get through the stress of your upcoming delivery? Why not consider hiring a doula (a professional labor-support worker)?

Studies have shown that women who use the services of doulas during labor are less likely to require cesareans, to require pain relief during labor, or to need a forceps delivery. They also tend to be more satisfied with their birth experiences than women who labor without this additional support.

While doulas were virtually unheard of just ten years ago, they're quickly gaining in popularity. In 1998, they attended 40,000 births in the United States. Their fees range from $300 to $600 for a delivery, and an increasing number of health insurance companies are agreeing to pick up the tab for their services.

While doulas aren't qualified to perform clinical tasks, such as checking your blood pressure or doing an internal exam, they can help to coach you and your partner through the process of giving birth. Typically, they will meet with you and your partner ahead of time to talk about your plans for the birth, provide continuous support during labor, and then provide you with plenty of hands-on help during the first hours or days of the postpartum period.

If you're interested in finding out more about using the services of a doula, you should contact Doulas of North America. You can find the organization's contact information listed in Appendix B.

IS EARLY INDUCTION A GOOD IDEA?

Obstetricians frequently disagree about whether it's a good idea to deliver a baby as soon as it's safe to do so, simply because the mother has had one or more babies die in the past.

Those who are in favor of early induction in this situation argue that it helps to reduce the anxiety of the pregnant woman—and often the obstetrician as well! Those who are opposed to early induction argue that it's best to leave the timing of the labor up to Mother Nature rather than arbitrarily intervening without just cause.

Your doctor will likely recommend that your labor be induced before your due date if:

- The fetus doesn't appear to be doing particularly well in the uterus and would likely be better off if it were to be delivered early.
- A stress test or nonstress test has indicated that the placenta is no longer functioning properly, and that it would be best for the baby to be born as soon as possible.
- Your membranes ruptured more than twenty-four hours ago, but labor has not yet started.
- You have developed preeclampsia or another serious medical condition, and an early delivery is necessary both for the sake of your own health as well as that of your baby.
- You have a history of rapid labor that puts you at risk of having an unplanned home birth.
- You live a considerable distance from a hospital and may not be able to make it to the hospital in time to deliver your baby once labor begins.

Note: A growing body of evidence suggests that it may be advisable to induce labor at forty-one weeks rather than forty-two weeks. Research combining eleven studies on the timing of induction indicated that the perinatal death rate drops from 2.5 per 1,000 births to 0.3 per 1,000 births when labor is induced at forty-one weeks, as opposed to being allowed to begin spontaneously.

Desirae, who experienced one infant death and three miscarriages prior to giving birth to her first healthy baby, was relieved that her doctor gave her the option of being induced early during that pregnancy. "Mentally I was about to go crazy and my doctor completely understood. He scheduled the induction with no problem. In fact, he had given me the option of induction back at the beginning of my pregnancy," she says.

Janann's doctor also agreed to induce her early. "My doctor induced me two weeks early," she recalls. "He had told me at our prepregnancy meeting that he would. He said that would be two less weeks that I would have to worry. At the time, I thought he was being overprotective. But after I was pregnant, I understood what he meant and I was so grateful.

"I thought it would get easier the farther I got in my pregnancy, but it was harder. Also, the nights were the worst. I would be scared and it was harder to make my fears go away in the middle of the night," she says.

Here are some questions to consider concerning induction.

Is your body ready for labor?

Inducing labor is a much more complicated process than many women realize. In order for an induction to proceed as smoothly as possible, your body has to be ready to go into labor. More often than not, those horror stories you hear about labor inductions involve women whose bodies weren't quite ready to go into labor, and who consequently required more than one attempt to get their labor started on its own.

Your doctor may use the Bishop Scoring System to assess your body's readiness for labor (following is an explanation of the system). As you can see, five factors are scored between 0 and 3. If your Bishop score is 8 or higher, you are considered a good candidate for an induction.

Bishop Scoring System

SCORE	0	1	2	3
Cervical dilation (how much the cervix has opened up)	Cervix is closed	Cervix is 1 to 2 cm dilated	Cervix is 3 to 4 cm dilated	Cervix is more than 5 cm dilated
Effacement (how much the cervix has thinned out)	Cervix is 0 percent to 30 percent effaced	Cervix is 40 percent to 50 percent effaced	Cervix is 60 percent to 70 percent effaced	Cervix is more than 80 percent effaced
Station (an estimate of the baby's descent into the birth canal)	- 3	- 2	-1, 0	+1, +2
Consistency of the cervix	Firm	Medium	Soft	
Position of the cervix	Posterior (pointing backward)	Midposition	Anterior (pointing forward)	

Of course, there are situations in which it may not be appropriate to induce labor at all:

- If the placenta is blocking the cervix (placenta previa).
- If the baby is in a presentation that would make a vaginal delivery inadvisable or impossible (e.g., transverse or breech).
- If the baby is believed to be too big to make its way through the mother's pelvis (cephalo-pelvic disproportion).
- If the mother has an active genital herpes infection.
- If the mother is carrying multiples (induction may be appropriate in selected cases).
- If there is evidence of fetal distress requiring emergency delivery.
- If the uterus is abnormally large and therefore at risk of a uterine rupture.
- You have had five or more previous births.

- You have a vertical uterine scar (not skin scar) from a previous cesarean delivery.

Is your baby ready for labor?

Your doctor doesn't just need to be concerned about your body's readiness for labor. He also needs to determine whether your baby is ready for life outside the womb. In addition to looking through your prenatal records to confirm that your due date is, in fact, accurate, your doctor may want to assess the maturity of your baby's lungs through amniocentesis. The risks of accidentally delivering a baby before he or she is ready are too great for your doctor to make this important decision without weighing all the appropriate factors.

What can you expect during an induction?

Despite what you may have heard, induced labors aren't always difficult. In fact, studies have shown that women who opt for inductions are no more likely to use epidurals than women who go into labor on their own.

If you opt for an induction, your doctor will likely use one or more of the following five methods of inducing labor:

Artificial rupture of membranes (amniotomy): If you opt to have your membranes ruptured, a piece of obstetrical equipment that resembles a crochet hook is inserted through your cervix and used to tear a small hole in the amniotic sac. The procedure is virtually painless if your cervix has already begun to dilate, but can be quite painful if you are dilated by less than one centimeter. If the amniotomy fails, you'll have to have your labor induced using another method. There's no turning back once your membranes have been ruptured.

Prostaglandin E suppositories or gel: Prostaglandin E suppositories or gel are used to help ripen the cervix. In 50 percent of cases, the suppository or gel will cause a woman to go into labor spontaneously and to deliver her baby within twenty-four hours.

Misoprostol tablets: Misoprostol tablets are inserted high into the vagina to help ripen the cervix and initiate labor. The drug has not yet been officially sanctioned for this use by the FDA, but many caregivers find it a safer, more effective, and easier-to-use alternative to Prostaglandin E.

Pitocin: Pitocin is simply the synthetic form of oxytocin, the naturally produced hormone that is responsible for causing your uterus to contract during labor. Pitocin is injected via an intravenous drip, and the strength of your contractions will be monitored. If your cervix is not yet ripe, it can take a couple of attempts to get labor started.

Cervical dilators: Cervical dilators are used to manually dilate the cervix. Sticks of compressed and dried seaweed or synthetic materials are placed in your cervix. As these sticks begin to absorb moisture and to expand, they force your cervix to dilate.

While some caregivers may suggest that you stimulate your nipples in an attempt to get labor started, this can actually be quite dangerous. It's impossible to control the amount of oxytocin that is released by your body as your nipples are stimulated, something that can, in rare cases, lead to excessively strong uterine contractions that could impair fetal/placental blood flow and lead to fetal distress.

HOW TO STAY SANE IF YOUR BABY IS OVERDUE

Forty weeks is more than long enough to be pregnant at the best of times. It can seem like an eternity if you're spent most of those weeks fretting and worrying about whether you're going to end up with a healthy baby in your arms! Is it any wonder, then, that many women become extremely anxious and depressed if their due date comes and goes and there's still no sign of labor?

There are, of course, many good reasons for concern if a pregnancy drags on and on. Most caregivers agree that it's best to induce labor when a mother starts the forty-second week of pregnancy (approximately a week after her due date has passed). Here's why:

- By this point in pregnancy, the placenta may have started to deteriorate. This complex organ is designed to work for about forty weeks from the time of conception but, in some cases, it can begin to deteriorate sooner rather than later.

- Your baby will continue to grow after your due date, something that puts you at increased risk of experiencing complications with your delivery if the baby's size is excessive.
- The amount of amniotic fluid may begin to drop, something that increases the likelihood of an umbilical cord compression problem and can indicate placental insufficiency or ruptured membranes.
- Your baby could inhale meconium. The longer a baby remains in the uterus, the greater the likelihood that he will pass his first bowel movement (meconium) before birth. Because inhaled meconium can lead to breathing problems in the newborn, it's best to avoid going too far overdue.

It can be easy to lose your marbles if you find yourself in the unenviable position of going overdue with your subsequent baby. Here are some tips that will help you to hold on to what's left of your sanity:

- Stay in regular contact with your caregiver. He or she may want to send you for a nonstress test, a contraction stress test, or a biophysical profile to ensure that your baby is continuing to thrive inside the uterus; he or she will also want to keep tabs on how you're feeling about being overdue.
- Keep yourself busy so that you'll have less time to fixate on the date on the calendar. Don't worry about having to cancel your plans at the last minute: Going into labor is the best excuse you'll ever have for standing someone up!
- Let the answering machine pick up all those annoying "Haven't you had that baby yet?" calls. They're the last thing that you need to deal with at this stage of the game. If you're not already feeling frustrated about being overdue, you will be by the time your twenty-fifth friend or relative has called to check in.
- Accept the fact that your caregiver can't look into a crystal ball to magically pinpoint the day and hour of your delivery.
- Remind yourself that you won't be pregnant forever—even if it feels that way. Only 10 percent of babies have yet to be born by the time their mothers reach the forty-second week of pregnancy, and most of these remaining babies are delivered very soon after that time.

WHAT LABOR MAY BE LIKE

Just when you think you're never going to go into labor, you'll begin to experience some of those tell-tale signs your baby's about to arrive. (See "The Signs of Labor" following.)

By this stage of the game, you're more than ready to meet your baby, but you may find yourself being hit with some last-minute stage fright. You may worry that you're not up to coping with the physical and emotional demands of labor, or you may feel reluctant to let your baby leave the safe environment of the womb. Obviously, the nature of your history will affect how you feel about this last point: If your baby died prior to birth, you may not feel that your body is able to offer a particularly safe haven, whereas if your baby died after birth, you may feel that the womb offers a far safer environment than the outside world.

The Signs of Labor

You can expect to experience one or more of the following signs of impending or actual labor during the days or weeks leading up to your baby's birth.

SIGN	WHAT TO EXPECT
Lightening ("dropping")	Your baby descends into the pelvis, resulting in an increased need to urinate but decreased pressure in the upper abdomen. This can happen weeks before you go into labor or right as labor is beginning. Despite what some pregnancy books will tell you, you can't predict which pattern will hold true for you simply based on whether this is your first or subsequent labor.
Increased pressure in your pelvis and rectum	You may experience cramping, groin pain, and persistent lower backache. You're likely to notice these symptoms more if this is your second or subsequent baby.
Slight weight loss or reduced weight gain	Your weight gain tends to decrease near term.
A change in your energy level	You may feel totally exhausted or highly energetic at this stage of pregnancy.

Passage of mucus plug	Your mucus plug—the thick sticky mucus that seals off the cervix during pregnancy, thereby protecting your baby from infection—begins to dislodge as your cervix begins to dilate and efface (thin out).
Pink or bloody show	As the cervix begins to thin out and open up, capillaries can rupture, causing a small amount of bleeding. This generally indicates that labor will begin shortly.
Increasingly painful Braxton-Hicks contractions	The so-called "practice contractions" that you've felt during the last half of your pregnancy become stronger. In some cases, they become as painful as "real" labor contractions.

Note: You should call your caregiver immediately if you:

- Experience a lot of bleeding (something that can indicate placenta previa or a placental abruption).
- Notice thick, green fluid coming from your vagina (an indication that your baby has passed meconium into the amniotic fluid and may be in distress).
- Can see or feel a loop of umbilical cord protruding into your vagina (an indicating that the umbilical cord may have prolapsed, disrupting the flow of oxygen to your baby). If you suspect that you have experienced a cord prolapse, lie with your head and chest on the floor and your bottom in the air. This will help to prevent the weight of your baby from blocking the flow of oxygen through the cord.

Is It "the Real Thing"?

Don't be surprised if you end up with a few "false starts" before your actual labor starts up. Most women experience a bout or two of false labor before the real thing kicks in. While there's nothing false about the way these false labor contractions feel—they can be every bit as painful as true labor contractions—they're categorized as false because they don't help to dilate the cervix, nor to they result in the birth of a baby.

As a rule of thumb, you should suspect that you're dealing with false labor if your contractions are irregular and are not increasing either in frequency (the length of time between the start of one contraction and the next) or severity; the contractions stop when you change position or have two large glasses of water; the pain from the contractions can be felt in your lower abdomen rather than your lower back; and the show (blood-tinged mucus) that you pass is brownish rather than reddish, and therefore is consequently more likely to have been caused by an internal examination or sexual intercourse rather than the bursting of cervical capillaries due to the onset of labor.

On the other hand, you should suspect that you're dealing with true labor if your contractions seem to be falling into a regular pattern, are getting longer, stronger, and more frequent, intensify with activity, and don't subside when you change position or drink two large glasses of water; the pain from the contractions starts in your lower back and then spreads to your abdomen and possibly your legs, too; you feel cramping like what you'd experience if you had a gastrointestinal upset, and it's accompanied by diarrhea; you've passed some pinkish or blood-streaked show; and your membranes have ruptured.

The Three Stages of Labor

Once you've determined that you are, in fact, experiencing true labor, you can expect your labor to progress through three basic stages: the first ends when the cervix is fully dilated; the second ends with the birth of the baby; and the third stage ends once the placenta has been delivered. These three stages of labor typically last for seven hours in a mother who has previously given birth, and twelve to fourteen hours in a mother who is giving birth for the first time. See a full detailing of the three stages of labor on pages 251–253.

WHAT TO EXPECT DURING A CESAREAN DELIVERY

Of course, not all babies are delivered vaginally. Approximately 15 percent to 20 percent of U.S. babies are delivered by cesarean section. While the media sometimes like to get carried away talking about the evils of cesareans, what gets lost in the all the rhetoric is the fact that cesareans play an important role in preventing a large number of infant deaths and birth-related injuries each year.

The Three Stages of Labor

WHAT HAPPENS DURING THIS STAGE	HOW YOU MAY BE FEELING PHYSICALLY	HOW YOU MAY BE FEELING EMOTIONALLY	WHAT TO DO DURING THIS STAGE
	FIRST STAGE (FROM THE ONSET OF LABOR UNTIL THE CERVIX IS FULLY DILATED)		
Early or latent labor (when your cervix dilates from 0 to 3 cm)	Backache, menstrual-like cramping, indigestion, diarrhea, a feeling of warmth in the abdomen, bloody show (the passage of blood-tinged mucus), and a trickling or gushing sensation if your membranes have ruptured	Excitement, relief, anticipation, uncertainty, anxiety, fear	Eat lightly, continue with your normal activities as long as possible, ask your partner or labor-support person to help you to time contractions and to pack any last-minute items before you leave for the hospital or birthing center (unless, of course, you're having a home birth)
Active labor (when your cervix dilates from 4 to 7 cm)	Increased discomfort from contractions (it's more difficult to talk or walk through a contraction), pain and aching in your legs and back, fatigue, increased quantities of bloody show	Anxiety, discouragement, highly focused on getting through this stage of labor	Remain upright and active as long as possible, experiment with positions until you find one that works best for you when a contraction hits (e.g., "slow dancing" with partner, squatting, supported squat, on hands and knees, leaning on a chair or table, and so on), rest in between contractions, empty your bladder regularly (at least once an hour), allow your partner or labor-support person to help you with labor breathing and/or relaxation techniques, continue to consume light fluids (with your caregiver's approval)

WHAT HAPPENS DURING THIS STAGE	HOW YOU MAY BE FEELING PHYSICALLY	HOW YOU MAY BE FEELING EMOTIONALLY	WHAT TO DO DURING THIS STAGE
Transition (when your cervix dilates from 8 to 10 cm	Increased quantities of show, pressure in your lower back, perineal and rectal pressure, hot and cold flashes, shaky legs, intense aching in your thighs, nausea or vomiting, belching, heavy perspiration	Irritable, disoriented, restless, frustrated	Change positions frequently to see if that will provide any pain relief, apply a hot water bottle or cold pack to your back to see if that helps with the pain, have your partner or labor-support person apply counter-pressure on the part of your back that is hurting by using either the palm of his hand or a tennis ball or a rolling pin, or have him/her apply strong finger pressure below the center of the ball of your foot.

SECOND STAGE (PUSHING)

Now that your cervix is fully dilated, your body is ready for the pushing stage.	You'll experience a series of sixty- to ninety-second contractions at two- to five-minute intervals. You may not feel the urge to push right away, because your baby's head needs to stretch the vaginal and pelvic-floor muscles before this reflex is triggered. You can expect to experience increased rectal pressure, an increase in bloody show, an urge to grunt as you bear down, a burning or stretching sensation	Excited and energetic or tired, discouraged, and overwhelmed, depending on how your labor is going	Have your partner or labor-support person help you to move into a squatting or semisquatting position to make it easier for you to push your baby out, push when you feel the urge, take short breaths rather than holding your breath and pushing through an entire contraction, be prepared to stop pushing (pant or blow instead) if your caregiver tells you that your perineum needs time to stretch gradually in order to avoid an episiotomy or a tear.

as your baby's head
crowns in the vagina,
and a slippery feeling
as your baby is born.

THIRD STAGE (DELIVERY OF THE PLACENTA)

Your uterus expells the placenta.	Mild contractions lasting for one minute or less will gently push the placenta out of your body. Your caregiver will examine the placenta to make sure that it's complete, since retained placental fragments can cause hemorrhaging. You will experience heavy bleeding from the vagina and you may pass some large blood clots when you go to the bathroom. (Be sure to tell your caregiver if they're any larger than a lemon.)	Distracted, happy, excited to finally be meeting your baby, exhausted from the delivery, cold, hungry.	Your caregiver may give you a shot of oxytocin or methylergonovine to try to prevent any problems with postpartum hemorrhaging.

Of course, as we noted in our other book, *The Unofficial Guide to Having a Baby,* the 25 percent or higher cesarean rate at some institutions isn't exactly anything to cheer about: Cesareans continue to be four times riskier than vaginal deliveries, posing such potential complications as infection, blood loss, problems related to the anesthesia, blood clots caused by reduced mobility after surgery, and bladder and bowel injuries.

One piece of misinformation about cesarean sections causes pregnant women a lot of unnecessary worry, so we'd like to set the record straight right now: There's no evidence that babies born by cesarean section receive any less "squeezing" than babies who are born vaginally (a process that is said to help to clear amniotic fluid from the lungs and stimulate the baby's circulation). As any obstetrician can tell you, a fair bit of squeezing occurs as a baby is delivered through the incision in your uterus. Hopefully, that will help to ease your anxiety level a little if you're scheduled for a cesarean section.

One other controversial issue needs to be tackled before we leave our discussion of cesarean deliveries: the pros and cons of attempting a vaginal birth after cesarean (VBAC).

Studies have shown that the success rate for such procedures (in other words, the number of women who end up being able to deliver their babies vaginally rather than requiring another cesarean section) is 50 percent to 80 percent. While there are a number of advantages to attempting a VBAC—vaginal deliveries are generally less risky than cesareans, take less time to recover from, and allow you to pay a more active role in your baby's birth—a VBAC also poses some risks. There's always the risk, however slight, that the uterine scar tissue from your previous incision may split, a potentially life-threatening complication for both you and your baby. Since there's a higher risk of experiencing this problem if you had a vertical uterine incision rather than a horizontal uterine incision, you'll need to check with your doctor to find out which type of incision was made in your uterus. (*Note:* It won't necessarily match the direction of the incision that was made in your skin.)

You'll also want to talk to your caregiver about whether you're a good candidate for a VBAC—in other words, someone who is carrying one baby, whose baby is neither breech nor transverse, who isn't likely to run into problems with the baby's head fitting through her pelvis, who will be delivering in a setting where an anesthetist is on call and a cesarean can be performed on short notice, and who is giving birth to a baby who isn't showing any signs of distress.

Don't feel like you need to attempt a VBAC in order to have the "ultimate" birthing experience. Delivering your baby through a cesarean section can be every bit as meaningful as delivering your baby vaginally. After all, all that matters at the end of the day is that you get what you want most of all: a healthy baby.

Here's what you can expect during a cesarean delivery.

Before the delivery   You may be given medication to dry the secretions in your mouth and upper airway and an antacid to reduce the acidity of your stomach contents (important in case you end up inhaling some of the contents of your stomach). Your lower abdomen will be washed and possibly shaved as well. A catheter will be inserted into your bladder so that it can be emptied to minimize the chance of injury. An intravenous needle will be inserted into your hand or arm so that you can be given medications and fluids during the delivery. You will be given an anesthetic (an epidural or a spinal or—in certain circumstances—a general anesthetic). Your abdomen will be swabbed with antiseptic solution and covered with a sterile drape. A screen will be put in place to keep the surgical field sterile, thereby blocking your view of the delivery.

During the delivery   An incision will be made through both the wall of your abdomen and the wall of your uterus once the anesthetic has taken effect. (You may be able to feel some pressure, but not any pain.) The amniotic sac will be opened up and amniotic fluid will pour out. Your baby will be lifted from your body. You may feel a slight tugging sensation if you've had an epidural, but you probably won't feel anything other than the doctor's hands on your upper abdomen if you've had a spinal. The umbilical cord will be clamped and cut and the placenta will be removed.

After the delivery   Your baby's nose and mouth will be suctioned and a doctor or nurse will assess the baby by performing the APGAR test, which involves assessing the baby's appearance, pulse (heartbeat), grimace (response to stimulation), activity (movements), and respiration (breathing). The test is performed twice, at one minute and five minutes after birth. The baby is given up to two points for each attribute. A baby with a score of seven or over is doing well; a baby with a score of five or six may require resuscitation; and a baby with a score of four or less may be in serious trouble.

Your uterus and abdomen will be stitched up and you may be given the opportunity to hold your baby in the delivery room, provided that both you and your baby are feeling up to it. You will then be taken to the recovery room so that your vital signs can be monitored and you can be watched for excessive bleeding and other complications. You may be given antibiotics and/or pain medications at this time.

Next, you will be moved on to the postpartum floor. Six to eight hours after the delivery, your catheter will be removed and you will be encouraged to get out of bed. You will be given intravenous fluids for one to two days, until you're able to start eating again. You will be able to leave the hospital after three to five days.

HOW YOU MAY FEEL ABOUT BEING IN LABOR AGAIN

Regardless of what type of delivery you attempt, you're likely to experience some powerful emotions while you are in labor. In addition to coping with the usual emotional challenges of labor—anxiety, frustration, exhaustion, and so on—you'll also likely be dealing with your fears about having another baby die and your grief about the baby who died.

Renee, who experienced two miscarriages and who had one twin die at term, found her subsequent labor to be extremely challenging. "I was an emotional mess and constantly worried if he was okay or not. I made the nurse turn the volume on the monitor way up so that I could hear his heartbeat loud and clear, and I watched it constantly. Being in the same hospital where I had lost my previous baby, I kept having images of the time before and I was so afraid that we would lose this baby, too. I think that my emotional state made it more difficult for me to cope with the pain," she says.

Nancy experienced similar challenges when she labored with her subsequent baby. "I constantly worried about Cody during labor, especially after a scare when his heart rate dropped when they first tried to induce me. The sound of his heartbeat on the monitor almost drove me insane. I would go berserk if he moved and the monitor wasn't picking it up," she recalls.

Nancy had to make a conscious effort to focus on the delivery rather than allow herself to think back to her stillbirth eleven months earlier—something she felt terribly guilty about doing: "I was trying to force myself to 'forget' what had happened with Kali. And blocking it out was like trying to put her in the back of my mind, which I can never do. But on the other hand, I wanted to be lost in the wonder and joy of giving birth to a living child, so I had to stop thinking of her. It was torment."

Monique experienced similar feelings of anxiety as the time for her son's cesarean delivery approached. She found herself becoming so panicked that he would die during the delivery, just as her daughter had two years earlier, that she decided to be put under a general anesthetic for the delivery. When she woke up, she was greeted with the news that she was the mother of a healthy baby boy.

Like Monique, Sarah felt that it was important to trust her gut instincts in deciding what would—and wouldn't—work for her during her subsequent birth. She felt quite strongly that she couldn't go through labor in the same room in which her second child had been stillborn, but, unfortunately, that was the only room available when she showed up at the hospital. Fortunately, the nursing staff took her concerns to heart once she filled them in about her situation. "The nurse explained that I would have to wait in the lobby while they moved someone out of another room so I wouldn't have to be in the room I had delivered in before. I was willing to wait and was touched that they were taking my request seriously," she says.

Jayne found that the worst time for her was the time that she spent waiting for the start of her cesarean section: "This was our sixth pregnancy and I had lost babies at different stages in the past, so I never really relaxed throughout the pregnancy. It was horrible. I wanted to be excited, but I couldn't be. The morning of the delivery was the worst, though. I really felt like I was on death row!"

Of course, not all women who have had a baby die find their subsequent deliveries to be especially difficult. Julie found that because all of her miscarriages had occurred during early pregnancy and she had previously given birth to healthy babies, she felt confident that her current delivery would result in a similarly happy outcome.

Amber felt similarly ready to tackle the challenges of labor because of all the groundwork she had laid during her pregnancy. In addition to talking to a counselor about her fears ahead of time so that the emotions of labor wouldn't hit her quite so hard, she decided to hire a professional labor-support person, or doula ("doula" is a Greek word meaning "woman's helper"), to help her and her partner to get through the delivery. "She helped me stay focused on the work of labor. That helped me so much."

Regardless of how you feel about the delivery, it's important to keep in mind that your partner will also be dealing with a wide range of emotions. Michael describes the truckload of different emotions that he found himself hit by as his wife, Judy, was giving birth: "So much anticipation, anxiety, love, fear, and pain welled up in me that I burst into tears when the baby arrived—with both of our subsequent pregnancies. It took me a long time to summon the emotional energy just to take a picture of the baby. I just wanted to hold the baby and Judy. It occurred to me just after Gregory was born that I had witnessed a miracle."

Here are some suggestions that may make it easier for you and your partner to deal with the emotional challenges of labor:

- Create a nurturing, comforting birthing environment for yourself and your partner. Even if you're giving birth in a high-tech environment, complete with fetal monitors, resuscitation equipment, and so on, you can make the atmosphere feel more homelike by turning the lights down or off and playing music that you find particularly calming.
- Put technology to work for you. If you think that it would be reassuring for you to hear your baby's heartbeat throughout labor, ask the hospital or birthing center staff to provide you with a fetal monitor and to turn the volume up so that you can hear it. If, on the other hand, the heartbeat accelerations and decelerations that occur during contractions are going to drive you crazy with worry, you might ask that they use the fetal monitor only if it's medically necessary, and that they turn the volume down so that it's less upsetting to you.
- Don't be afraid to ask for the reassurance you need. If you're concerned about your baby's well-being, ask the doctor or nurse to check the baby's heartbeat again. This is no time to worry about being a bother to the nursing staff. You've earned the right to be treated like a queen!

WELCOMING YOUR SUBSEQUENT BABY

Suddenly, after months of anticipation, it's all over. Your baby is finally here. You may feel euphoric and filled with joy—or you may feel exhausted and just plain numb.

Nancy remembers feeling on top of the world when her subsequent baby was born. "I was crying, but they were tears of joy! And the relief, oh, the relief, of having him in my arms, hearing him cry, seeing him kick his little legs around. I felt as if a huge burden had been lifted as he sounded his birth cry. It was that immediate for me. I was in heaven. He was here to stay. I was finally sure of it."

Janann found that she reacted with total disbelief when her baby arrived safely. "When his head came out, I wouldn't look at him. They kept saying, 'Can you see him?' I was waiting for what seemed like forever to hear him cry. I just couldn't look. I finally asked if he was breathing and just then he cried. Then I just sat there and watched him cry. I really couldn't believe that he was all right," she says.

Kim remembers feeling panic-struck during those first few seconds after the birth. "My first fear was that she wouldn't cry. The silence when Molly [her stillborn baby] was born was one of those 'What's wrong with the universe?' moments. On Meg's birth announcement, we led off with the words, 'The most amazing sound our ears can hear is the sound of a newborn baby.' Once she cried, our concerns shifted to 'Is everything okay?'"

Renee remembers experiencing a variety of different emotions as she processed the fact that her baby was here safe and sound. "Right after the birth, I think I first felt relief that he was alive and appeared to be healthy. Then I felt such tremendous joy," she says. "It was the first time I'd really experienced any happiness or true joy in two years, and it was wonderful to feel that again. But at the same time, I felt sadness that I had lost James (the twin who had died at term) nearly two years before and had missed out on so much with him. I didn't get to do all the natural things you get to do with your baby right after birth, like bathe and breast-feed him."

Lisa found that the birth of her subsequent baby also served to remind her of what she had missed when her first child died as a result of a placental abruption. "Nothing could have prepared me for the birth of my subsequent baby," she insists. "I was raw with emotions after he was born. I was so happy that he was alive and well, yet so deeply saddened by my previous loss because now I knew exactly what I had missed with my first son. I remember holding my new son, awed by his very presence. The fierce love I felt for him only served to make me feel guilty about his dead brother. How could I be so happy at the birth of this child when his brother was dead? In some ways, I felt as if I were betraying my first son by loving my second son. Having a living child did not erase any of the pain of my loss. In reality, it increased that pain. This new baby was in no way a replacement for his dead brother, whom I was still grieving. It was the hardest time emotionally in my entire life."

Christi felt similarly torn as she welcomed her new baby daughter. "I was ecstatic because I was holding a live, breathing baby who was completely healthy. I was just in awe of her and so in love. I was sad, too, however, because I was reminded of my firstborn and how much I loved her and how wonderful it was to hold her the first time. I missed her incredibly and it was very difficult to be happy. I had a lot of mixed emotions," she says.

Jayne found it hard to believe that the nightmare was actually over and became hysterical when her son had to be taken to the special care nursery after the delivery. "They then brought his crib into my room for a few minutes to reassure me. I had had a C-section with a spinal, so I couldn't go to him."

Jenn found herself in for a similar scare when her son Jaden was born prematurely. "They took him to NICU right after he was born. I didn't even get a chance to hold him. John went with him and I couldn't move, because I had a reaction to the epidural and had been given a Benadryl injection. I was pretty much numb from the waist down so I had to wait," she recalls. "All I could think of was Jaden dying and me not even getting to hold him first. When I finally got to see him, he was on a ventilator. It was so hard to watch a machine breathing for him. It was like all the sad stories I had heard. I was never given any steroid injections to mature his lungs so he didn't have that extra help he needed to breathe on his own. I felt totally helpless."

FEELINGS ABOUT LOSING ANOTHER BABY

While Jayne and Jenn were soon able to take their babies home, not all of the parents we interviewed for this book enjoyed such a happy outcome to their pregnancies. Some of them went on to experience the death of another baby.

Lisa remembers feeling filled with rage when her second baby died. Her first baby died shortly after birth as a result of complications arising from fetal hydrops; her fourth baby was stillborn at term for unknown reasons.

"After we lost our second son, Connor, one day after his due date, I was angry—angrier than after we lost Tyler. I just couldn't believe that I had lost another child. Connor's loss devastated both of us. We had no warning: He was perfect one day and then gone the next. I just couldn't believe we had to do it all again," she says.

"Coming home and seeing everything ready for my son was too much to bear. I destroyed the room. After we put everything away and cleaned up some broken glass, we shut the door and locked it. It was hard enough that my heart and my life felt empty at times: I just couldn't bear having an empty room to look at."

Laure also found the death of her second baby much more difficult to cope with than her first: "It was the most devastating thing I had ever experienced. My self-esteem was at an all-time low and I wondered what was wrong with me. Everyone else got pregnant and had their babies. What was so wrong with me?"

Jennifer found that her optimism took a beating after she experienced her second loss: "After my first loss, I kept telling myself I could still go on and have a baby and have everything be 'normal.' After the second, that idea seemed much farther away."

Mary found herself feeling increasingly isolated over time. "With each loss, the feelings of grief were more intense, the depression lasted longer, and my family became less understanding and supportive. When I lost my first baby, we came home from the hospital to a lot of flowers, phone calls, and cards. The cards kept coming for weeks," she remembers. "By the time I lost Nicholas—my fifth loss—no one even sent a card. No one knew what to say or do to help. Since my family—my mom in particular—didn't want us to try again, there was a big fat 'I told you so' hanging in the air."

Deb, on the other hand, found that the loss of her second baby was far less difficult for her to cope with than her first had been. "I think the emotions were less raw the second time around. It was like going through a familiar dark tunnel. I didn't like it in the horrible dark tunnel, but it wasn't as scary because I had been there before," she says.

Tammy had a similar experience: "I was much more analytical and less emotional the second time around. I had a much better understanding of my grief and what was okay in grief. I describe my first loss as one hundred percent pain: We learned nothing from Adam's birth and death. But Andrew's birth and death was, in my mind, so much more powerful: His loss gave us the knowledge that the problem was an incompetent cervix. He gave us the hope of a future successful pregnancy. He made Claire [her next baby, who lived] possible."

You may feel convinced that you won't be able to survive the death of another baby. Don't underestimate your own strength and resilience. You can take what you've learned about grieving, coping, and remembering, and use those skills to survive this tragedy. You can survive. You're not alone. And you will probably find the courage to try again.

$\mathscr{A}15$ *Life After Baby*

THE POSTPARTUM PERIOD can be an emotional minefield for parents who have just given birth to their subsequent baby, coming on the heels of nine months of worry and anxiety. Not only do you have to deal with the massive number of physical changes that your body undergoes as it begins to return to its prepregnant state, but you also have to get used to the idea that the baby you've been dreaming about holding for the past nine months is actually here in your arms.

In this final chapter, we will look at the unique challenges that couples with a history of miscarriage, stillbirth, and infant death face during the first few weeks following the arrival of their subsequent baby.

WHAT TO EXPECT AFTER THE BIRTH

It's a lesson that most parents end up learning through the School of Hard Knocks: Life with a new baby isn't quite as blissful and perfect as what the baby powder commercials would have you believe. As wonderful as it is to hold a precious newborn baby in your arms, caring for a newborn baby can be just plain exhausting. Add to that the fact you may have a tender episiotomy site or cesarean incision, hemorrhoids the size of golf balls, and breasts that seem to have taken on a life of their own, and you can see why many parents describe the weeks after the birth of their subsequent baby as the best of times and the worst of times all wrapped into one!

If you're already feeling a bit emotionally fragile—a completely understandable state of affairs for anyone who has just lived through a subsequent pregnancy—you may find yourself experiencing a variety of conflicting emotions as you attempt to adjust to life after baby. Here are just a few of the emotions that you can expect to experience during this challenging period in your life.

Inadequacy

After months of waiting to meet your new baby, he or she is finally here. You may be shocked to discover how woefully unprepared you may feel for the challenges of parenting. Jennifer—whose first pregnancy ended in stillbirth, but who subsequently gave birth to a healthy baby girl—remembers feeling totally unprepared for what lay ahead after her baby daughter arrived: "I remember thinking, 'I actually have a baby to take home. What do I know about babies? I know everything about being pregnant, but I'm not at all prepared for being a mommy with a baby at home.'"

Marilyn experienced similar emotions after the birth of her first living child. Her fears were compounded when her daughter was born seven weeks prematurely and had to spend the first few weeks of her life being cared for in the NICU. "I became so accustomed to her being well taken care of in the hospital by people who knew exactly what they were doing that, when it came time to bring her home, I was petrified!" she recalls. "She weighed barely five pounds and looked premature. Her skin still had that translucent quality, she was scrawny, her ears were mere cartilage—my husband called them 'bat ears'—and her face often made weird, involuntary, jerky movements. I felt unable to care for a normal baby, let alone one who needed to be force-fed every two hours and kept bundled up even in the ninety-degree heat wave we were having."

Unreality

You might have a hard time believing that the worst of your nightmare is now behind you—that you can actually relax and enjoy your new baby.

Lisa has vivid memories of a nightmare she experienced after the birth of her second child. (Her first child died as a result of a placental abruption.) "The first night he was born, I had terrible nightmares that a nurse would come in to my room and say, 'I'm sorry, but there's been a mistake. Your baby is dead.' It was such a realistic dream and scared me so much that I insisted that the baby be brought to me immediately," she says.

Anxiety

You've already mastered the art of worrying. After all, you've just completed a nine-month-long apprenticeship! Chances are, you'll find plenty of opportunities to put this newly developed skill to good use during the postpartum period.

Sara, whose first child died shortly after birth, found that she began to worry about her subsequent baby the moment he arrived. In fact, she was so afraid that something would happen to him that she stayed awake for the first four days after his birth. "I was terrified that I would miss out on his short life, and I didn't want to miss one moment. It was just awful—I was so stressed and tired and in pain. It was months before I felt any kind of confidence that he would still be alive when I woke up," she says.

Like Sara, Jennifer, whose first child was stillborn, has found plenty to worry about since her subsequent baby arrived a few months ago. "I was scared of everything at first," she recalls. "Scared that he would choke to death, scared that he would stop breathing and I wouldn't be able to save him, scared that he wasn't eating enough and was going to die from starvation right before my eyes. I was so busy being scared that I don't think I got to enjoy his first few weeks.

"I am very scared of SIDS now and don't sleep at night hardly at all. I am up every thirty minutes or so checking on him to be sure that he is still breathing. If I happen to sleep for several hours, I always dread going into his room because I am scared he will be dead. This sounds ridiculous to me, even as I say it, but it really is how I feel. I guess maybe it is normal but I wish I could learn to put it behind me. I want to be able to enjoy this baby, but it is so hard when I am so scared of losing him," she admits.

Pandora found that she tended to play—and replay—one particular nightmare in her mind: having her new baby die in her arms, just as her previous baby had. "I had one peculiar reaction," she recalls. "I could not hold the baby on my left shoulder, only on my right shoulder. My baby Rhiannon had died on my left shoulder and if I put my newborn there, I started feeling uneasy and shaking. Oddly, it was my new baby herself who overcame this fear for me. One day when she was six months old, she rolled to my left side and nestled the back of her head in my left shoulder and snuggled against me. I started to feel the tears falling, but I finally felt safe to hold her there."

Torn Feelings

As if it weren't challenging enough to have to deal with all your worries about something happening to your new baby, you may also find yourself being flooded with memories of the baby who died, or worried about not bonding enough with your new baby.

Nancy felt like she had to apologize to her newborn son for not being joyful enough after his birth and to her stillborn daughter for not visiting her gravesite as regularly because she was so busy with the new baby: "I felt as if I was being pulled in different directions and my heart couldn't choose."

Sarah remembers feeling similarly torn when her subsequent baby was born: "I grieved our son and also felt guilty for not being able to feel happy, appreciate, and enjoy our beautiful daughter. It was a horrible feeling to feel like I was not giving our wonderful newly arrived baby the welcome she deserved."

While you may be worried that your preoccupation with your other baby is stopping you from bonding with your new child, it's important to remind yourself that your reactions are perfectly normal and likely temporary. It takes time for your heart to make room for another baby, but as any mother with more than one child can tell you, you *will* find a place in your heart for your new baby over time. Remember, bonding doesn't happen in an instant: It happens over time.

Christi—whose first baby died shortly after birth, but who subsequently went on to give birth to another healthy baby—offers these words of wisdom to parents who are afraid that they will never love the new baby as much as the one they lost: "Know that you will love that subsequent baby just as much as you loved the one you lost—and don't feel guilty for that. Also, if you don't feel that bond right away with the subsequent baby, don't worry: It will happen. Finally, remember this: Your subsequent baby is the closest you will ever get to watching the baby you lost grow up. Treasure that always."

Grief

It's not unusual for your feelings of grief for the baby who died to intensify after your new baby arrives. While most parents find that this period of "regrieving" eventually ends, it can be extremely painful while it lasts.

Laura found that the most difficult period for her was when the new baby moved out of the newborn stage. Because her other baby had lived for only eight days, Laura never had the opportunity to see that baby pass through the same milestones her subsequent baby passed: "I found that as Ian hit milestones, my grief about Sarah would increase. I found it particularly difficult when Ian stopped looking like a newborn baby. I couldn't look at his face and pretend I was looking at Sarah anymore."

Christi—whose daughter died shortly after birth, but who subsequently gave birth to another healthy baby—feels that parents who have experienced the death of a baby need to realize that their grief will never entirely leave them, not even after the new baby arrives. "I want the world to know that when you have a subsequent baby, it doesn't take the memories of your lost child away," she insists. "You don't stop thinking about the baby, dreaming of him or her, and wondering what that child would be like, etc. Your subsequent baby is a constant reminder of what you lost and that is difficult to deal with. I wish people would realize this and know that even though it has been three years since the birth/death of my firstborn, I still cry, I still get angry, I still miss her, love her incredibly, and wish she was here. I will always feel this way and nothing will change that. No matter how many children I have, I will always be missing and loving my Alyssa Raine and reminiscing about those four short days I had to spend with her—the most beautiful four days of my life."

Not all women experience an intensification of their grief for the baby who died after the new baby arrives. This was certainly Janann's experience. "I actually was surprised that I wasn't terribly upset and sad for the baby I had lost after I gave birth to my next child. I thought that it would bring back memories and make me sad that Dawson hadn't lived," she says. "But actually I only had joy for the new blessing in my life. It was so wonderful to experience the wonder of life and to see this beautiful baby that my heart was only filled with joy. It was really a surprise to me. I had thought there would be tears for Dawson, and had prepared myself for those feelings. Then they never came."

Longing for Another Baby

Some parents find that their grief for the baby who died is expressed through a longing for another baby—a feeling that they may find difficult to understand when they're already cradling a newborn baby in their arms.

Kendra was surprised to discover how strongly she wanted to be pregnant again, even after her subsequent baby arrived. "I find that while logically it wouldn't make sense for me to put my body through another pregnancy and that I don't really feel that I have the resources to parent more than two living children, I am left longing for another baby. I'm sure that no matter how many more children I have, I will forever have this longing," she says. "When I think about it, I know that what I want is the baby I lost, but there's a strong desire to go through pregnancy again and have another newborn to hold."

Sarah, who gave birth to a healthy baby after losing her second child through stillbirth, found herself experiencing similar emotions: "I felt like I wanted to go ahead and have another baby, and then I came to the realization that I would always feel one baby short."

Joy

Up until now, we have focused on the more negative emotions that can arise during the postpartum period. Now it's time to focus on the emotion that most parents also report experiencing when they finally get the chance to meet their new babies: joy.

Cindy remembers feeling flooded with happiness when she gave birth to a healthy baby after her first child was stillborn. "Once she was here, my world seemed to be okay. I had worried and scared myself for nine long months and was ready to stop doing that. She was actually in my arms—safe and sound and truly perfect—and that's all I was concerned about," she says.

Janann had a similar reaction: "Now that Bronson is here, I am no longer consumed with grief about Dawson's death. I am still sad from time to time, but life is so much easier to deal with now. Bronson does not replace Dawson in any way. He is not the cure for my grief, but he is like a really strong painkiller for what is hurting me. My pain is still there. It will never go away. It was lessening with time, and now Bronson has lessened that pain so much more."

SURVIVING THE POSTPARTUM PERIOD

Wondering how you're going to get through the postpartum period without completely losing your marbles? Here are some tips from women who've weathered the postpartum storms and lived to tell.

Cut yourself some slack. Realize that you've got a lot of emotions to work through and that this could very well be one of the most challenging times in your life. Don't worry about washing the dishes or scrubbing the pots and pans. Let someone else do that for you or else eat off paper plates for a while! Your top priorities at this stage are your baby and yourself.

Accept the fact that you may feel anxious and overprotective. "Given what you've been through, it is normal—not abnormal—to feel overprotective," explains Deborah Davis, author of *Empty Cradle, Broken Heart.* "As time goes on and your baby becomes less dependent and vulnerable, you'll be able to relax more. What's more, you'll learn to live with the fact that you can't have total control over what happens to your new baby. In the meantime, you can find a balance between keeping your baby safe and close to you and also encouraging your baby to grow and explore and not be afraid of the world. Find the balance that works for you and your baby. The key is to learn how to distinguish between fears that arise from your imagination and fears that arise from what's actually happening around you or to your baby. Let go of the former and heed the latter."

Don't be overly hard on yourself for being a less-than-perfect parent. It can be quite draining to try to get by on four hours sleep or to pace the floor with a fussy baby. Instead of allowing yourself to run on empty, learn how to take care of your own needs as well. Allowing other people to step in and give you a break from the demands of caring for a new baby will allow you to recharge your batteries so that you'll be better able to nurture and care for your new baby.

Stay connected. Keep in touch with other parents you know who have been through the birth of a subsequent baby. It can be reassuring to be able to compare notes about how you're feeling and to ask any questions you may have about newborn care.

Get out of the house. Nothing can add to your stress level more than being housebound with a new baby—particularly if your baby happens to be fussy. Whether you decide to take your baby for a brisk walk outdoors or a leisurely stroll through the mall, it's important to do whatever it takes to avoid cabin fever.

Don't worry about spoiling your baby. This is a common fear of many parents who have recently welcomed their subsequent baby. Ignore any well-meaning (or not-so-well-meaning!) relatives who warn you against the evils of nurturing your baby. It simply isn't possible to spoil a newborn. Responding quickly to your baby's cries simply teaches him to trust the world around him, something that will ultimately lead to a much happier baby.

Discover your baby's likes and dislikes. If your baby tends to be fussy at a particular time of day, try to figure out what works best to soothe him. Since no two babies are exactly alike, plan on engaging in some heavy-duty detective work until you solve the mystery of your baby's likes and dislikes.

Accept any and all offers of help. This is no time in your life to go into martyr mode. If friends and family members offer to help, take them up on the offer. Keep a running list of jobs that need to be done so that you'll always have a task or errand to delegate to a willing body. **Hint:** Put them to work taking care of domestic chores, such as cooking and cleaning, so that you'll have more time to relax and enjoy your new baby.

Don't force yourself to dress your new baby in clothing that belonged to the baby who died. Some parents like the idea of their other baby being able to "hand down" clothing to the new baby, much as any two siblings would do; others prefer to pack that clothing away along with other mementos of their baby who died.

Forgive yourself if you don't have time to go to the cemetery as often as you used to. The fact that you're insanely busy taking care of a new baby doesn't mean that you're being disloyal toward or forgetting about your baby who died.

Allow yourself to love your new baby. Remind yourself that you have an infinite supply of love to give. It's not as if you are given a certain "quota" of love that you are then forced to divide between the baby who died and your new baby.

No what-ifs. Don't be surprised if you find yourself dwelling on the fact that you might not have had this baby if your other baby had survived. "Playing 'what if' is a natural facet to your grief," Davis explains. "Eventually, as you mull over the possibilities, cry about it, and work through it, you will be able to let go of what might have been and turn to face what is."

Get help if you are dealing with anything more serious than a mild case of "baby blues." Postpartum depression is far more common—and far more debilitating—than most people realize. One new mother found that she needed to go on antidepressants in order to make it through this difficult period. "Between worrying about the new baby, grieving for my stillborn son, and starting back to work when my baby was eight weeks old, the stress and anxiety were too much. I finally had to go on antidepressants for a short while. It really helped," she says.

PARENTING YOUR NEXT BABY

Parents who have experienced both the heartache of losing a baby and the joy of welcoming another baby into their lives often consider their new baby to be one of the greatest gifts they have ever been given: a reason to be joyful again.

Some parents also report that the tragedies that they have faced have strengthened them, allowing them to be better parents—and better people—than they might otherwise have been.

"I am sure that both my husband and I are better parents to our wonderful son because of what we have been through," says Suzy, who experienced two miscarriages and two pregnancy terminations as well as the birth of one living child. "We treasure him. Surprisingly to some, the losses have reenergized us each time. We enjoy every day. Our attitude to life has been positively affected. We are very aware of the good things in our lives: our marriage, our son, our friends, our careers, and so on."

Michael feels that the fact that he and Judy managed to live through the nightmare of losing a child has given the two of them greater confidence in their ability to cope with whatever other challenges parenthood throws their way. "We have lived through the worst possible outcome of parenting. We are confident that we can survive almost anything else," he says.

Tammie—who experienced the deaths of two babies before subsequently gaving birth to a healthy baby—feels the tragedies she experienced have made her appreciate what a gift it truly is to be blessed with a living child. "I know that I am the kind of mother to Claire that I am only because I lost Adam and Andrew. I have an appreciation for motherhood that I'm sure those who have not lost cannot possibly have," she says.

There's no guarantee that the road that lies ahead will be easy for you and your child. The road that leads from infancy to adulthood is notoriously full of potholes, after all. But because you have experienced the death of a child, you already know the importance of treasuring those magic moments that occur between parent and child—a lesson that far too many people learn too late, if at all.

We wish you a lifetime of magic moments between you and your subsequent baby.

Epilogue

A DIFFERENT CHILD

A different child,
People notice
There's a special glow around you.
You grow
Surrounded by love,
Never doubting you are wanted;
Only look at the pride and joy
In your mother and father's eyes.

And if sometimes
Between the smiles
There's a trace of tears,
One day
You'll understand.
You'll understand
There was once another child
A different child
Who was in their hopes and dreams.
That child will never outgrow the baby clothes
That child will never keep them up at night

In fact, that child will never be any trouble at all.
Except sometimes, in a silent moment,
When mother and father miss so much
That different child.
May hope and love wrap you warmly
And may you learn the lesson forever
How infinitely precious
How infinitely fragile
Is this life on earth.
One day, as a young man or woman
You may see another mother's tears
Another father's silent grief
Then you, and you alone
Will understand
And offer the greatest comfort.
When all hope seems lost,
You will tell them
With great compassion,
"I know how you feel.
I'm only here
Because my mother tried again."

For Madoka Marietta Rosalie, from your mother, Pandora Diane Waldron, March 4, 1999.

Remembering, with love, and not with sadness, our Special Angel, Rhiannon Roxane, who left this world two years ago today.

Appendix A: Number of Infant Deaths and Infant Mortality Rates for 1997

	Number	Rate per 100,000 live births
All causes	28,045	722.6
Certain intestinal infections	200	5.2
Whooping cough	6	—
Meningococcal infection	46	1.2
Septicemia	196	5.1
Vital diseases	111	2.9
Congenital syphilis	4	—
Remainder of infections and parasitic diseases	158	4.1
Malignant neoplasms	91	2.3
Benign neoplasms	63	1.6
Diseases of thymus gland	3	—
Cystic fibrosis	10	—
Diseases of blood and blood-forming organs	81	2.1
Meningitis	97	2.5
Other diseases of nervous system and sense organs	334	8.6
Acute upper respiratory infections	12	—
Bronchitis and bronchiolitis	106	2.7
Pneumonia and influenza	421	10.8
Pneumonia	409	10.5

	Number	Rate per 100,000 live births
Influenza	12	—
Remainder of diseases of respiratory system	274	7.1
Hernia of abdominal cavity and intestinal obstruction without mention of hernia	77	2.0
Gastritis, duodenitis, and noninfective enteritis and colitis	76	2.0
Remainder of diseases of digestive system	187	4.8
Congenital anomalies	6,178	159.2
Anencephalus and similar anomalies	344	8.9
Spina bifida	48	1.2
Congenital hydrocephalus	146	3.8
Other congenital anomalies of central nervous system and eye	290	7.5
Congenital anomalies of heart	1,760	45.4
Other congenital anomalies of circulatory system	332	8.6
Congenital anomalies of respiratory system	973	25.1
Congenital anomalies of digestive system	94	2.4
Congenital anomalies of genitourinary system	302	7.8
Congenital anomalies of musculoskeletal system	424	10.9
Down's syndrome	102	2.6
Other chromosomal anomalies	805	20.7
All other and unspecified chromosomal anomalies	558	14.4
Certain conditions originating in the perinatal period	12,935	333.3
Newborn affected by maternal conditions that may be unrelated to present pregnancy	164	4.2
Newborn affected by maternal complications of pregnancy	1,244	32.1
Newborn affected by complications of placenta, cord, and membranes	960	24.7
Newborn affected by other labor and delivery complications	76	2.0
Slow fetal growth and fetal malnutrition	39	1.0
Disorders related to short gestation and unspecified low birthweight	3,925	101.1

Disorders related to long gestation and high birthweight	—	—
Birth trauma	185	4.8
Intrauterine hypoxia and birth asphyxia	452	11.6
Fetal distress in liveborn infant	123	3.2
Birth asphyxia	329	8.5
Respiratory distress syndrome	1,301	33.5
Other respiratory conditions of newborn	1,734	44.7
Infections specific to the perinatal period	777	20.0
Neonatal hemorrhage	339	8.7
Hemolytic disease of newborn, due to isoimmunization and other perinatal jaundice	14	—
Syndrome of "infant of a diabetic mother" and neonatal diabetes mellitus	11	—
Hemorrhagic disease of newborn	1	—
All other and ill-defined conditions	1,713	44.1
Symptoms, signs, and ill-defined conditions	3,773	97.2
Sudden Infant Death Syndrome	2,991	77.1
Symptoms, signs, and all other ill-defined conditions	782	20.1
Accidents and adverse effects	765	19.7
Inhalation and ingestion of food or other object causing obstruction of respiratory tract or suffocation	76	2.0
Accidental mechanical suffocation	303	7.8
Other accidental causes and adverse effects	386	9.9
Homicide	317	8.2
Child battering and other maltreatment	98	2.5
Other homicide	219	5.6
All other causes (residual)	1.524	39.3
Human Immune Virus infection	19	—

SOURCE: *National Vital Statistics Reports*, vol. 47, no. 19, June 30, 1999. This was the most recent data available as of January 2000. NOTE: Some figures may not add up to whole numbers due to rounding of data.

Appendix B: Directory of Organizations — United States and Canada

Adoption

Adoptive Families of America
2309 Como Avenue
St. Paul, MN 55108
Phone: 651-645-9955
Fax: 651-645-0055
Web: www.adoptivefam.org
E-mail: info@adoptivefam.org

American Academy of Adoption Attorneys
Box 33053
Washington, DC 20033-0053
Phone: 202-862-2222
Fax: 202-293-2309
Web: adoptionattorneys.org
E-mail: trustees@adoptionattorneys.org

Concerned United Birthparents
2000 Walker Street
Des Moines, IA 50317
Phone: 515-263-9558

National Adoption Center
1500 Walnut Street, Suite 701
Philadelphia, PA 19102

Phone: 800-TO-ADOPT or 215-735-9988
Fax: 215-735-9410
Web: www.adopt.org
E-mail: nac@adopt.org

National Adoption Information
 Clearinghouse
330 C Street SW
Washington, DC 20447
Phone: 888-251-0075 or 703-352-3488
Fax: 703-385-3206
Web: www.calib.com/naic
E-mail: naic@calib.com

North American Council on Adoptable
 Children
970 Raymond Avenue, Suite 106
St. Paul, MN 55114-1149
Phone: 612-644-3036

Birth centers

The National Association of Childbearing
 Centers
3123 Gottschall Road
Perkiomenville, PA 18074-9546
Phone: 215-234-8068

Fax: 215-234-8829
Web: www.birthcenters.org
E-mail: reachnacc@birthcenters.org

Breastfeeding

Global Maternal/ Child Health Associations
P.O. Box 1400
Wilsonville, OR 97070
Phone: 503-682-3600
Fax: 503-682-3434
E-mail: waterbirth@aol.com

International Board of Lactation Consultant
  Examiners
7309 Arlington Boulevard, Suite 300
Falls Church, VA 22042
Phone: 703-560-7330
Fax: 703-560-7332
Web: www.iblce.org
E-mail: IBLCE@erols.com

International Lactation Consultant
  Association
4101 Lake Boone Trail, Suite 201
Raleigh, NC 27607
Phone: 919-787-5181
Fax: 919-787-4916
Web: www.ilca.org
E-mail ilca@erols.com

La Leche League International
1400 North Meacham Road
P.O. Box 4079
Schaumberg, IL 60168-4079
Phone: 800-LA LECHE or 847-519-7730
Fax: 847-519-0035
Web: www.lalecheleague.org
E-mail: PRDept@llli.org

Caregivers

American College of Nurse-Midwives
818 Connecticut Avenue NW, Suite 900
Washington, DC 20006
Phone: 888-MIDWIFE or 202-728-9860
Fax: 202-728-9897
Web: www.acnm.org
E-mail: info@acnm.org

American College of Obstetricians and
  Gynecologists (ACOG)
Resource Center
409 12th Street SW
P.O. Box 96920
Washington, DC 20090-6920
Phone: 202-638-5577
Web: www.acog.org
E-mail: resources@acog.org

Cesarean birth

International Cesarean Awareness
  Network Inc.
1304 Kingsdale Avenue
Redondo Beach, CA 90278
Phone: 310-542-6400
Fax: 310-542-5368
Web: www.childbirth.org/section/
  ICAN.html
E-mail: ICANinfo@aol.com

Childbirth education

The Academy of Certified Childbirth
  Educators
2001 East Prairie Circle, Suite I
Olathe, KS 66062
Phone: 800-444-8223

The Bradley Method
P.O. Box 5224
Sherman Oaks, CA 91413-5224
Phone: 800-4-A-Birth
Web: www.bradleybirth.com

Lamaze International
1200 19th Street NW, Suite 300
Washington, DC 20036-2412
Phone: 800-368-4404 or 202-857-1128
Fax: 202-857-1102
Web: www.lamaze-childbirth.com
  E-mail: lamaze@DC.sba.com

Association of Labor Assistants and
  Childbirth Educators (ALACE)
P.O. Box 382724
Cambridge, MA 02238-2724
Phone: 617-441-2500
Web: www.server4.hypermart.net/alacehq

Association of Women's Health, Obstetric,
and Neonatal Nurses
2000 L Street NW, Suite 740
Washington, DC 20036
Phone: 202-261-2400
Fax: 202-728-0575
Web: www.aiawhonn.org

Childbirth Without Pain Education
Association
20134 Snowden
Detroit, MI 48235-1170
Phone and Fax: 313-341-3816
E-mail: cat-flora@juno.com

Coalition for Improving Maternity Services
2120 L Street NW, Suite 400
Washington, DC 20037
Phone: 202-478-6138
Fax: 202-223-9579
Web: www.motherfriendly.org
E-mail: info@motherfriendly.org

International Childbirth Education
Association & Bookcenter (ICEA)
P.O. Box 20048
Minneapolis, MN 55420
Phone: 612-854-8660 or 800-624-4934
(Bookcenter)
Fax: 612-854-8772
Web: www.icea.org
E-mail: info@icea.org

Doulas

Doulas of North America
13513 North Grove Drive
Alpine, UT 84004
Phone: 801-756-7331
Fax: 801-763-1847
Web: www.dona.org
E-mail: Doula@dona.org or
referrals@dona.org or
certification@dona.org

Endometriosis

Endometriosis Association
8585 North 76th Place
Milwaukee, WI 53223
Phone: 800-992-3636 (United States) or
800-426-2363 (Canada)

Genetic Counseling

Alliance of Genetic Support Groups
4301 Connecticut Avenue NW, Suite 404
Washington, DC 20008
Phone: 800-336-4363
Web: www.medhelp.org

March of Dimes Birth Defects Foundation
1275 Mamaroneck Avenue
White Plains, NY 10605
Phone: 914-428-7100 or 888-663-4637
Web: www.modimes.org
E-mail: resources@modimes.org

National Society of Genetic Counselors
233 Canterbury Drive
Wallingford, PA 19086-6617
Phone: 610-872-7608
Fax: 610-872-1192
Web: www.nsgc.org
E-mail: nsgc@aol.com

Spina Bifida Association of America
4590 MacArthur Boulevard NW, Suite 250
Washington, DC 20009-4226
Phone: 800-621-3141
Fax: 202-944-3295
E-mail: spinabifida@aol.com

High-risk Pregnancy

The Confinement Line
P.O. Box 1609
Springfield, VA 22151
Phone: 703-941-7183

DES Action USA
1615 Broadway, Suite 510
Oakland, CA 94612
Phone: 800-DES-9288
Fax: 510-465-4815
Web: www.desaction.org
E-mail: desact@well.com

Epilepsy Foundation
4351 Garden City Drive
Landover, MD 20785
Phone: 301-459-3700
Information and referral: 800-332-1000
Fax: 301-577-2684
Web: www.epilepsyfoundation.org
E-mail: Webmaster@efa.org

Intensive Caring Unlimited (ICU)
P.O. Box 563
Newton Square, PA 19073
Phone: 610-876-7872

Sidelines National Support Network
P.O. Box 1808
Laguna Beach, CA 92652
Phone: 949-497-2265
Fax: 949-497-5598
Web: www.sidelines.org
E-mail: sidelines@sidelines.org

HMOs

The American Association of Health Plans
1129 20th Street, NW, Suite 600
Washington, DC 20036-3421
Phone: 202-778-3200
Fax: 202-331-7487
Web: www.aahp.org

Joint Commission on Accreditation of
   Healthcare Organizations
One Renaissance Boulevard
Oakbrook Terrace, IL 60181
Phone: 630-792-5000
Fax: 630-792-5005 or 630-792-5645
Web: www.jcaho.org
E-mail: Addresses consist of the first letter
   of the contact person's first name and the
   entire last name @jcaho.org

National Committee for Quality Assurance
2000 L Street NW, Suite 500
Washington, DC 20036
Phone: 202-955-3500
Fax: 202-955-3599
Web: www.ncqa.org
E-mail: Webmaster@ncqa.org

Infant Health

American Academy of Pediatrics
141 Northwest Point Boulevard
Elk Grove Village, IL 60007
Phone: 847-228-5005
Fax: 847-228-5097
Web: www.aap.org

Association for the Care of Children's
   Health (ACCH)
7910 Woodmont Avenue, Suite 300

Bethesda, MD 20814-3015
Phone: 301-654-6549 or 800-808-2224
Fax: 301-986-4553

Back to Sleep Campaign
National Institute of Child Health and
   Human Development (NICHD)
31 Center Drive
Building 31 Room 2A32
Bethesda, MD 20892-2425
Phone: 301-496-5133 or 800-505-CRIB
Fax: 301-496-7101
Web: www.nichd.nih.gov

National Association of Pediatric Nurse
   Associates and Practitioners
1101 Kings Highway North, Suite 206
Cherry Hill, NJ 08034-1912
Phone: 856-667-1773
Fax: 856-667-7187
Web: www.napnap.org
E-mail: info@napnap.org

Infertility

American Society of Andrology
74 New Montgomery, Suite 230
San Francisco, CA 94105
Phone: 415-764-4823
Fax: 415-764-4915
E-mail: asa@hp-assoc.com

American Society for Reproductive
   Medicine
1209 Montgomery Highway
Birmingham, AL 35216
Phone: 205-978-5000
Fax: 205-978-5505
Web: www@asrm.org
E-mail: asrm@asrm.org

American Urological Association
   Headquarters
1120 North Charles Street
Baltimore, MD 21201
Phone: 410-727-1100
Fax: 410-468-1835
Web: www.auanet.org
E-mail: aua@auanet.org

DES Action USA
1615 Broadway, Suite 510
Oakland, CA 94612
Phone: 800-DES-9288
Fax: 510-465-4815
Web: www.desaction.org
E-mail: desact@well.com

Fertility Research Foundation
875 Park Avenue
New York, NY 10021
Phone: 212-744-5500
Fax: 212-744-6536
E-mail: frfbaby@msn.com

International Council on Infertility
    Information Dissemination Inc.
P.O. Box 6836
Arlington, VA 22206
Phone: 520-544-9548 or 703-579-9178
Fax: 703-379-1593
Web: www.inciid.org
E-mail: INCIIDinfo@inciid.org

RESOLVE Inc.
1310 Broadway
Somerville, MA 02144-1731
Business office: 617-623-1156
Help Line: 617-623-0744
Fax: 617-623-0252
Web: www.resolve.org
E-mail: resolveinc@aol.com

Surrogates by Choice
P.O. Box 05257
Detroit, MI 48205
Phone: 313-839-4946

Maternal-Infant Health

Association of Maternal and Child Health
    Programs
1220 19th Street NW, Suite 801
Washington, DC 20036
Phone: 202-775-0436
Fax: 202-775-0061
Web: www.amchp.org
E-mail: info@amchp.org

California Family Health Council
3600 Wilshire Boulevard, Suite 600
Los Angeles, CA 90010-0605

Phone: 213-386-5614
Fax: 213-368-4410
Web: www.cfhc.org

Healthy Mothers, Healthy Babies Coalition
121 North Washington Street, Suite 300
Alexandria, VA 22314
Phone: 703-836-6110
Fax: 703-836-3470
Web: www.hmhb.org
E-mail: info@hmhb.org

Maternity Center Association
281 Park Avenue South, 5th Floor
New York, NY 10010
Phone: 212-777-5000
Fax: 212-777-9320
Web: www.maternity.org
E-mail: mcabirth@aol.com

National Center for Education of Maternal
    and Child Health
2000 15th Street N, Suite 701
Arlington, VA 22201-2617
Phone: 703-524-7802
Fax: 703-524-9335
Web: www.ncemch.org
E-mail: info@ncemch.org

National Maternal and Child Health
    Clearinghouse
2070 Chain Bridge Road, Suite 450
Vienna, VA 22182-2536
Phone: 703-356-1964 or 888-434-4624
Fax: 703-821-2098
Web: www.nmchc.org
E-mail: nmchc@circsol.com

Public Citizen's Health Research
1600 20th Street NW
Washington, DC 20009
Phone: 202-588-1000

Midwifery Organizations

Association for Childbirth at Home
    International
14140 Magnolia Boulevard
Sherman Oaks, CA 91423
Phone: 323-663-4996

Midwives Alliance of North America
(MANA)
4805 Lawrenceville Highway, Suite 116-
279
Lilburn, GA   30047
Phone: 800-923-MANA (6262)
Fax: 801-720-3026
Web: www.mana.org
E-mail: info@mana.org

Multiple Births

Center for the Study of Multiple Birth
333 East Superior Street, Room 464
Chicago, IL 60611
Phone: 312-266-9093
Fax: 312-908-5800
Web: www.multiplebirth.com
E-mail: lgk395@nwu.edu

Minnesota Center for Twin and Adoption
Research
University of Minnesota
Department of Psychology
75 East River Road
Minneapolis, MN 55455
Phone: 612-625-4067
Fax: 612-626-2079

MOST (Mothers of Supertwins)
[Triplets or more]
P.O. Box 951
Brentwood, NY 11717-0627
Phone: 631-859-1110
Fax: 631-859-3580
Web: www.mostonline.org
E-mail: Maureen@mostonline.org

National Organization of Mothers of Twins
Clubs Inc.
P.O. Box 438
Thompson Station, TN 37179-0438
Phone: 877-540-2200
Web: www.NOMOTC.org
E-mail: NOMOTC@aol.com

Triplet Connection
P.O. Box 99571
Stockton, CA 95209
Phone: 209-474-0885
Fax: 209-474-2233

Web: www.tripletconnection.org
E-mail: tc@tripletconnection.org

Twin Services
P.O. Box 10066
Berkeley, CA 94709
Phone and Fax: 510-524-0863
E-mail: twinservices@juno.com

The Twins Foundation
P.O. Box 9487 or 6043
Providence, RI 02940-9487 or 02940-6043
Phone: 401-274-8946 or 401-751-4642

Twins Magazine
5350 South Roslyn, Suite 400
Englewood, CO 80111-2125
Phone: 800-328-3211
Fax: 303-290-9025
Web: www.twinsmagazine.com
E-mail: twins.editor@businessword.com

Twin to Twin Transfusion Syndrome
Foundation
411 Longbeach Parkway
Bay Village, OH 44140
Phone: 440-899-TTTS or 440-899-8887
Fax: 440-366-6148
Web: www.TTTSFoundation.org
E-mail: TTTSFound@aol.com

Natural Family Planning Organizations

Couple to Couple League
P.O. Box 111184
Cincinnati, OH 45211-1184
Phone: 513-471-2000
Fax: 513-557-2449
Web: www.ccli.org
E-mail: ccli@ccli.org

Diocesan Development Program for NFP
3211 4th Street NE
Washington, DC 20017-1194
Phone: 202-541-3240
Fax: 202-541-3054
Web: www.nccbuscc.org/prolife/issues/nfp
E-mail: nfp@nccbuscc.org

Parent Support

National Association of Mothers' Centers
64 Division Avenue
Levittown, NY 11756
Phone: 516-520-2929 or 800-645-3828
Fax: 516-520-1639
Web: www.motherscenter.org
E-mail: info@motherscenter.org

Postpartum Support International
927 North Kellogg Avenue
Santa Barbara, CA 93111
Phone: 805-967-7636
Fax: 805-967-0608
Web: www.postpartum.net
E-mail: jhonikman@earthlink.net

Pregnancy/Infant Loss

Abiding Hearts
P.O. Box 5245
Bozeman, MT 59717
Phone: 406-388-8001
Fax: 406-587-7197
E-mail: hearts@imt.net

AMEND (Aiding a Mother and Father
  Experiencing Neonatal Death)
4324 Berrywick Terrace
St. Louis, MO 63128-1908
Phone: 314-487-7582

Bereavement Services (Resolve through
  Sharing)
1910 South Avenue
La Crosse, WI 54601-5400
Phone: 800-362-9567, ext. 4747
Web: www.gundluth.org/bereave
E-mail: berservs@gundluth.org

CLIMB
Center for Loss in Multiple Birth Inc.
P.O. Box 91377
Anchorage, AK 99509
Phone: 907-222-5321
Web: www.climb-support.org
E-mail: climb@pobox.alaska.net

The Compassionate Friends
National Office
P.O. Box 3696
Oak Brook, IL 60522-3696

Phone: 630-990-0010
Fax: 630-990-0246
Web: www.compassionatefriends.org
E-mail:
  nationaloffice@compassionatefriends.org

National SIDS Resource Center
2070 Chain Bridge Road, Suite 450
Vienna, VA 22182
Phone: 703-821-8955
Fax: 703-821-2098
Web: www.circsol.com/sids
E-mail: sids@circsol.com

Pails of Hope Newsletter
Pregnancy and Parenting After Infertility
  and/or Loss Support
Pen Parents Inc
P. O. Box 8738
Reno, NV 89507-8738
Phone: 775-826-7332
Web: www.penparents.org
E-mail: penparents@aol.com

Parent Education Program
Abbott Northwestern Hospital
800 East 28th Street
Minnesota, MN 55407
Phone: 612-863-4427

Perinatal Loss
2116 NE 18th Avenue
Portland, OR 97212
Phone: 503-284-7426
Fax: 503-282-8985
Web: www.tearsoup.com
E-mail: grieving@tearsoup.com

A Place to Remember
de Ruyter-Nelson Publications Inc.
1885 University Avenue, Suite 110
St. Paul, MN 55104
Phone: 651-645-7045 or 800-631-0973
Fax: 651-645-4780
Web: www.aplacetoremember.com
E-mail: aptr@aplacetoremember.com

Pregnancy and Infant Loss Center
1421 E. Wayzata Boulevard, #70
Wayzata, MN 55391
Phone: 952-473-9372

Pregnancy Loss Support Program
National Council of Jewish Women
New York Section
9 East 69th Street
New York, NY 10021
Phone: 212-535-5900

SHARE Pregnancy & Infant Loss Support
    Inc.
St. Joseph Health Center
300 First Capitol Drive
St. Charles, MO 63301-2893
Phone: 800-821-6819 or 636-947-6164
Fax: 636-947-7486
Web: www.nationalShareOffice.com
E-mail: share@nationalshareoffice

SIDS Alliance
1314 Bedford Avenue, Suite 210
Baltimore, MD 21208
Phone: 800-638-SIDS or 410-653-8226
Fax: 410-653-8709
Web: www.sidsalliance.org
E-mail: sidshq@charm.net

Twinless Twins Support Group
    International
11220 St. Joe Road
Fort Wayne, IN 46835
Phone and Fax: 219-627-5414
Web: www.fwi.com/twinless
E-mail: twinworld1@aol.com or
    twinless@iserv.net

Wintergreen Press
3630 Eileen Street
Maple Plains, MN 55359
Phone: 612-476-1303

Premature Infants

Parent of Premature and High Risk Infants
    International Inc.
c/o Sherri Nance, M.O.M.
22940 West Frisca Drive
Valencia, CA 91355
Phone: 661-254-2426

Prenatal Health

Registry of Pregnancies Exposed to
    Chemotherapeutic Agents
Department of Human Genetics

University of Pittsburgh
Pittsburgh, PA 15261
Phone: 412-624-9951
E-mail: bgettig@helix.hgen.pitt.edu

Reproductive Health

American Society for Colposcopy and
    Cervical Pathology
20 West Washington Street, Suite 1
Hagerstown, MD 21740
Phone: 800-787-7227
Fax: 301-733-5775
Web: www.asccp.org

Safety

The Danny Foundation
12901 Alcosta Boulevard, Suite 2C
San Ramon, CA 94583
Phone: 800-83-DANNY
Fax: 925-327-1443
Web: www.dannyfoundation.org
E-mail: dannycrib@earthlink.net

Consumer Product Safety Commission
Washington, DC 20207
Phone: 800-638-2772, 800-628-8326 in
    Maryland and Alaska, 800-492-8363 in
    Hawaii

Juvenile Products Manufacturers
    Association
236 Route 38 West, Suite 100
Moorestown, NJ 08057
Web: www.jpma.org

Sexually Transmitted Diseases (STDs)

American Social Health Association
    (ASHA)
P.O. Box 13827
Research Triangle Park, NC 27709-3827
Phone: 919-361-8400
Fax: 919-361-8425
Web: www.ashastd.org

Centers for Disease Control
Division of STD/HIV Prevention
1600 Clifton Road, NE
Atlanta, GA 30333
Phone: 404-639-3311
Web: www.cdc.gov

National Herpes Hotline
P.O. Box 13827
Research Triangle Park, NC 27709
Phone: 919-361-8488

Special Needs/Birth Defects

Cleft Palate Foundation
104 South Estes Drive, Suite 204
Chapel Hill, NC 27514
Phone: 800-24-CLEFT
Fax: 919-933-9604
Web: www.cleft.com

Association of Birth Defect Children
  (ABDC)
930 Woodcock Road, Suite 225
Orlando, FL 32803
Phone: 800-313-2232 or 407-245-7035
Fax: 407-895-0824
Web: www.birthdefects.org
E-mail: abdc@birthdefects.org

Federation for Children with Special Needs
1135 Treemont Street, Suite 420
Boston, MA 02120
Phone: 617-236-7210 or 800-331-0688
  (Massachusetts only)
Fax: 617-572-2094
Web: www.fcsn.org
E-mail: fcsninfo@fcsn.org

Juvenile Diabetes Foundation
120 Wall Street, 19th Floor
New York, NY 10005
Phone: 800-223-1138
Fax: 212-785-9595

National Down's Syndrome Congress
7000 Peachtree-Dunwoody Road
Building #5, Suite 100
Atlanta, GA 30328
Phone: 800-232-NDSC or 770-604-9500
Fax: 770-604-9898
Web: www.NDSCcenter.org
E-mail: NDSCcenter@aol.com

National Down's Syndrome Society (NDSS)
666 Broadway
New York, NY 10012-2317
Phone: 800-221-4602
Fax: 212-979-2873

Web: www.ndss.org
E-mail: info@ndss.org

National Information Center for Children
  and Youth with Disabilities (NICHCY)
P.O. Box 1492
Washington, DC 20013-1492
Phone: 202-884-8200 (V/TTY) or 800-695-
  8441 (V/TTY)
Fax: 202-884-8441
Web: www.nichy.org
E-mail: nichcy@aed.org

National Organization for Rare Disorders
  (NORD)
100 Route 37
P.O. Box 8923
New Fairfield, CT 06812-8923
Phone: 800-999-6673
Fax: 203-746-6481
Web: www.rarediseases.org
E-mail: orphan@rarediseases.org

National Reye's Syndrome Foundation
P.O. Box 829
Bryan, OH 43506
Phone: 800-233-7393
Fax: 419-636-9897
Web: www.bright.net/~reyessyn
E-mail: reyessyn@mail.bright.net

Parents Helping Parents
3041 Olcott Street
Santa Clara, CA 95054
Phone: 408-727-5775
Fax: 408-727-0182
Web: www.php.com

CANADIAN ORGANIZATIONS

Adoption

Adoption Council of Canada
Box 8442
Station T
Ottawa, Ontario K1G 3H8
Tel: 613-235-1566 or 888-54-ADOPT
Fax: 613-235-1728
Web-site: www.adoption.ca
E-mail: jgrove@adoption.ca

Breastfeeding

INFACT Canada
(Infant Feeding Action Coalition)
6 Trinity Square
Toronto, Ontario M5G 1B1
Phone: 416-595-9819
Web: www.infactcanada.ca
E-mail: infact@ftn.net

La Leche League Canada
18C Industrial Drive
Box 29
Chesterville, Ontario K0C 1H0
Phone: 613-448-1842
Breastfeeding referral: 800-665-4324
Fax: 613-448-1845
E-mail: laleche@igs.net

Caregivers

The College of Family Physicians of Canada
2630 Skymark Avenue
Mississauga Ontario L4W 5A4
Phone: 905-629-0900
Fax: 905-629-0893
Web: www.cfpc.ca
E-mail: info@cfpc.ca

Community Health Nurses Association
P.O. Box 85232 Albert Park Postal Outlet
Calgary, Alberta T2A 7R7
Phone: 403-207-0334
Fax: 403-207-0340

Contraception

The Bay Centre for Birth Control
790 Bay Street, 8th Floor
Toronto, Ontario M5G 1N8
Phone: 416-351-3700
Fax: 416-351-3727

Planned Parenthood Federation of Canada
1 Nicholas Street, Suite 430
Ottawa, Ontario K1N 7B7
Phone: 613-241-4474
Fax: 613-241-7550
Web: www.ppfc.ca
E-mail: admin@ppfc.ca

Doulas

Doula CARE (Canadian Association,
Registry and Education)
Maple Grove Village
P.O. Box 61058
Oakville, Ontario L6J 6X0
Phone: 905-842-3385
Fax: 905-844-9983
Web: www.globalserve.net/~martensn
E-mail: Martensn@globalserve.net

Endometriosis

Endometriosis Association of Canada
74 Plateau Crescent
Don Mills, Ontario M3C 1M8
Phone: 800-426-2363
Fax: 416-447-4384

High-risk Pregnancy

Canadian Diabetes Association
15 Toronto Street, Suite 800
Toronto, Ontario M5C 2E3
Phone: 416-363-3373
Fax: 416-363-3393
Web: www.diabetes.ca
E-mail: info@cda-nat.org

DES Action Canada
5890 Monkland Avenue, Suite 203
Montreal, Quebec H4A 1G2
Phone: 514-482-3204
Fax: 514-482-1445
Web: www.web.net/~desact
E-mail: desact@web.net

Epilepsy Canada
1470 Peel Street, Suite 745
Montreal, Quebec H3A 1T1
Phone: 514-845-7855
Fax: 514-845-7866
Web: www.epilepsy.ca
E-mail: epilepsy@epilepsy.ca

Lupus Canada
Box 64034,
5512 4th Street NW
Calgary, Alberta T2K 6J1
Phone: 1-800-661-1468 (Canada)
Phone/Fax: 403-274-5599
Web: www.lupuscanada.org
E-mail: info@lupuscanada.org

Sidelines Canada Prenatal Support Network
31 Iona Street
Ottawa, Ontario K1Y 3L6
Phone: 877-271-SIDE or 613-792-3633
Web: www.sidelinescanada.org
E-mail: info@sidelinescanada.org

Thyroid Foundation of Canada
96 Mack Street
Kingston, Ontario K7L 1N9
Phone: 613-544-8364
Fax: 613-544-9731
Web: www.home.ican.net/~thyroid/
   canada/html
E-mail: thyroid@kos.net

Infant Health

Canadian Foundation for the Study of
   Infant Deaths
586 Eglinton Avenue East, Suite 308
Toronto, Ontario M4P 1P2
Phone: 416-488-3260 or 800-END-SIDS
   (outside Toronto)
Fax: 416-488-3864
Web: www.sidscanada.org/sids.html
E-mail: sidscanada@inforamp.net

Canadian Institute of Child Health
885 Meadowlands Drive East, Suite 512
Ottawa, Ontario K2C 3N2
Phone: 613-224-4144
Fax: 613-224-4145
Web: www.cich.ca
E-mail: cich@igs.net

Canadian Paediatric Society (CPS)
2204 Walkley Road, Suite 100
Ottawa, Ontario K1G 4G8
Phone: 613-526-9397
Fax: 613-526-3332
Web: www.cps.ca
E-mail: info@cps.ca

Parent to Parent Link
c/o The Easter Seal Society
1185 Eglinton Avenue East, Suite 706
Toronto, Ontario M3C 3C6
Phone: 416-421-8377 or 800-668-6252
   (outside Toronto)
Web: www.easterseals.org
E-mail: info@easterseals.org

Provincial IODE Genetics Resource Centre
Children's Hospital of Western Ontario
800 Commissioners Road East
London, Ontario N6C 2V5
Phone: 519-685-8140
Fax: 519-685-8214

Infertility

Infertility Awareness Association of Canada
   Inc.
201–396 Cooper Street
Ottawa, Ontario K2P 2H7
Phone: 613-234-8585 or 800-263-2929 (all
   North America)
Fax: 613-244-8908
Web: www.iaac.ca
E-mail: iaac@fox.nstn.ca

Maternal/Infant Health

Canadian Mothercraft Association
32 Heath Street West
Toronto, Ontario M4V 1T3
Phone: 416-920-4054 (120)
Fax: 416-920-5983

National Institute of Nutrition
265 Carling Avenue, Suite 302
Ottawa, Ontario K1S 2E1
Phone: 613-235-3355
Fax: 613-235-7032
Web: www.nin.ca
E-mail: nin@nin.ca

YWCA Canada
590 Jarvis Street, 5th Floor
Toronto, Ontario M4Y 2J4
Phone: 416-962-8881
Fax: 416-962-8084
Web: www.ywcacanada.ca
 E-mail: national@ywcacanada.ca

Midwifery Associations

Alberta Association of Midwives
1616–20A Street NW
Calgary, Alberta T2N 2L5
Phone: 403-932-7777

Association des Sage-femmes du Quebec
54 Boulevard Chambord
Lorraine, Quebec J6Z 1P5
Phone: 514-965-8673

Association of Manitoba Midwives
Norwood Post Office
P.O. Box 83
Winnipeg, Manitoba R2H 3B8
Phone: 204-897-8672

Association of Nova Scotia Midwives
P.O. Box 968
Wolfville, Nova Scotia B0P 1X0
Phone: 902-582-3151

Association of Ontario Midwives
562 Eglinton Avenue East, Suite 102
Toronto, Ontario M4P 1B9
Phone: 416-481-2811
E-mail: midwives@interlog.com

College of Midwives of Ontario
2195 Yonge Street, 4th Floor
Toronto, Ontario M4S 2B2
Phone: 416-327-0874
Fax: 416-327-8219
E-mail: admin@cmo.on.ca

Les Sage-femmes du Quebec
BP 354 Station Cote-des-neiges
Montreal, Quebec H3S 2S6
Phone: 514-738-8090

Midwives Association of British Columbia
219–1675 West 8th Avenue
Vancouver, BC V6J 1V2
Phone: 604-736-5976

Midwives Association of Saskatchewan
2836 Angus Street
Regina, Saskatchewan S4S 1N8
Phone: 306-653-1349

New Brunswick Midwives
200 Inglewood Drive
Fredericton, New Brunswick E2B 2K6

Newfoundland and Labrador Midwives
  Association
132 Cumberland Crescent
St. John's, Newfoundland A1B 3M5
Phone: 709-739-6319

Northwest Territories Community Health
  Centre
Keewatin Regional Health Board
Rankin Inlet, Northwest Territories X0C
  0G0
Phone: 819-645-2816

Prince Edward Island Midwives Association
P.O. Box 756
Cornwall, PEI C0A 1H0
Phone: 902-566-3102

Multiples

Parents of Multiple Births Association of
  Canada (POMBA Canada)
P.O. Box 234
Gormley, Ontario L0H 1G0
Telephone: 905-888-0725
Fax: 905-888-0727
Web: www.pomba.org
E-mail: office@pomba.org

Natural Family Planning Organizations

Serena Canada
151 Holland Avenue
Ottawa, Ontario K1Y 0Y2
Phone: 613-728-6536
Fax: 613-724-1116
Web: www.mlink.net/~serena
E-mail: serena@on.aibn.com (Ottawa) or
  serena@mlink.net (Montreal)

Other Resources

The Consumer Health Information Service
Toronto Reference Library
789 Yonge Street
Toronto, Ontario M4W 2G8
Phone: 416-393-7056 or 800-667-1999
Web: www.tpl.toronto.on.ca/TRL/centres/
  chis/index.html

Postpartum depression

Canadian Association of Family Resource
  Programs
101–30 Rosemount Avenue
Ottawa, Ontario K1Y 1P4
Phone: 613-728-3307
Fax: 613-729-5421

Postpartum Adjustment Support Services–
  Canada (PASS–CAN)
P.O. Box 7282, Station Main
Oakville, Ontario L6J 6L6
Phone: 905-844-9009
Fax: 905-844-5973

Pregnancy/Infant Loss

Bereaved Families of Ontario
562 Eglinton Avenue East, Suite 401
Toronto, Ontario M4P 1P1
Phone: 800-BFO-6364 or 416-440-0290
Fax: 416-440-0304
Web: www.inforamp.net/~bfo
E-mail: bfo@inforamp.net

Canadian Foundation for the Study of
  Infant Deaths
586 Eglinton Avenue East, Suite 308
Toronto, Ontario M4P 1P2
Phone: 800-END-SIDS or 416-488-3260

The Compassionate Friends
685 William Avenue
Winnipeg, Manitoba R3E 0Z2
Phone: 204-787-4896

Perinatal Bereavement Services Ontario
6060 Highway #7 East, Suite 205
Markham, Ontario L3P 3A9
Phone: 905-472-1807 or 1-888-301-PBSO
Fax: 905-472-4054
Web: www.digitalrain.com/pbso

Reproductive Health

The Canadian Pelvic Inflammatory Disease
  (PID) Society
Box 33804, Station D
Vancouver, BC V6J 4L6
Phone: 604-684-5704

Sunnybrook & Women's College Health
  Sciences Centre
Women's College Campus
Regional Women's Health Centre
790 Bay Street, 8th Floor
Toronto, Ontario M5G 1N8
Phone: 416-586-0211
Fax: 416-351-3727
Web: www.utl1.library.utoronto.ca/www/
  wch/index.htm

Vancouver Women's Health Collective
1675 West 8th Avenue, Suite 219
Vancouver, BC V6J 1V2
Phone: 604-736-5262
Fax: 604-736-2152
E-mail: vwhc@axionet.com

Women's Health Office
Faculty of Health Sciences
Room 2B11
McMaster University
1200 Main Street W
Hamilton, Ontario L8N 3Z5
Phone: 905-525-9140, ext. 22210
Fax: 905-522-6898
Web: www-fhs.mcmaster.ca/women
E-mail: who@mcmaster.ca

Safety

Infant and Toddler Safety Association
  (ITSA)
385 Fairway Road South, Suite 4A-230
Kitchener, Ontario N2C 2N9
Phone: 519-570-0181
Fax: 519-894-0739

Safe Start
B.C.'s Children's Hospital
4480 Oak Street, Room B227
Vancouver, BC V6H 3V4
Phone: 604-875-3273 or 888-331-8100
Fax: 604-875-2440
Web: www.cw.bc.ca/safestart
E-mail: amckendrick@cw.bc.ca

Transport Canada
Road Safety and Motor Vehicle Regulation
Place de Ville, Tower C
330 Sparks Street
Ottawa, Ontario K1A 0N5
Phone: 800-333-0371
Fax: 613-998-4831
E-mail: roadsafetywebmail@tc.gc.ca

Special Needs/Birth Defects

Canadian Coalition for the Prevention of
  Developmental Disabilities
c/o Canadian Institute of Child Health
885 Meadowlands Drive, Suite 512
Ottawa, Ontario K2C 3N2
Phone: 613-224-4144

Fax: 613-224-4145
Web: www.cich.ca
E-mail: cich@cich.ca

Canadian Council of the Blind
396 Cooper Street, Suite 200
Ottawa, Ontario K2P 2H7
Phone: 613-567-0311
Fax: 613-567-2728
E-mail: ccb.national@on.aibn.com

Canadian Cystic Fibrosis Foundation
2221 Yonge Street, Suite 601
Toronto, Ontario M4S 2B4
Phone: 416-485-9149
Fax: 416-485-0960
Web: www.ccff.ca
E-mail: info@ccff.ca

Canadian Down's Syndrome Society
811 14th Street NW
Calgary, Alberta T2N 2A4
Phone: 800-883-5608
Fax: 403-270-8291
Web: www.cdss.ca
E-mail: dsinfo@cdss.ca

Canadian Hemophilia Society
625 President Kennedy Avenue, Suite 1210
Montreal, Quebec H3A 1K2
Phone: 514-848-0503
Fax: 514-848-9661
E-mail: chs@microtec.net

Canadian Spinal Research Organization
120 Newkirk Road Unit 1
Richmond Hill, Ontario L4C 9S7
Phone: 905-508-4000
Fax: 905-508-4002
Web: www.csro.com
E-mail: csro@globalserve.net

Lower Mainland Down's Syndrome Society
14740 89A Avenue
Surrey, BC V3R 7Z9
Phone: 604-581-5609
Fax: 604-930-1113
Web: www.lmdss.bc.ca
E-mail: lmdss@vcn.bc.ca

Spina Bifida and Hydrocephalus
   Association of Canada
388 Donald Street, Suite 220
Winnipeg, Manitoba R3B 2J4
Phone: 800-565-9488
Fax: 204-925-3654
Web: www.sbhac.ca
E-mail: spinab@mts.net

Turner's Syndrome Society
814 Glencairn Avenue
Toronto, Ontario M6B 2A3
Phone: 800-465-6744
Fax: 416-781-7245
Web: www.turnersyndrome.ca
E-mail: tssincan@web.net

Appendix C: Directory
of Internet Resources

Please note: To save space, we have not repeated the numerous Web site addresses that can be found in Appendix B: Directory of Organizations, so be sure to check through that part of the book as well for leads on many other excellent sources of online support and information.

FERTILITY/INFERTILITY

American Society for Reproductive Medicine's "Selecting an IVF/GIFT Program"
www.asrm.org/current/press/select.html
Provides couples who are experiencing infertility with advice on choosing an IVF/GIFT program.

Atlanta Reproductive Health Center
www.ivf.com
Contains detailed information on fertility and infertility, including an online photo gallery that illustrates various high-tech fertility methods.

Centers for Disease Control and Prevention's Assisted Reproductive Technologies Success Rates
www.cdc.gov/nccdphp/drh/arts/index.htm
Contains the text of the first-ever government report on fertility clinics.

Fertile Thoughts
www.fertilethoughts.com
Information on a variety of fertility and pregnancy-related topics.

Fertility Infertility Treatment
www.fertilitext.org
Detailed information on a variety of fertility-related topics.

Infertility Resources
www.ihr.com/infertility/index.html
Online articles, links to newsgroups, and more.

HIGH-RISK PREGNANCY

Hannah's Prayer
www.hannah.org/risk.htm
A list of helpful resources related to high-risk pregnancy.

INFANT HEALTH-RELATED
INFORMATION

Adam.com
www.adam.com
A good source of information on infant and child health.

American Academy of Pediatrics
www.aap.org
Find out about where the academy stands on a variety of issues related to infant health.

Centers for Disease Control and Prevention–"Group B Streptococcal Infections"
www.cdc.gov/ncidod/diseases/bacter/strep_b.htm
Contains detailed and accurate information about what group B strep can mean to a pregnant woman and her baby.

U.S. Consumer Product Safety Commission
www.cpsc.gov
A great place to go to stay up-to-date on product recalls on a range of consumer goods, including juvenile products.

PREGNANCY INFORMATION
(GENERAL)

American College of Obstetrician and Gynecologists
www.acog.com
Contains accurate information on a variety of pregnancy and gynecology-related topics.

American Dietetic Association
www.eatright.org
Contains useful information on prenatal nutrition.

BabyCenter
www.babycenter.com
One of the leading pregnancy and baby web sites. Packed with useful information on a variety of pregnancy and parenting-related topics. Also home to a very active "Pregnancy After Miscarriage/Stillbirth" bulletin board.

Canadian Parents Online
www.canadianparents.com
An excellent source of pregnancy and parenting information for Canadian parents.

DrKoop.com.
www.drkoop.com
A good source of information on a variety of health-related topics, including pregnancy.

Fit Pregnancy
www.fitpregnancy.com
Contains articles from the publication of the same name. A good source of information on prenatal fitness.

Having a Baby.com
www.having-a-baby.com/tryingagain.htm
The official web site for this book. Drop by for Web site updates and other important information.

Intelihealth
www.intelihealth.com
The health web site developed by Johns Hopkins University. Contains plenty of useful pregnancy-related information.

Mayo Health O@sis
www.mayohealth.org
The official web site of the Mayo Clinic. Contains detailed information on a variety of health-related topics, including pregnancy.

MedicineNet
www.medicinenet.com
Contains detailed information on a variety of health-related topics, including pregnancy. Features an online medical dictionary and more.

Mediconsult.com
www.mediconsult.com
One of the leading health information web sites. Contains detailed information on a variety of pregnancy-related topics.

Medscape
www.medscape.com
Another major health web site that offers detailed information on a variety of health-related topics, including pregnancy.

The Merck Manual
www.merck.com
www.merck.com/pubs/mmanual/section18/sec18.htm
Contains the entire text of this highly respected medical manual. Includes detailed information on a variety of pregnancy-related topics.

Motherrisk
http://motherisk.org
Maintained by the Motherisk Clinic at the Hospital for Sick Children in Toronto, Ontario, Canada. An excellent source of information on prenatal health.

National Center for Health Statistics
www.cdc.gov/nchs/
The best place to search for pregnancy- and infant-health related statistics.

National Library of Medicine–Grateful Med database
http://igm-01.nlm.nih.gov/
A searchable database of abstracts for leading medical journals. A quick way to find out if there have been any recent breakthroughs concerning particular types of pregnancy- and infant-losses.

New York Times on the Web's Women's Health—Pregnancy
www.nytimes.com/specials/women/whome/pregnancy.html
Packed with numerous articles and book excerpts of interest to pregnant women and their partners.

Obgyn.net
www.obgyn.net
A useful source of information on topics related to obstetrics and gynecology.

Obstetric Ultrasound
www.ob-ultrasound.net/
A web site that allows you to view ultrasound photos of babies at various stages of fetal development.

Pregnancy Calendar.com
www.pregnancycalendar.com
Type in your due date and this site will immediately produce a customized pregnancy calendar for you. A fun site for those times when you're actually able to let yourself relax and breathe a little.

U.S. Equal Opportunity Commission
www.eeoc.gov
A good source of information about pregnancy discrimination on the job.

WebMD
www.webmd.com
Another major health Web site. Frequently contains articles and other materials written by the authors of this book.

PREGNANCY INFORMATION (LOSS-RELATED)

Learn2.com–"Learn2 Avoid Junk Mail"
www.learn2.com/05/0514/0514.php3
Contains step-by-step instructions on how to get yourself off baby- and pregnancy-related junk mail lists—something you'll definitely want to do if you're unfortunate enough to experience another loss.

SIDS Network
www.sids-network.org
Contains information on topics related to pregnancy and infant loss. An excellent source of leads on online support groups dealing with these issues.

Subsequent Pregnancy After a Loss Support Group
www.inforamp.net/~bfo/spals
Explains how you can subscribe to the Subsequent Pregnancy After a Loss Support Group. Also contains a number of useful links to other related resources.

Wisconsin Stillbirth Service Program
www.wisc.edu/wissp/when.htm
Contains information on coping with stillbirth.

The links in this directory were accurate at the time this book was published. Because content on the World Wide Web is constantly changing, it's possible that some of the links may be outdated by the time you decide to visit. We will post updates at our web site, www.having-a-baby.com/tryingagain, from time to time, so be sure to let us know if you discover a missing or relocated link.

NOTE: Because we have no control over the content on these web sites, we can't vouch for their medical accuracy. What we can tell you, however, is that these sites are the crème de la crème of the literally hundreds of pregnancy-related Web sites that we visited while researching this book.

References

Books

Barnes, Belinda, and Suzanne Gail Bradley. *Planning for a Healthy Baby.* London: Vermillion, 1990.

Barrett, Joyce, and Teresa Pitman. *Pregnancy and Birth: The Best Evidence.* Toronto: Key Porter Books, 1999.

Beers, Mark H., and Robert Berkow, eds. *The Merck Manual of Diagnosis and Therapy.* 17th ed. Whitehouse Station, NJ: Merck & Co., 1999.

Bramblett, John. *When Good-Bye Is Forever: Learning to Live Again After the Loss of a Child.* New York: Ballantine, 1991.

Brown, Judith E. Ph.D., and Howard N. Jacobson, M.D. *Nutrition & Pregnancy: A Complete Guide from Preconception to Postdelivery.* Lost Angeles: Lowell House, 1998.

Cunningham, F. Gary, et al. *Williams Obstetrics,* nineteenth edition. Norwalk, CT: Appleton and Lange, 1993.

Davis, Deborah L. *Empty Cradle, Broken Heart: Surviving the Death of Your Baby.* Golden, CO: Fulcrum Publishing, 1996.

Douglas, Ann, and John R. Sussman. *The Unofficial Guide to Having a Baby.* New York: Macmillan, 1999.

Gilbert, Elizabeth Stepp, and Judith Smith Harmon. *Manual of High Risk Pregnancy and Delivery.* New York: Mosby, 1998.

Herman, Barry, and Susan K. Perry. *The Twelve-Month Pregnancy. What You Need to Know Before You Conceive to Ensure a Healthy Beginning for You and Your Baby.* Los Angeles: Lowell House, 1997.

Katz, Jane. *Water Fitness During Your Pregnancy.* Champaign, IL: Human Kinetics, 1995.

Kohner, Nancy, and Alix Henley. *When a Baby Dies: The Experience of Late Miscarriage, Stillbirth and Neonatal Death.* London: Pandora Press, 1991.

Lanham, Carol Cirulli. *Pregnancy After a Loss: A Guide to Pregnancy After a Miscarriage, Stillbirth, or Infant Death.* New York: Berkley Books, 1999.

Lauersen, Neils H., and Colette Bouchez. *Getting Pregnant: What Couples Need to Know Right Now.* New York: Ballantine Books, 1992.

Luke, Barbara, and Tamara Eberlein. *When You're Expecting Twins, Triplets, or Quads.* New York: Harper Perennial, 1999.

Manginello, Frank P., and Theresa Foy Di Geronimo. *Your Premature Baby: Everything You Need to Know about Childbirth, Treatment, and Parenting.* New York: John Wiley and Sons, 1991.

Mullens, Anne. *Missed Conceptions: Overcoming Infertility.* Toronto: McGraw-Hill Ryerson, 1990.

Pasquariello, Patrick S. Jr. (ed.). *The Children's Hospital of Philadelphia Book of Pregnancy and Child Care.* New York: John Wiley and Sons, 1999.

Paulson, Richard J., and Judith Sachs. *Rewinding Your Biological Clock: Motherhood Later in Life.* New York: W. H. Freeman, 1999.

Peoples, Debby, and Harriette Rovner Ferguson. *What to Expect When You're Experiencing Infertility.* New York: W. W. Norton, 1999.

Peppers, Larry G., and Ronald J. Knapp. *How to Go on Living After the Death of a Baby.* Atlanta, GA: Peachtree Publishers, 1985.

Powning, Beth. *Shadow Child: An Apprenticeship in Love and Loss.* Toronto: Viking, 1999.

Pullen, Heather, and Jocelyn Smith. *Making Babies: A Complete Guide to Fertility and Infertility.* Toronto: Random House of Canada, 1990.

Sanders, Catherine M. *How to Survive the Loss of a Child.* Rocklin, CA: Prima Publishing, 1992.

Schiff, Harriet Sarnoff. *The Bereaved Parent.* New York: Penguin, 1977.

Silber, Herman J. *How to Get Pregnant.* New York: Warner Books, 1980.

Sussman, John, and B. Blake Levitt. *Before You Conceive.* New York: Bantam Books, 1989.

Vaughan, Christopher. *How Life Begins: The Science of Life in the Womb.* New York: Dell Publishing, 1996.

Warland, Jane. *Pregnancy After Loss.* Adelaide, Australia: Jane and Michael Warland, 1996.

Weschler, Toni. *Taking Charge of Your Fertility: The Definitive Guide to Natural Birth Control and Pregnancy Achievement.* New York: Harper Collins, 1995.

YMCA of the USA, with Thomas W. Hanlon. *Fit for Two: The Official YMCA Prenatal Exercise Guide.* Champaign, IL: Human Kinetics, 1995.

Articles

Adler, Jerry, and Robina Riccitiello. "Your Baby Has a Problem." *Newsweek* special edition (Spring-Summer 1997): 46.

"Aftermath of Loss." *U.S. News and World Report* (17 February 1997): 66.

Ahner, Regine, et al. "The Fast-Reacting Fetal Fibronectin Test: A Screening Method for Better Prediction of the Time of Delivery." *American Journal of Obstetrics and Gynecology* 177 (1997): 1478.

"Amniocentesis Alert. Early Amniocentesis May Increase Risk of Miscarriage and Clubfoot." *Maclean's* (2 February 1998): 58.

"Analysis of Risk Factors for Occurrence of Fetal Death." *American Family Physician* 51, 1 (1995): 245.

Andolsek, Kathryn M. "Risk of Ectopic Pregnancy Following Tubal Ligation." *American Family Physician* 56 (1997): 1460.

———. "Antidepressant Treatment During Breast Feeding." *American Family Physician* 55 (1997): 692.

———. "Chlamydial Infection and Risk of Ectopic Pregnancy." *American Family Physician* 56 (1997): 258.

———. "Cost Analysis of Procedures Used in Ectopic Pregnancy." *American Family Physician* 54 (1996): 2560.

———. "Early Postpartum Discharge with Nurse Visitation." *American Family Physician* 55 (1997): 2832.

Beatty, Denise. "Healthy Mommy, Healthy Baby: Follow Health Canada's New Prenatal Nutrition Guidelines to Benefit Yourself and Your Baby." *Canadian Living* (October 1999).

Begley, Sharon. "The Baby Myth." *Newsweek* (4 September 1995).

Berkowitz, Richard L. "From Twin to Singleton: If 'Psychological Stress' Is Accepted for Terminating Singletons, It Ought to Be for Reducing Twins As Well." Editorial. *British Medical Journal* 313 (1996): 373.

"Best Delivery Time Different for Single, Multiple Births." *American Medical News* 39, 18 (1996): 73.

Blohm, Febe, et al. "Fertility After a Randomized Trial of Spontaneous Abortion Managed by Surgical Evacuation or Expectant Treatment." *The Lancet* 349 (1997): 995.

Blumenfeld, Louis C., et al. "Retinopathy of Prematurity in Multiple-Gestation Pregnancies." *American Journal of Ophthalmology* 125, 2 (1998): 197.

Bodin, Melissa Moore. "The Eggs, Embryo, and I." *Newsweek* (28 July 1997): 14.

Bolumar, F., et al. "Hold the Coffee: Studies Link Caffeine Intake to Delayed Conception and Low Birth Weight." *Consultant* 37 (1997): 1248.

Braun, Wendy, and Patrick Perry. "Misconceptions about Conception." *Medical Update* 19, 10 (1996): 1.

"Caffeine and Spontaneous Abortion." *Nutrition Research Newsletter* (October 1996): 109.

Centers for Disease Control and Prevention. *1995 Assisted Reproductive Technology Success Rates: National Summary and Fertility Clinic Reports* (1997).

Chapman-Sheath, P., et al. "Iatrogenic Ileal Obstruction: a Complication of Umbilical Cord Clamping." *British Medical Journal* 313 (1996): 613.

Clifford, K., et al. "Does Suppressing Luteinising Hormone Secretion Reduce the Miscarriage Rate?" *British Medical Journal* 312 (1996): 1508.

Cnattingius, Ragnhild, R.N.M., Francis C. Notzon, Ph.D., and Sven Cnattingius Ph.D. "Obstacles to Reducing Cesarean Rates in a Low-Cesarean Setting: The Effect of Maternal Age, Height, and Weight." *Obstetrics and Gynecology* 92 (1998): 501–506.

Cogswell, Mary E., Sara Beck Fein, Kelley Scanlon, and Lura A. Schieve. "Medically Advised, Mother's Personal Target, and Actual Weight Gain During Pregnancy." *Obstetrics and Gynecology* 94 (1999): 616–622.

Coney, Sandra. "Auckland Inquest into Death After IVF." *The Lancet* 345 (1995): 849.

de Jonge, E. T. M., et al. "Randomized Clinical Trial of Medical Evacuation and Surgical Curettage for Incomplete Miscarriage." *British Medical Journal* 311 (1995): 662.

Denton, Jane. "The Nurse's Role in Treating Fertility Problems." *Nursing Times* (14 January 1998): 60–61.

Derrick, Rachel Christmas. "Natural Family Planning." *Essence* (27 August 1996): 28.

"Diagnostic Hysteroscopy for Habitual Miscarriage." *Clinical Reference Systems* (December 1997): 2504.

Douglas, Ann. "Making Babies: How to Make Sure Your Reproductive System Works When You Want It to, from What You Should Eat to When to Do the Deed." *Chatelaine* (June 1999): 51.

Dulitzki, Mordechai, Angela Chetrit, Shlomo Mashiach, Eyal Schiff, Daniel Seidman, and David Soriano. "Effect of Very Advanced Maternal Age on Pregnancy Outcome and Rate of Cesarean Delivery." *Obstetrics and Gynecology* 92 (1998): 935–939.

Dutton, Gail. "Genetic Testing: Should You Pay?" *Business and Health* (April 1996): 4.

Dyer, Claire. "Selective Abortions Hit the Headlines." *British Medical Journal* 313 (1996): 380.

Eberlein, Tamara. "Too Many Babies?" *Redbook* (August 1996): 88.

"Ectopic Pregnancy." *Morbidity and Mortality Weekly Report* 44 (1995): 46.

"Ectopic (Tubal) Pregnancy." *Clinical Reference Systems* (December 1997): 2430.

Fisher, Adam. "The Sperm Scrimmage: Dept. of Motility." *Esquire* (January 1997): 33.

"Folic Acid Decreases Neural Tube Defects." *Peterborough County-City Health Unit* (18 October 1993).

"Folic Acid, Miscarriages, and Birth Defects." *Nutrition Research Newsletter* (October 1997): 101.

Forster, Jeff. "Two Ways to Prevent Neonatal Group B Strep." *Patient Care* (15 July 1996): 22.

Garfein, Jennifer L. "The Patient's Perspective (Medical Student Becomes a Patient.)." *Journal of the American Medical Association* 275 (1996): 1371.

Gianelli, Diane M. "Anesthesiologists Question Claims in Abortion Debate." *American Medical News* 39 (1996): 4.

Giussani, Dino A. "Evidence for Link for Prenatal and Adult Health Grows." *The Lancet* 348 (1996): 535.

Grady, Denise. "How to Coax New Life." *Time Canada* (Fall 1996).

Graham, Janis. "How to Get Pregnant." *Redbook* (January 1998): 78.

Grim, Pamela. "Emergency Deliveries: High-Risk Pregnancies Shouldn't Show up in the ER. But They Do, and They Are Never Simple." *Discover* (April 1997): 28.

Grossman, Charles M., et al. "Hypothyroidism and Spontaneous Abortions Among Hanford, Washington, Downwinders." *Archives of Environmental Health* (May–June 1996): 175.

Hannah, M., and W. Hannah. "Caesarean Section or Vaginal Birth for Breech Presentation at Term: We Need Better Evidence As to Which Is Better." *British Medical Journal* 312 (1996): 1433.

"Healthy Eating." *American College of Obstetricians and Gynecologists* (December 1999).

Haupt, Donna. "Saving Babies: Why C-Section Is Not a Dirty Word." *Redbook* (October 1996): 102.

"HIV Increases Miscarriage." *AIDS Alert* (March 1996): 36.

Hollander, D. "Fetal Death Surveys." *Family Planning Perspectives* (March–April 1996): 86.

Hook, Ernest B., and Andrew E. Czeizel. "Can Terathanasia Explain the Protective Effect of Folic-Acid Supplementation on Birth Defects?" *The Lancet* 350 (1997): 513.

"How His Health Affects Your Baby." *Redbook* (December 1996): 42.

Hueston, William J., and Richard R. McClaflin. "Variations in Caesarian Delivery for Fetal Distress." *Journal of Family Practice* 43 (1996): 461.

Hughes, P. M., P. Turton, and C.D.H. Evans. "Stillbirth as risk factor for depression and anxiety in the subsequent pregnancy: Cohort study." *British Medical Journal* 318 (1999): 1721–1724.

Jovanovic-Peterson, Lois. "Control Is the Key to Successful Family Plannning." *Diabetes in the News* (January–February 1995): 34.

Kase, Lori Miller. "How Hormones Rule Your Moods." *American Health for Women* (May 1997): 54.

Klebanoff, M. A., R.J. Levine, R. DerSimonian, J. D. Clemens, and D. G. Wilkins. "Maternal serum paraxanthine, a caffeine metabolite, and the risk of spontaneous abortion." *New England Journal of Medicine* 341, 22 (November 25, 1999): 1639–1644.

Kluger, Jeffrey, Lawrence Mondi, and Alice Park. "Eggs on the Rocks." *Time* (27 October 1997): 105.

Larson, Beverly. "Childbirth in the '90s." *Prevention* (April 1995): 86.

Luke, Barbara, et al. "Date of Delivery in Multifetal Pregnancies." Letter and reply. *Journal of the American Medical Association* 276 (1996): 452.

Lynch, Denis J., et al. "Major Depressive Disorder Following Miscarriage." Letter. *Journal of the American Medical Association* 277 (1997): 1517.

Mackworth-Young, Charles, and Munther A. Khamashta. "Antiphospholipid (Hughes') Syndrome: A Treatable Cause of Recurrent Pregnancy Loss." *British Medical Journal* 314 (1997): 244.

"Making Better Babies." *Prevention* (July 1996): 40.

Mandl, Kenneth D. "Maternal and Infant Health: Effects of Moderate Reductions in Postpartum Length of Stay." *Journal of the American Medical Association* 279 (1998): 40.

Mandl, Kenneth D., et al. "Maternal and Infant Health: Effects of Moderate Reductions in Postpartum Length of Stay." *Archives of Pediatrics and Adolescent Medicine* 151 (1997): 915.

Mascarenhas, Lawrence, et al. "The Changing Face of Ectopic Pregnancy: Laparoscopic or Medical Treatment Should Now Replace Laparotomy." *British Medical Journal* 315 (1997): 141.

McCord, Holly, et al. "How to Get the Folate You Need." *Prevention* (December 1996): 50.

McMahon, C. A., et al. "Anxiety During Pregnancy and Fetal Attachment After In-Vitro Fertilization Conception." *Human Reproduction* 12 (January 1997): 176–182.

"Medical Care Expenditures Attributable to Cigarette Smoking During Pregnancy." *Journal of the American Medical Association* 278, 23 (1997): 2058.

Meniru, Godwin I., and Ian Craft. "Assisted Conception Options for Patients with Good Prognosis Cervical Cancer." *The Lancet* 349 (1997): 542.

"Methotrexate Therapy for Unruptured Ectopic Pregnancy." *American Family Physician* 51, 8 (1995): 1986.

Meyers, Carole, Rony Adam, Jeffrey Dungan, and Valerie Prenger. "Aneuploidy in Twin Gestations: When is Maternal Age Advanced?" *Obstetrics and Gynecology* 89 (1997): 248–251.

Mills, James L. "Protecting the Embryo from X-Rated Drugs." *New England Journal of Medicine* 333 (1995): 124.

Minakami, Hisanori, and Ikuo Sato. "Reestimating Date of Delivery in Multifetal Pregnancies." *Journal of the American Medical Association* 275 (1996): 1432.

"Miscarriage." *Clinical Reference Systems* (December 1997): 2566.

Mitchell, Alana. "New Surgical Procedure Can Help Many Couples with Previously Untreatable Forms of Infertility." *PR Newswire* (21 May 1996).

Monif, Gilles R. G., M.D. "The Great Douching Debate: To Douche, or Not to Douche." *Obstetrics and Gynecology* 94 (1999): 630–631.

Moore, Peter. "Tackling Autoantibody-Linked Pregnancy Loss." *The Lancet* 350 (1997): 269.

"Morning Sickness." *Clinical Reference Systems* (December 1997): 2496.

Nathanielsz, Peter W. "The Timing of Birth (Role of the Fetal Brain in the Birth Process)." *American Scientist* (November–December 1996): 562.

National Vital Statistics Report 47, 19 (30 June 1999).

Nelson, Maureen R., and Adrienne G. Tilbor. "Birth Brachial Plexus Injury." *Western Journal of Medicine* 162, 2 (1995): 154.

Nemeth, Mary. "Looking for Moral Anchors." *Maclean's* (19 August 1996): 18.

Neugebauer, Richard, et al. "Major Depressive Disorder in the Six Months After Miscarriage." *Journal of the American Medical Association* 277 (1997): 383.

Nofzinger, Margaret. "Margaret Nofzinger on Tracking Fertility." *Nutrition Health Review* (Spring 1996): 6.

"Nutrition During Pregnancy." *American College of Obstetricians and Gynecologists* (September 1999).

O'Connor, Amy. "'Genius' Advice." *Vegetarian Times* (January 1996): 18.

Pearson, Susan. "Nutrition in Pregnancy." *Nursing Times* (8 April 1998): 52–53.

Peterson, Herbert B. "Challenging Preconceived Ideas about Pregnancy." *Consultant* 37 (1997): 2004.

Pisacane, Alfredo. "Neonatal Prevention of Iron Deficiency: Placental Transfusion Is a Cheap and Physiological Solution." Editorial. *British Medical Journal* 312 (1996): 136.

Porter, T. Flint, M.D.; Alison M. Fraser, M.P.H.; Cheri Y. Hunter, Ryk H. Ward, Ph.D., and Michael W. Verner, M.D. "The Risk of Preterm Birth Across Generations." *Obstetrics and Gynecology* 90 (1997): 63–67.

"Postpartum Disorders." *Harvard Mental Health Letter* (September 1997): 1.

Powell, Megan P., and Jana R. Spellman. "Medical Management of the Patient with an Ectopic Pregnancy." *Journal of Perinatal and Neonatal Nursing* 9, 4 (1996): 31.

Rai, R., et al. "Randomized Controlled Trial of Aspirin and Aspirin Plus Heparin in Pregnant Women with Recurrent Miscarriage Associated with Phospholipid Antibodies." *British Medical Journal* 314 (1997): 253.

Raloff, Janet. "DES Sons Face No Fertility Problems." *Science News* (27 May 1995): 324.

"Risks of Motherhood." *Maclean's* (24 June 1996): 29.

Roberts, Richard J. "Trial of Labour or Repeated Cesarean Section: The Woman's Choice." *Journal of the American Medical Association* 278 (1997): 464.

Rosenbaum, Joshua. "Beat the Clock." *American Health* (December 1995): 70.

"Roundtable: The Politics of Genetic Testing." *Issues in Science and Technology* 13, 1 (1996): 48.

Ryder, Bob, and Hubert Campbell. "Natural Family Planning in the 1990s." *The Lancet* 346 (1995): 233.

Sadovsky, Richard. "Accuracy of Methods Used in Diagnosing Ectopic Pregnancy." *American Family Physician* 54 (1996): 2094.

Shea, Katherine M., et al. "Post-Term Delivery: A Challenge for Epidemiologic Research." *Epidemiology* 9, 2 (1980): 199.

Snyder, Karyn. "New Concept on Conception." *Drug Topics* (8 January 1996): 65.

"Spontaneous Abortions Possibly Related to Ingestion of Nitrate-Contaminated Well Water—LaGrange County, Indiana, 1991–94." *Morbidity and Mortality Weekly Report* 45 (1996): 569.

"State-Specific Variation in Rates of Twin Births—United States, 1992–1994." *Journal of the American Medical Association* 277 (1997): 878.

Stover, Anne McPherren, and Janet Griffith Marnejon. "Postpartum Care." *American Family Physician* 52 (1995): 1465.

Sundberg, K., et al. "Randomized Study of Risk of Fetal Loss Related to Early Amniocentesis versus Chorionic Villus Sampling." *The Lancet* 350 (1997): 697.

"Surgery to Close the Cervix." *Clinical Reference Systems* (December 1997): 2355.

"Taking the Low Tech Road to Conception." *Nutrition Health Review* (Spring 1996): 2.

"Timing of Sexual Intercourse and Probability of Pregnancy." *American Family Physician* 53 (1996): 2164.

"Tracking Fertility through Bodily Changes." *Nutrition Health Review* (Spring 1996): 3,4.

"Transdermal Estrogen Therapy in Severe Postnatal Depression." *American Family Physician* 54 (1996): 753.

Travis, John. "Hormonal Clock Predicts Premature Births (Maternal Blood Concentrations of Corticotropin-Releasing Hormone Predicts When Birth Will Occur.)." *Science News* (29 April 1995): 260.

Van Look, Paul F. A. "Lactational Amenorrhoea Method for Family Planning: Provides High Protection from Pregnancy for the First Six Months After Delivery." *British Medical Journal* 313 (1996): 893.

Walling, Anne D. "Flouxetine and Counseling for Postpartum Depression." *American Family Physician* 56 (1997): 946.

———. "Risk of Fetal Death Among Women Over Age 35." *American Family Physician* 55 (1997): 1382.

Whitmore, Barbara. "Musical Birth: Sound Strategies for Relaxation." *Mothering* (Fall 1997): 56.

Wild, Jennifer, et al. "Prevention of Neural-Tube Defects." *The Lancet* 350 (1997): 30.

Wolfelt, Alan D. "Helping Yourself Heal When a Baby Dies." *Thanatos* (Spring 1992): 30–32.

Wolff, Kristen M., M.D., Jeffrey A. Kuller, M.D., Michael J. McMahon, M.D., William R. Meyer, M.D., and David K. Walmer, M.D., Ph.D. "Advanced Maternal Age and Perinatal Outcome: Oocyte Recipiency versus Natural Conception." *Obstetrics and Gynecology* 89 (1997): 519–523.

Wolkomir, Michael S. "Managing Nausea in Pregnancy: Your First and Second-Line Options." *Consultant* 36 (1996): 298.

"Womb for Improvement." *Economist* (18 November 1995): 89.

Wood, Chris. "Beyond Abortion: Advances in Science Leave an Old Debate in the Dust." *MacLean's* (19 August 1996): 14.

Worth, N. J. "Reaction of Fathers to a Stillborn Child." *Clinical Nursing Research* 6, 1 (1997): 71–89.

Index